Gas

Gastronaut

Adventures in Food
for the Romantic,
the Foolhardy,
and the Brave

Stefan Gates

Photography by Mrs. Gates

Harcourt, Inc.
Orlando Austin New York San Diego Toronto London

Requests for permission to make copies of any part of the work should be mailed to the following address: Permissions Department, Harcourt, Inc., 6277 Sea Harbor Drive, Orlando, Florida 32887-6777.

www.HarcourtBooks.com

First published in Great Britain by BBC Books.

Library of Congress Cataloging-in-Publication Data
Gates, Stefan.
Gastronaut: adventures in food for the romantic, the foolhardy, and the brave / Stefan Gates; photography by Georgia Glynn Smith.
p. cm.
Includes bibliographical references and index.
1. Gastronomy. 2. Cookery. I. Title.
TX631.G38 2006
641'.013—dc22   2005026699
ISBN-13: 978-0-15-603097-7   ISBN-10: 0-15-603097-7

Text set in Aries
Designed by Kaelin Chappell Broaddus

Printed in the United States of America
First U.S. Harvest edition

K J I H G F E D C B A

What are little boys made of?
What are little boys made of?
Frogs and snails,
And puppy-dogs' tails,
That's what little boys are made of.

What are little girls made of?
What are little girls made of?
Sugar and spice,
And all things nice,
That's what little girls are made of.

To my girls, Georgia, Daisy, and Poppy

Contents

Hello   xi
The Gastronaut's Creed   xiv

Chapter 1   The Gastronaut's Toolbox   1
Let Them Eat Gold   3
Teaching Grandmothers To Suck Eggs   9
How To Make Your Own Moonshine (Almost)   13
How To Make Your Own Biltong   15
How To Make Your Own Cheese   18
How To Make Your Own Margarine   21
A Biscuit-tin Smokery   25

Chapter 2   Adventures In Dining   27
The Last Supper and Other Memorable Meals   29
How To Stage a Bacchanalian Orgy   38
Why Not Eat Insects?   47
How Britain Lost Its Culinary Edge   50

Chapter 3   Food and the Body   53
Our Secret Cannibal Desires   55
A Personal Journey Into Cannibalism   58
Cannibal Recipes   61
The Human Harvest   65
Aphrodisiacs   73
Flatulence   79
A Personal Journey Into Extreme Flatulence   84
Physiological Fun   87

Chapter 4   Exhibitionism for the Romantic   93

Cooking with Aftershave   95
Fanny Sandwich   98
Red and White Soup   101
Mumbled Mushrooms   103
Homemade Gravlax   105
Smug Homemaker Iced Pea and Lemon Grass Soup   106
King Edward's Chippenham Cheese Savory   108
Chicken-foot Stew   109
Laver Bread   111
Mackerel Tartare   113
Heartbreaker   116
Lumpydick   117
Buckinghamshire Bacon Badger   118
Nettle Soup and Nettle Haggis   120
Rabbit Pie   123
Gruel   125
Monkey Gland Steak   127
Carpetbagger Steaks   129
Clapshot   130
Picasso's Poussin   133
Interactive Pizza Engineering   135
Andy Warhol's Chocolate Balls   138
Hasty Pudding   139
Flummery   141
Deep-fried Mars Bar   143
Toffee Fondue   144
Frumenty   146

Chapter 5   Adventures for the Bold
             and the Brave   147

Sea Urchin Gonads   148
Cow-heel Soup   149
Pigeon Pie   151
Mock Turtle Soup   152
Fish Sperm on Toast   157

The World's Oldest Recipes   158

Cooking with Insects   160

Frogs' Legs   163

Testicles   166

Rhinoceros Soup   167

Drisheen   170

Ears   171

Reindeer Stew   174

Stargazey Pie   176

Stuffed Fish Heads   179

Stone, Stepladder, and Bucket Cream   181

Fourteenth-century Blancmange   182

Chapter 6   *Grands Projets* for Men and Women of Destiny   185

Headcheese   187

Suckling Pig   194

Turducken   199

Imu   203

Brillat-Savarin's Truffled Turkey   215

Guinea Pig   219

Chapter 7   Leftovers   223

A Beginner's Guide to Gastronautics   225

Beef Carpaccio   226

Ten-hour Leg of Lamb   226

Roast Partridge   226

Chicken with Forty Cloves of Garlic   226

Calf's Liver   227

Whole Roasted Pineapple   227

Seasonal Oddments   228

Rhubarb Shortcake   228

Pickled Eggs   229

Sweetbreads   229

Carrot Jam   230

Elderflower Cordial   231

Herring Sperm on Horseback   232
Pickled Walnuts   233
Marsh Samphire   233
Dandelion Coffee   234
Fragolina Grapes   234
Mushroom Ketchup   235
Homemade Ginger Beer   235
A Brief History of Washing-up   237

Useful Web Sites and Suppliers   241
Bibliography   244
The Gastronautical Survey   248
Index   252
Acknowledgments   258

Hello

You hold in your hands a gastronautical questbook, a practical guide for the adventurous cook and a personal journey through the crazy, twisted, mixed-up world of food. If you see it as a manual for culinary show-offs, I can live with that. I just want to encourage you to play with your food.

The first half of this book is for your bedside: a mixture of essays and tales of culinary adventure. If that inspires you, then I hope the second half will travel to your kitchen to join you on some wild gastronomic projects. Barring a handful of recipes that I've included because I thought they'd tickle you or because I just couldn't stop myself, everything here is real and practical. That said, I don't expect you to cook from this book every day or even every week, but rather when you have the time and inclination to have some fun, to make something spectacular and to explore the culinary hinterland.

But why bother playing with food? Well, bear this in mind: you will eat twenty-two tons of food in your lifetime, and you'll spend 2,946.62 days eating, shopping, cooking, queuing, or hunting for it. That's 16 percent of your entire waking life. You could spend that time making comfort food, eating burgers, or fussing over canapés, but Christ alive, what a waste of a life. We're a race of dreamers, alchemists, poets, and explorers; and my guess is that you, dear reader, are one of those and you're not willing to see life slip through your fingers. Much better to maximize your excitement-to-mastication ratio by every now and then spending an inordinate amount of time slaving away over a crazy recipe in search of a moment of epiphany.

Whenever I've been asked what my moment of culinary epiphany was, I've lied through my teeth trying to make up something clever. The truth of the matter is that I fell in love with cooking first, and for two very simple reasons. The first was named Jane and the second, Denise. These were two highly fanciable girls in my home economics class when we were thirteen years old, and whenever the teacher wasn't looking, we'd play a game whose rules were completely incomprehensible, but which invariably ended up with us fondling each other's bottoms with floury hands. It quickly dawned on me that great things could be achieved through food.

Food is so much more than fuel—it's a catalyst for emotion, a historical journey, a rite, a celebration, a three-times-daily act of giving and receiving love, and a fine opportunity for exhibitionism. For myself, I wouldn't claim that I dive into the culinary unknown every day, but most weekends I like to destroy my kitchen (with my two-year-old daughter as my wingman) in a flight of gastronomic fancy, and I hope that once in a while you will, too.

Experimenting with food is more than just fun—it's essential. In the 1580s the potato was an obscure poisonous tuber, but some gastronaut persevered until it became one of the world's most successful crops, sustaining life for billions. But then by relying on this miracle discovery, we failed a nation by creating a monoculinary culture. Ireland's tragic potato famine was mostly due to over-dependence on a single strain of that selfsame crop.

We are omnivores with a diverse diet and, in our primitive state, an insatiable culinary curiosity, and this is one of the reasons why, in evolutionary terms, our species has been so successful. We are highly adaptable in times of want, unlike the koala, for instance, which lives exclusively on eucalyptus. If the eucalyptus season is a bad one, whole populations of koalas are wiped out. We have the ability to move on to other crops (annoyingly, we can't actually digest eucalyptus—the koala has had to develop a special stomach to cope with such a poisonous herb, but you get my drift). We must avoid the temptation to stick with what we know, and continue to experiment, to take risks in order to survive.

But is over-reliance on a small set of foods really a problem in the modern age? Absolutely. Our current problems with obesity are caused by a dietary dependence on specific food types, and it's killing people right now. A reliance on powdered baby milk causes terrible problems, especially in the developing world. Richer nations have a long history of maneuvering farmers across the world into growing commercial crops that create a devastating lack of adaptability, and modern agribusiness offers the joys of the GM (genetically modified) seed-to-chemical cycle of financial dependence. There are strong arguments for and against GM crops (and organic foods, for that matter), but none of it sits well with me yet.

We may hate GM, but we still need to find a way to feed a hungry, changing world, so we must keep experimenting with both new and ancient foods. I'm not saying that we'll be the ones to save the world, but who knows what you and I will find on our adventures?

I ought to dish out some apologies here: I'm sorry to all my friends and family who've been guinea pigs as I gambled recklessly with their appetites; who're rarely served their food before midnight and smile even though they're too pissed to taste it. And above all for their enthusiasm—together we've discovered a whole encyclopedia of successes and a fair few disasters.

I'd also like to apologize to you, dear reader, for having to endure the many moments of indulgence in this book that I have failed to cull. In my defense, they are inextricably linked to the exhilaration of culinary adventure, so I thought I might just get away with them. I hope that this book heralds a few adventures for you, helps you have a little fun, and perhaps unlocks some secrets. And if you stumble across anything new and wonderful, or have any glorious failures, I want to know all about it.

When are you free for supper?

The Gastronaut's Creed

Food will consume 16 percent of my life. That life is too precious to waste, therefore:

- ℂ I resolve, whenever possible, to transform food from fuel into love, power, adventure, poetry, sex, or drama.

- ℂ I will never turn down the opportunity to taste or cook something new.

- ℂ I will never forget: canapés are evil.

- ℂ I will remember that culinary disaster does not necessarily equal culinary failure.

- ℂ I will always keep a jar of pesto on hand in case of the latter.

Chapter 1
The Gastronaut's Toolbox

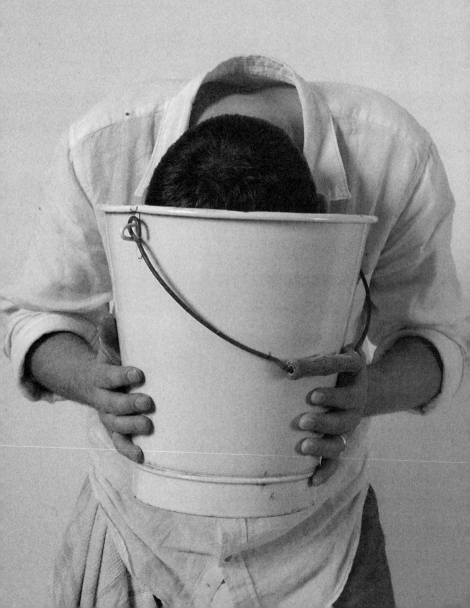

Let Them Eat Gold

In the pantheon of unnecessary, over-elaborate, and time-consuming recipes, there's surely no greater waste of time and money, no more pointless and recklessly prodigal a task than cooking with gold. Let's give it a go. Gold has traditionally been used to decorate namby-pamby fancy foods, such as chocolates, gingerbread, and cakes. So we're going to make bangers and mash with golden sausages, fish and chips with golden chips, and gilded Cheetos.

Why bother cooking with gold? It's tasteless, odorless, infuriating to handle, entirely devoid of nutrients and cripplingly expensive. But that's precisely why it's so exciting. It's an alchemical elevation of food from fuel to wonder, an escape from reality, a flight of decadent fancy. And it's all the more decadent if, like me, you can't actually afford it. Like going shopping to ease the misery of your overdraft, or eating chocolate to forget how overweight you are. In fact, if you're rich, cooking with gold is no fun at all. Gauche, even. A bit like putting a big sign in front of your mansion saying, I'M RICH.

There's an interesting, if slight, history to gilded food. It was very popular in medieval Britain, especially among the clergy. Elizabeth Grey's 1653 *Secrets in Physick and Chyrugery* explains how to gild candied flowers, the fifteenth-century *Ordinance of Pottage* shows how to gild walnuts, and in 1769 Elizabeth Raffald wrote a recipe for gilded fish in jelly. Bols Distilleries still makes Gold Wasser de Danzig, which they claim dates back to Louis XIV's time and features flocculent shavings of gold lurking at the bottom—so flocculent, in fact, that it looks like there's been a fault with the bottling machine, but it's a nice idea. In India and Pakistan gold is used on special occasions for handmade sweets and is occasionally mixed, with a glorious sense of abandon, with rice. Unsurprisingly, gold is also reputed to have aphrodisiac qualities. These days it's pretty much confined to the odd dusting on a bourgeois chocolate truffle, and the European Union has classified it—rather unromantically—as food coloring E175 (silver is E174 and aluminum E173).

Once you have decided to throw caution to the wind, you must procure some gold. Unless you are a complete squandermaniac, the only reasonable approach is to buy gold leaf, usually available from art shops. At this point, you may be tempted to try cooking with silver leaf, which does indeed behave in a similar way but is infinitely cheaper. Perhaps the appallingly named Luster Dust or Gold Luster Dust aerosols have caught your eye. Don't even think about it. You'd only be cheating yourself. If you're going to celebrate life by doing something truly pointless and unnecessary, you have to throw in your lot completely. It's got to be real gold or nothing at all.

There are three main types of gold that you can use for food: gold leaf, gold ribbon, and gold powder. By far the most cost-effective is gold leaf, but it is a tricky substance to deal with.

Two of the leading gilding specialists in Great Britain are E. Ploton, with a shop in north London, and Habberley Meadows, which boasts BY APPOINTMENT TO HER MAJESTY THE QUEEN and is based in Birmingham. For those of you not in these neighborhoods, visit www.cheftools.com. I stopped by Ploton's and spoke to an affecting young scallywag by the name of James, who was wonderfully helpful and patient. He had once tried gilding some profiteroles, a confession that surprised and pleased me, coming from a young man of grunge-rocker appearance.

Ploton's advises that only 24 ct gold (i.e. 100 percent pure) is edible, though other sources say that 22 ct is okay. Anything below 24 ct is mixed with copper and nickel, so the choice is yours. Gold leaf is sold by the book of 25 leaves, each mere molecules thick, which makes it a flighty, extremely delicate substance to handle. It tears easily and if you pick it up with your fingers it will stick and probably disintegrate. You can buy it as "transfer" leaf, which sits conveniently on a piece of parchment, or "loose," which is great for uneven surfaces but a swine to control.

So how much does it cost? At the time of writing, a book containing 25 leaves of 24 ct transfer gold 3.25" x 3.25" was $27.25 from Ploton's, which is pretty good value for a book of dreams even after converting the price to U.S. dollars. It costs $25.40 loose, while the 22 ct was $18.81 loose or $21.62 for transfer. If you want to go crazy, gold powder would cost about $98.45 for .07 ounce. (All prices fluctuate, often on a daily basis, as the price of gold shifts.) Most of it seems to be made in Germany or Italy. It's also a good idea to buy some inedible faux gold leaf for practicing with before you use the real stuff. Try some No. $2\frac{1}{2}$ Schlag loose leaf at $5.19 for a larger 5.5" x 5.5" book, but bear in mind that it's still thicker than real gold. If you're feeling flush, you might also want to invest in a special gilding brush made from squirrel hair, 3.5" wide and $19.60 to you, squire.

When you buy the gold, a warm feeling sweeps through you. Enjoy it—that's decadence setting in. It feels rather sparkling and splendid to own sheets of pure gold. Once you get home, find a couple of artist's paintbrushes (if you didn't buy the squirrel version), a pair of tweezers, some sharp scissors, and a good, smooth chopping board. Close the windows—any breeze at all is likely to destroy wafer-thin gold—and pour a small amount of vegetable oil into a bowl. Have a go with the faux gold first—try gilding a few Cheetos and you'll see how delicate and tricky it is. You'll need to coat the Cheeto with a thin layer of oil to make the leaf stick, then roll it across the gold, pressing it down with the brush. You'll make a hash of the first few, but then you should get the hang of it.

Before you start, clean and dry your hands. If at any stage a gold leaf floats free, don't try to catch it as it may break and probably stick disastrously to your fingers. Let it settle wherever it wants to, then pick it up very gently with tweezers or with a paintbrush dabbed with the lightest amount of oil. When you're ready to do the real thing, make sure you have a little bowl ready to keep all the gold shavings that you muck up or don't use. These can be used later to scatter on top of cappuccinos or for gilding a nifty gin and tonic.

I thoroughly recommend that you try this. Cooking with gold lends you a gentle magical aura that lasts for a couple of days afterward—similar to that blessed feeling of waking up with no hangover when by rights you should be enduring waves of alcoholic nausea and nihilism. And just so you know, your guests are likely to ask you the following questions:

❧ *Will the gold hurt my fillings in the way that a stray piece of foil will?*
The answer is NO.

❧ *Is it bad for you?*
Again, NO.

⟨ *Will I have gold poo in the morning?*
Well, you might find some flecks, if you're lucky and observant, but during my own investigations, none has been found.

⟨ *Will I be able to lay golden eggs?*
Of course you will, dear.

Gilded Sausages and Mash

I suggest that you gild just one sausage for each person to serve with some ungilded ones, otherwise you'll be there all day. Use good sausages that aren't overly thick—no bigger than the usual eight-to-the-pound banger. Breakfast sausages are even better. I won't waste time with the recipes for mash and gravy—I'm sure you've got your favorites.

Heat your oven to 325°F. Slowly roast rather than fry your sausages (this seems to keep the shape better) for anything up to an hour (check after thirty minutes), and while they are cooking make your mash and perhaps a red onion gravy. When the sausages are nicely done, let them cool a little, and as soon as you can handle them easily, take the ones that are least curly—one for each person—and dab as much of the fat off with paper towels as you can. Don't skip this bit otherwise the fat will go straight through the gold and fasten it to the parchment.

Turn the oven off and put the rest of the sausages in to keep them warm. Shut all doors and windows and set yourself up on the kitchen table with all your tools and an aura of calm. Having put all the time and effort into preparing yourself for this moment, it should now only take you about ten minutes to gild the sausages if you have all the tools assembled. Take one leaf of transfer gold and lay it on the chopping board. Then simply roll your sausage across the gold leaf and it will pick up the gold as you roll. The leaf will probably not be long enough to entirely cover the sausage so either cover one end fully and bury the other into the mash for serving or use two leaves per banger. You may need to use a dry paintbrush (*not* the oily one) to dab the leaf onto the sausage if it hasn't stuck, and then carefully pull the parchment away, if it hasn't come away already. It probably won't be that neat, and you may have left some gaps, but it's best not to worry too much.

Put a neat pile of mash on each plate and stick the plain sausages into the mash in Yosemite Sam style. Pick up the (admittedly slightly colder) gold one—you should be able to use your fingers without destroying them. Serve, without drawing any attention to the gold, and crack open a very expensive bottle of wine. Luxuriate in the warmth of your fellow man.

Golden Cheetos

Very slowly and carefully, cut your gold to the approximate size needed for each Cheeto. Paint a little oil (olive or sunflower will do) onto each Cheeto just before you are ready to gild it, then roll it across the leaf, as you did with the sausages. This is a tricky number as Cheetos are uneven and difficult to roll. Persevere. Use your dry paintbrush to dab the gold onto the delicious, cheesy, corn-based puff product. As with the sausages, it would be madness to gild all the Cheetos, so do just a few and scatter them among some ungilded ones. Incidentally, it's best not to prepare these too far in advance as Cheetos turn stale very quickly, often within the hour.

Golden Fries

This is basic but fussy. This time, you should try to cut the gold leaf (while still on the parchment) to a shape that's slightly bigger than the french fry. It's a bit of guesswork, really. Very sharp scissors are a great help here. Again, the fries shouldn't be too hot or they will be a nightmare to handle. Follow the same principle as with the sausages, draining as much of the grease from the fries as you can before gilding. Again, serve just a few gold french fries among the normal ones.

You should be feeling slightly mucky from all this decadence by now. I suggest you pick up the phone and call Oxfam to make a hefty donation. It might not solve your guilt, but it's a redemption of sorts.

MUSIC SUGGESTIONS
While carrying out the actual gilding, it's useful to play something appropriately ethereal, such as the collection of pieces by Hildegard von Bingen, *A Feather on the Breath of God*, the delicious "Song to the

Siren" from This Mortal Coil's *It'll End in Tears* album or "Trying to Find a Home" from the Tinderstick's *Waiting for the Moon*. For serving, however, perhaps Quincy Jones's *Big Band Bossa Nova*, for the simple reason that it's splendid.

Teaching Grandmothers To Suck Eggs

I love old ladies. I've rarely met a bad one. In fact, if I didn't relish the prospect of being a pipe-smoking, Boo Radleyesque, grumpy, slightly stinky old man quite so much, I would like to have been an old lady when I grow up. One thing has always troubled me, though: the idea that you can't teach them (or, specifically, grandmothers) to suck eggs. This is one of a family of wide-ranging culinary assumptions such as "Too many cooks spoil the broth" and "A watched pot never boils." These really ought to be proven before they are allowed to become aphorisms (I presume there's an aphorism council that decides such things), so I've taken my favorite one to test.

The aphorism "You can't teach a grandmother to suck eggs" is generally used to imply that what you are saying is obvious, that you're telling someone a fact that they already know. It works on the assumption that our elder folk are wise and sage about everything. Now, I love a granny as much as the next man, but to grant them omniscience is pushing it a bit. So I decided to test the theory in an unbiased, strictly controlled study. First, I needed to become an expert at egg-sucking, then I needed to get me some grandmothers (a quorum of twenty, say) and try teaching them.

The body of literature on egg-sucking is small. So small that I couldn't find anything. I bet there's a church pamphlet on creating Easter displays that contains everything you need to know, but luckily in the absence of written guides there is a strong word-of-mouth history, which reveals that egg-sucking is mainly used to remove the insides of eggs so that you can preserve the shells for painting, like the brightly decorated eggs traditionally produced at Easter. Eggs are, of course, a potent symbol of new life in lots of religions, including paganism, Christianity and Judaism.

So how do you suck an egg? I had to ask . . . well . . . a grandmother. Grandma Gates, my long-suffering mum and grandmother to my daughters, Daisy and Poppy, has sucked eggs in the past—not for any religious occasion, but because she wanted to preserve some wild birds' eggs (we'll skip lightly over the legality of this—in mitigation, it was some time ago) and was taught by my grandfather, Wilfred. The technique seemed pretty obvious: Take your egg and, using a needle or thin point of a knife, make a small hole in the top and bottom. Then suck the egg out.

I resolved to become an expert, so I sat down with half a dozen eggs and gave it a try. It quickly became apparent that if you use unwashed eggs donated by your friend's chickens you are apt to get a shitty mouth. I washed the second egg but the process was still disgusting. Having a mouthful of cold, raw egg made me want to vomit. It also struck me that raw eggs aren't the best things to ask people to eat, especially people who are old and, quite possibly, infirm. I put this to my mum. "Oh yes," she said, "I think we actually blew the eggs rather than sucked." Thanks, Mum.

After extensive experimentation, I ascertained the following:

◁ Take the eggs out of the fridge to let them warm a little, making the insides less viscous and more manageable.

◁ Use a pin to make the hole and then widen it with the point of a knife.

◁ Don't make too small a hole otherwise the pressure of the exiting egg will cause more damage, collapsing your egg.

I may be particularly malcoordinated, but one third of the eggs cracked too much to be useable.

It took me five eggs to get it right. Now I needed some grandmas. I originally had visions of going to a retirement home and gathering a group of willing, lovely ladies to teach. I realized, however, that this might be seen as patronizing—who would ever agree to that? So I got hold of the phone numbers of eighteen grandmas through friends and family, and called them up. Not quite my quorum of twenty, but near enough.

Out of my eighteen grandmas, seven of them politely declined to take part, and hence couldn't, indeed, be taught to suck eggs. One was just too talkative and managed with devilish skill to change the subject, so I never did get to the teaching. One was my mum, who taught me in the first place, and therefore couldn't be taught herself. This left nine grandmas, eight of whom claimed that they already knew how to suck eggs. There was, however, one wonderful lady, a friend of my mum's, who thought the whole thing hilarious, and I managed to teach her successfully, albeit over the phone, so I can't guarantee that she pulled it off to complete satisfaction.

So, from this I concluded that on the whole the idiom is *true*—you can't teach all grandmas to suck eggs. You can, however, teach one grandma to suck eggs, and if I found one, there might be others. But the idiom is one of those absolutist conceits—if even one grandmother can be taught, the whole thing goes out the window and hence the aphorism is proved *false* and should be struck from the aphorism register immediately.

But I won't stop playing with old ladies. If you know any grandmas who are in the dark about the egg-sucking thing, please send them to me complete with a box of half a dozen free-rangers, and we can suck some eggs and maybe drink some tea.

How To Make Your Own Moonshine (Almost)

If you're planning to make your own spirits, stop right there. I don't want to be the cause of your moral collapse, nor the collapse of your house: Home distillation is highly illegal and dangerous to boot. If, however, your interest is purely academic, or if you live in New Zealand (where, oddly enough, it's legal) you may read on.

Moonshine is illicitly distilled alcohol, traditionally synonymous with Wile E. Coyote and, by all accounts, very common in Scandinavia. It's also common in Bridgnorth, Shropshire, where in 2003 customs officers found six illegal stills on a remote farm, busy brewing moonshine under the name "Highland Game." They arrested a fellow called Peter Cox and put him away for two years.

At first, a sentimental part of me sympathized with Mr. Cox—surely moonshiners are survivalist freedom fighters kicking against taxation from greedy governments? All he needed was to have his hair tousled with an "On your way, scallywag." Then I read how much moonshine he was brewing at the time of Her Majesty's customs officers' visit: 9,246 gallons. Around 130,000 empty bottles had been supplied to the farm and Coxy pleaded guilty to evading $930,465 in excise duty. Not exactly *Good Neighbors*, is it?

The reason it's illegal is simple: cash. Evading duty equals "theft of vast sums from the public purse" (I've always imagined the public purse to be the size of a house, all purple velvet, brim-full of golden ducats, with a big drawstring at the top). I had protracted conversations with Customs and Excise about what exactly is illegal about home brewing. Apparently it's not the alcohol content—you can make home brew for your own use at any level of alcoholic content. It's all about owning and running the *still*. Basically, any still has to be licensed, and to get it licensed you need to meet a whole shedload of difficult criteria—it has to have a capacity of 476 gallons, for starters, and your premises need to have certain levels of security.

Moonshine is also potentially dangerous. If impurities or chemicals like methanol are left in, it can cause severe abdominal pain, drowsiness, dizziness, blurred vision leading to blindness, and the risk of coma with breathing difficulties. The customs folk warn that "If anyone has a bottle at home, or is unsure if it is a genuine product, they should contact their Environmental Health Officer." Yeah, right.

So bearing all this in mind (i.e., that you can't, mustn't, *won't*), how *would* you go about making the stuff? Well, very carefully and very quietly, that's for sure. There are, inevitably, several ways of going about this. You can make your own still but you'd need to be an engineer or survivalist fruitcake because it's rather complicated. Everyone else would buy their stills from legal suppliers in New Zealand or Germany, where they are sold as *water purifiers*. They helpfully break the equipment down into several inconspicuous packages to avoid prying eyes, if required.

The whole process starts off thoroughly legally, with the creation of a "wash"—an alcoholic base liquid up to 20 percent alcohol. You can make your own wash from pretty much any organic material—one combination is water, sugar, orange juice, and yeast, and you can make it in three weeks or so. But you can also buy complete kits to make a high-alcohol home brew. These kits work very well. I only wish I had a faster consumption rate for spirits—the kits tend to make 1.3 gallons in a batch.

You could, of course, stop here, which many people do, and add one of hundreds of different essences to your brew, including gin, vodka, rum or Scotch. They are surprisingly authentic but they are still only 20 percent alcohol. Happily, this brew can then be converted into the illegal stuff by distillation, which aficionados have taken to complex levels of expertise.

At this point I had hoped to put all the means to brew some potent hooch at your disposal. However, when the lawyers read my manuscript they had what I can only describe as a "fit," and banned the four pages that followed, despite my having struggled so hard to offset hardcore engineering with irreverent humor. Luckily, my burden of responsibility is lighter than my publisher's, so I have provided the entire set of instructions at www.thegastronaut.com. Ha.

How To Make Your Own Biltong

uring meat is good for the soul. It may seem a daunting prospect, but the childish sense of pride you get from making your first batch will get you straight on the phone telling your mum how proud she ought to be. Biltong is the ideal way to start your journey into home butchery—it's a very simple process and can be done on a small scale—and before you know it you'll be making *saucisson* and spending your weekends washing pigs' intestines.

Biltong is a strangely addictive, very chewy South African specialty made from cured and air-dried strips of meat, and it was developed as a good way of storing meat in a hot climate. The word comes from the Dutch—"bil" meaning "buttock" and "tong" meaning "strip." The temptation to delve into the sexual proclivities of the Boers is strong, but I've fought it—this is a book about food.

There are several versions of biltong including ostrich, kudu (a type of antelope), springbok, and fish, though the most common is undoubtedly beef. What's interesting is that, other than the fish one, they all seem to taste the same. Of course, try telling a South African that and they'll bite your head off.

The equipment involved is minimal—the most important thing is to knock out a contraption in which to dry the hanging strips of meat. It should allow a flow of air but not flies (if you're too lazy even for this, you can buy a ready-made biltong-maker with an integral heater). I've made one of these out of coat hangers and mosquito netting in the past, and even found an old cage in a secondhand shop and lined that with mosquito netting.

I don't need to give you full directions as it's pretty simple. First of all you need a box-shaped frame a bit bigger than a portable TV with slats or wires on the top that will allow you to tie strips of meat on with string, letting them hang without touching the bottom or sides. Then you need to cover the whole thing with netting for protection.

When you have assembled your biltong-maker you will need to find somewhere to hang it. If it's hot and dry, you can leave it hanging somewhere outside in the sunshine. You can also use a dry cellar, but failing that a window ledge will do. If you put it in your closet your laundry will smell of biltong for weeks, so you have been warned.

First, make your hanging contraption, then:

Makes About 1-3/4 Pounds

4-1/2 pounds of beef fillet

3/4 cup red wine vinegar

1/4 cup Worcestershire sauce

1 handful of coriander seeds, coarsely ground

1 tablespoon black pepper, coarsely ground

✐ Cut the beef into strips about 1-1/2 inches thick and as long as you fancy. Put the meat into a bowl so that it fits tightly and add the vinegar and Worcestershire sauce. Leave for thirty minutes.

✐ Meanwhile, mix the coriander and pepper together in another bowl.

✐ In a third bowl, mix the salt, sugar, and bicarbonate of soda together.

✐ Remove the meat from the liquid (but don't throw it away), drain briefly, and add to the bowl of spices, mixing it around for an even coating. Retain the spices that don't stick.

1 pound fine sea salt

5-1/3 ounces brown sugar

1 teaspoon bicarbonate of soda (this will help to soften the meat)

Bury the spiced beef in the salt and sugar mixture and leave it for three hours (it will draw in the brine mixture). Remove the beef from the brine and dip it back in the vinegar for another five minutes. Remove and, using the vinegar, wipe all the salt off (don't skip this bit or your biltong will be unbearably salty). Squeeze it to remove as much liquid as you can, roll it in the spices again, and it's ready for hanging.

To hang your biltong, cut lengths of string, and tie them tightly around one end of each beef strip. Tie these to the top of your hanging contraption and make sure that they don't touch the sides or bottom.

Leave the strips hanging for three to twenty days in a dry (and preferably warm) place. It's difficult to say exactly how long they'll need because it will depend on the temperature and humidity of your chosen drying place, but basically they're ready when the meat is as tough as old boots. When made in midsummer in South Africa, this is about three days.

MUSIC SUGGESTIONS
Anything by Miriam Makeba or Ladysmith Black Mambazo would fit the bill.

How To Make Your Own Cheese

I used to think cheese making was one of those arcane, magical things like wine making or horse whispering—an immensely complicated process that can't be taught, only known, and then only by besmocked country folk. I think of cheese as a living, breathing organism, the result of a symbiotic relationship between man and cow, and, along with wine, bread, and cured meat, possibly the most wonderful substance ever created. Then I stumbled across an old book that explained how to make your own cheese at home, and suddenly it all became clear.

A note on cheese loving: Apparently the UK now makes more types of cheese than they do in France—seven hundred as opposed to their five hundred and the U.S.'s four hundred. While I suspect a little Anglo-Saxon creative accountancy here, we definitely have an incredibly strong new culture of cheese making, which is very exciting. My favorite cheese changes from month to month, and my current favorites are Gorwydd Caerphilly, Flower Marie, and a gnarly old lump of moldy milk sold by a scrofulous old lady in the Saturday market at Gignac in the south of France. It has no name, but Madame claims it's made with ewes' milk.

I'll be honest: home cheese making is one of those tasks that brings little material benefit. It doesn't save you money and you can certainly buy better stuff in shops. But it's fascinating and enormously satisfying, and understanding the process has definitely made me enjoy cheese more. There's an element of childish pride in serving homemade cheese to your friends. You really ought to try it.

There are different levels of effort you can throw at the task, with correspondingly tasty results. At the top of the scale, hard cheese is time-consuming and requires quite a lot of gear. Either set aside some DIY time or, if you have $200 or so to spare, you can buy a rather posh-looking kit from a specialist supplier containing everything you need (barring the milk) to make hard cheese. Generally speaking, it takes four gallons of milk to produce two pounds of hard cheese. There are a few good books on the subject—try *Home Cheese Making* by Ricki Carroll, or Jocasta Innes's brilliant book *The Country Kitchen*.

Then there are soft cheeses, which are a lot quicker and easier to make. If you can lay your hands on some rennet, which costs only five to seven dollars for a bottle, you can start to indulge some fun projects, such as Innes's recipe for homemade mozzarella.

Lastly there's cream cheese, which is dead easy and takes about three days with minimal tinkering and can be made without rennet. It's a great way to start a cheese-making obsession as all the basic elements are there. Here's how you do it.

Makes 1 Small Cheese

Equipment

any ovenproof glass or ceramic jug or similar container that will hold 1/2 gallon

2 clean towels or muslin (even muslins for babies seem to work well)

an ovenproof bowl

another bowl

string

For the cheese

1/2 gallon full-fat milk (I've used unpasteurized milk to good effect)

4 tablespoons full-fat live yogurt

a sprig of rosemary or thyme

salt

Sterilize your container and towels (or muslin) in a saucepan of boiling water. Pour the milk into the jug and add the yogurt. Stir well, cover it with one of your damp towels, and leave it for two days. The bacteria in the yogurt will have grown in the milk, producing acid that starts souring it. Don't worry—this is a good thing.

Heat your oven to 225°F. Skim the cream off to leave behind the solidifying gloop, and place this gloop in an ovenproof bowl. Warm it in the oven for thirty minutes—this will encourage the solid curds and watery whey to separate.

Lay your second towel in a large mixing bowl with the corners hanging over the sides. Pour the curds and whey mixture on top, then carefully lift the four corners of the cloth and gently compress to squeeze out the liquid. Tie it up with a string and hang it from something to drip. Traditionally, it was suspended from the legs of an upturned stool, but use whatever you've got. It'll need to drip-dry for twelve hours, so make sure you put it somewhere out of the way.

After twelve hours, place your bundle on a plate. To add some flavor (because it doesn't taste of much) untie the bundle and place a washed sprig of rosemary or thyme on top of the cheese. Re-tie it and put another plate on top to gently compress it. Leave for another two hours or so, then serve it with a pinch of salt and a little pool of olive oil (in the Languedocian style) or in a pool of runny honey.

MUSIC SUGGESTION

Since making this cheese will take about three days, why don't you listen to Schoenberg's *Verklärte Nacht* (with Karajan and the Berlin Philharmonic Orchestra) over and over again? After about three days on constant rotation, you will finally understand the piece and enter a state of grace.

How To Make Your Own Margarine

t's all very well camping up mealtimes with arcane recipes but it hardly paints a balanced view of gastronomy, and for that I'm truly sorry. In recompense, I'd like to offer you this treatise on something that no one really likes to talk about other than to slate in broad "processed food" terms. Despite its reputation as an artificial foodstuff and gastronomic pariah, margarine gave us essential fats in times of need, especially during wars, and it still has an important place feeding our hungry nation. When I was a child we used to eat loads of it from vast plastic tubs that didn't really need to be kept in the fridge, and I remember being rather partial to it, especially when it was spread liberally on my toast. I can't escape the fact that I am, in part, made of margarine, so here is an honest, impartial view of it.

Marge was invented by the French (which always makes me chuckle) at the request of Napoleon III. The date was 1869, the Industrial Revolution had drawn people into cities, and food production wasn't keeping up with demand. Europe was running low on the edible fats, especially butter, that kept up energy and body warmth both for city workers and (more importantly) for an army on the brink of war. So Napoleon launched a competition for food scientists to develop an alternative to butter that was cheap, long-lasting and easy to produce.

Enter one Hippolyte Mège-Mouriès (1817–80), armed with a theory based on margaric acid. He mixed oleo (an oil made from beef fat), skimmed milk, and water with a piece of udder (he thought this would work in the same way that rennet helps turn milk into cheese), then he chilled the mixture and churned it. The resulting pearly white substance acted uncannily like butter. Bingo.

In actual fact, the theories that Mège-Mouriès used were wrong (margaric acid didn't exist, having been wrongly identified as a distinct substance that formed pearly drops in 1813 by a chemist called Chevreul, who named it after the Greek for "pearl," and which gave rise to the name "margarine"). But it didn't really matter that the science behind it was cockeyed because, in practice, Mège-Mouriès had achieved his original aim of making a butter substitute. In 1871 patents were flying and large-scale production started in 1880. In 1905 the process of hydrogenation for stiffening vegetable oils was developed.

But it wasn't all plain sailing for marge. The authorities hated it, defined it as a "harmful drug" and imposed heavy taxes, which gave rise to bootlegging, believe it or not. The public, however, couldn't get enough of it. Even now, we eat three times as much margarine as butter, not just because it's cheaper, but also because it contains less cholesterol and saturated fats. Although many people have reservations about its flavor and its artificiality it has been remarkably successful as imitation foods go.

What's interesting is that no one ever made a better name stick. In America they tried the rather ugly "oleomargarine" and then gave it up. I took a good look in my local supermarket, where they have all been renamed "spreads," which seems a little disingenuous—like the manufacturers feel a little guilty that they make marge. The only one that admits its provenance is Stork brand margarine, which boasts about its efficacy as a baking ingredient.

Marge is a water-in-oil emulsion (mayonnaise is the same kind of thing) but would you ever try making it? Well, to be quite frank, even the most committed gastronaut would be hard-pushed because of the complexity of the processes and the equipment involved. At first glance it seems strange that so involved a process could possibly make a substance that's cheaper than butter, which is simply made from churned cream, but on an industrial scale, creating margarine is remarkably cost effective. It will come as no surprise that a synthetic food needs a bit of science to be made (of course, if you break it down, the exact process by which milk is made in a cow involves a lot of complicated science, too, and butter production is actually a set of complex reactions, fermentations, and emulsifications) but get this:

✍ Procure some oil (sunflower, soya, groundnut, and palm oils are common, but animal fats are also used). Mix in 5 percent water and heat to 194°F, then use a centrifuge to remove impurities.

✍ Neutralize it by heating it with caustic soda to between 167°F and 205°F for half an hour to remove free fatty acids and their flavors by turning them into soap. Wash this soap out with water and remove this water by evaporation in a vacuum. Add 1 percent fuller's earth to bleach out any color and impurities from plant pigments. Heat to between 194°F and 230°F in a vacuum. Filter the earth out to clear the oil.

✍ To get a solid consistency, you need hydrogenation: Add hydrogen and a nickel catalyst in a sealed tank at 365°F.

✍ Neutralize and filter again.

✍ Heat the oil and blow steam through it at 356°F to deodorize.

✍ Blend liquid oils and solid fats to give the desired texture. Add water-soluble ingredients: For animal margarines, use skim milk cultured with *Streptococcus lactis* bacteria and pasteurized milk. Flora uses "whey, brine, and powdered ingredients, such as milk proteins or starches mixed with water."

✍ Add oil-soluble ingredients: vitamins A and D, natural or synthetic color, diacetyl, caproic acid, flavorings, butyric acid, and salt, along with the all-important emulsifiers, such as lecithin and monoglycerides. Emulsify that little lot by agitating at 122°F–140°F in a rotator, then pasteurize it at between 158°F and 185°F.

✐ Chill to crystallize the fat in the emulsion, working and kneading it at the same time.

✐ Pack the margarine and store it at between 36°F and 185°F.

So let's recap the raw materials used. Not all of these can be strictly termed ingredients—some are used as catalysts or facilitators, and different margarines have different lists—but here are the basics.

Oil	Animal margarines use:	Powdered ingredients, such as:	Caproic acid
Water			Flavorings (including delta lactones)
Caustic soda	Skim milk cultured with *Streptococcus lactis* bacteria	Milk proteins or starches mixed with water	
Fuller's earth			Salt
Hydrogen		Vitamin A	Lecithin
Nickel	Pasteurized milk	Vitamin D	Monoglycerides made from acids and glycerol
Steam	Vegetable margarines use:	Natural or synthetic color	
	Whey	Diacetyl	
	Brine		

Just thought you should know.

MUSIC SUGGESTION
If you make margarine, you are either a food scientist, a factory technician for a vast food conglomerate, or completely nuts. Either way, Herbie Hancock's *Head Hunters* album should cool your boots.

A Biscuit-tin Smokery

This unlikely-sounding cooking method is actually very simple, quick, and rather spectacular to boot, and comes courtesy of John Strike, at Quayside Fish in Porthleven, Cornwall. It's actually a cross between smoking, barbecuing, and poaching, and it has a nice survivalist feel to it. But it's important to realize that this doesn't make smoked salmon as you generally know it, which is cold-smoked for hours—this little fella takes only about three minutes to build, three minutes to heat up, three minutes to cook, and three minutes to clean up afterward. It does brew up a little smoke, but far less than you'd imagine, so it can be done inside on any type of cooker.

Constructing a Smokery

✐ Take your grill material and, using the pliers, bend and twist it to make a self-supporting platform that fits inside the tin and sits about 1-1/2 inches above the bottom.

✐ And that really is it. No holes, no oxygen supply. Just a tin with a platform. How it works is this: You scatter wood shavings on the base of the tin, lay your food on the grill, and put the lid on. Place the whole shebang on a medium heat and allow the wood shavings to smolder; you will create a mixture of smoke, steam, and convection but it won't burst

into flames (due to the lack of oxygen). It cooks the food very quickly and gives it a glorious smoky flavor and a golden hue. When you take the lid off, there will be a puff of smoke but it's not as asphyxiating as you'd imagine. It is, however, a bit smelly afterward.

Please be careful with this:

Equipment

a large biscuit tin or chocolate tin with its lid (mine is an old Danish butter cookie tin)

a piece of metal grill/thick chicken wire/steel mesh that's bigger than your biscuit tin (I use an old supermarket-bought single-use BBQ grill)

a pair of pliers

For smoking

a handful of hardwood shavings or dust (i.e., oak, birch, beech, or any fruit woods, but not pine as softwoods can give a nasty resinous taste)

Serves 4

4 fillets of good fresh salmon, skinned (or any skinless fish or meat fillets, e.g., mackerel, chicken; eggs are good, too)

a splash of vegetable oil

◖ Never leave a smokery unattended on the heat.

◖ Don't touch the tin with your bare hands as it gets very hot.

◖ And when you're done, replace the lid and put in a safe place to cool.

Biscuit-tin Smoked Salmon

✑ You must skin the salmon first because the cooking time is short and the flavor doesn't penetrate far into the fish.

✑ Take the grill out of your tin and lightly oil it (this will help to stop the fish from sticking to it). Scatter a handful of wood shavings in the bottom of the tin and put the grill back in. Place your salmon on the grill and put the lid on.

✑ Place the whole tin over a medium heat on your stove top for three minutes. Remove and rest for one minute. Carefully remove the lid, bearing in mind that it's probably very hot.

✑ Serve with a dollop of crème fraîche mixed with dill, small boiled potatoes, and some green beans, perhaps.

MUSIC SUGGESTIONS
The Veils' *The Runaway Found*, or *Fun* by the Candy-skins.

Chapter 2
Adventures In Dining

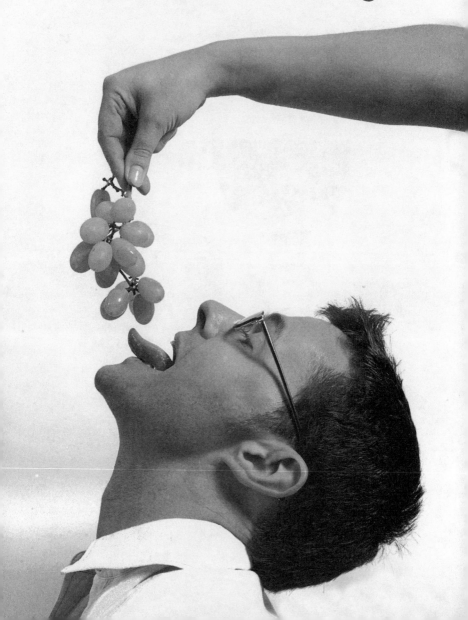

The Last Supper and Other Memorable Meals

How to secure your dinner party's place in history

F
ood is so much more interesting when laced with drama, emotion, and adventure. It's much better to cause an uproar by serving something brutally spectacular, unfathomably complex, or unbelievably disastrous than to host a formal dinner party where everyone eats sensibly and behaves themselves. But I've always wanted to go further. I secretly aspire to throwing a dinner party that becomes *legendary*. I'm not talking about people praising my napkin rings or asking for my *Paupiettes de Veau Belle Hélène* recipe, but rather the creation of a hold-the-front-page *convivium* that enters folklore—a dinner of such mythic proportions that everyone wishes they had been invited.

The trouble is that there's a fine line between spectacle and frippery, between inspiration and affectation. I can't bear domestic smugness of the Martha Stewart variety, or those gruesome aspirational features you read in lifestyle magazines—the ones where the nibbles are divine, the table settings are tasteful, and the food is exquisitely presented. I'd rather boil my head than make a canapé. But how do you know where the line is drawn?

The truth is, it's hard to engineer legendary dinners—they seem to be created by a combination of the right people, the right food, plus a major turning point in history. You may think that historical turning points may be out of our control, but what if you just happen to be in the right place at the right time? You must be ready to capitalize on fate. And the best way to do that? Study the classics: If we analyze the great meals of history, we should be able to throw together a passable equivalent of the Last Supper or an adequate Last Dinner on the

Titanic, perhaps, should circumstances present themselves. So here are some of the great dinners of all time.

The world's biggest single banquet

In terms of physical size, the biggest banquet is generally assumed to have been thrown by former French President Émil Loubet (1838–1929) to entertain France's 22,695 mayors on September 22, 1900, with all of them dressed in frock coats and crush hats. Huge tents were erected in the Tuileries gardens, with more than four miles of tables, and the waiters were forced to work on bicycles. The menu was: *Beef "Bellevue," Terrine of Rouen Duck*, roast chicken from Bresse and *Ballottine of Pheasant*. By all accounts, the event, organized by Maison Potel et Chabot, went remarkably smoothly.

What we learn from this is the function of sheer scale and civic pride. This is Power Eating. The French love a bit of local government and don't seem to mind their leaders making grandiose, expensive gestures, even if they end up paying for it themselves. And there's the rub: If you end up as president of France, you could happily bludgeon your way into culinary lore and get your employer, the French public, to pick up the tab.

The last dinner on the *Titanic*

The first-class menu on that last tragic day (April 14, 1912) included:

First course: Canapés à l'Amiral, Oysters à la Russe

Second course: Cream of Barley Soup

Third course: Poached Salmon with Mousseline Sauce

Fourth course: Chicken Lyonnaise

Fifth course: Roast Sirloin of Beef Forestière, Château Potatoes, Creamed Carrots

Sixth course: Chocolate Painted Eclairs with French Vanilla Cream

Seventh course: Assorted Fresh Fruits and Cheeses

After dinner: Coffee, Cigars

This meal is famous for everyone being in the wrong place at the wrong time. Hence I'm not sure that re-creating it is the best way to make a splash for yourself, though restaurants and dining clubs across the world seem to disagree: Anniversary re-enactments seem to be surprisingly common. You could try re-creating this meal with dinner jackets and a really, really big bag of ice, but that would probably be a bit sick.

The Gold Rush

In 1925 Charlie Chaplin ate his own boot in *The Gold Rush*, which became one of the classic scenes in movie history. It's Thanksgiving and he's in a remote cabin with Big Jim. Charlie cooks his own boot and serves it up as a grand-scale delicacy, laces, hobnails, and all. In reality, the boot was made out of licorice and after three days and sixty-five takes, Mack Swain (the actor playing Big Jim) and Chaplin both felt the laxative effects of the licorice.

Awesome stuff. A powerful combination of strength of purpose, conceptual feasting, and the triumph of spectacle over appetite.

The feast of the archbishop of York

When George Neville was appointed archbishop of York in 1466 the occasion was marked by a spectacular feast. The inventory lists 41,833 different items of meat and poultry, including 5,000 geese, 7,000 capons and 504 assorted stags, bucks, and roes (but only six wild bulls). This was washed down with 75,000 gallons of ale and 25,000 gallons of wine. Not for the faint-hearted. After the Reformation, the dissolution of the monasteries and all that, the Church found it hard to pick up the tab for shindigs of this scale.

What George had done here was use the classic approach of throwing money at the problem and, frankly, it worked. This meal has been quoted in so many books (like the one you're reading now) that it will never be forgotten.

The palace-warming feast of Assurnasirpal II

Assurnasirpal II (883–859 BC) had a simple approach to spectacular dining. Here's a man who just invited as many people as he could—69,574 to be precise. And then they partied for ten days solid.

This does sound a bit *nouveau riche*, but a ten-day-long party would take some forgetting.

Mitterrand's last meal

François ate ortolan, along with oysters, foie gras, and capon for his last ever meal on December 31, 1995. It's illegal to hunt or eat ortolans in France. Possibly because it's traditional to force these tiny birds to overeat in total darkness until they are unnaturally distended, then to drown them in brandy before cooking. But when you're the president of France, people seem to turn a blind eye. Ortolans are supposed to be eaten from underneath a napkin to hide your shame from God.

An interesting way to enter the history books—as a naughty eater— but once again, a testament to the power of the politician in France, and this story only serves to strengthen the legend. The most shocking element of the meal was that he ate *two* ortolans, flying in the face of tradition. Needless to say, he died a week later, apparently without any other food passing his lips.

A last supper

Mama Cass, the legendarily vast singer from the Mamas and the Papas, did not choke on a ham sandwich bought in London, as is famously assumed. She did, indeed, have a ham sandwich as her last meal, but her death on July 29, 1974, was due to a heart attack assumed to be linked to the effects of long-term obesity.

And here lies the most important lesson of all: Much as you shouldn't wear dirty knickers in case you get run over and the nurse sees them at the hospital, so you also shouldn't eat crap food in case you die swiftly afterward and are remembered for what you ate rather than what you did.

Trimalchio's feast

The most notorious feast of all time, this was a shockingly tasteless display of wealth and power, complete with absurd ceremony, public urination, humiliation of slaves, endless singing, and spectacular food. The vast menu included wild boar stuffed with live thrushes, pigs stuffed with sausages, and a multitude of birds and fish. The orgiastic excess ended with everyone wildly drunk and Trimalchio, the dissolute host, lying as if dead, reading out his will while musicians played the death march. Fabulous stuff.

It was, sadly, fiction; but by all accounts it was a pretty accurate description of many Roman feasts—Nero often hosted dinners along these lines. Written sometime before AD 65 by Petronius, the story of Trimalchio was a part of his *Satyricon*, a pornographic novel.

Before I die I hope to re-enact this gloriously tacky extravaganza. It's all about display, nothing about soul, and a complete waste of money; but I've always thought it would be a transcendental experience, and what a great way to write yourself into history. The basic meal is just about feasible, if cripplingly expensive, but the tricky bit is finding people willing to be slaves who will allow you to wipe your hands on their hair. For further reading and the original menu take a look at "How to stage a bacchanalian orgy" (see page 38).

The Last Supper

The original all-round dinner party triumph. The benchmark, if you will, against which all subsequent suppers have been judged. But when you pull it apart, Jesus took a simple entertaining format and added a twist of his own. Let's remind ourselves of the key elements . . .

The event

You will remember from your Bible reading that the Last Supper was a Passover meal, which is itself a meal replete with symbolism. (Passover is the most important festival in the Jewish year, celebrating the Jews' escape from captivity in Egypt; and Jesus was, obviously, a Jew.) The Bible is actually pretty scant on detail, but the basics are that he and the twelve apostles sat down to eat in an upstairs room in Jerusalem. For reasons I've never been able to fathom, a great deal of foot washing ensues. Jesus reveals that one of his guests will betray him, refusing to elaborate, then he does the most extraordinary thing: He breaks bread and gives it to his disciples, saying, "Take it; this is my body." Then he does the same with wine, saying, "This is my blood of the covenant." (See Matthew 26:17–35, Mark 14:1–26, Luke

22:7–38—these three all tell the story pretty much identically—and John 13:1–17:26, who goes on a bit about who loves whom.) The books of the New Testament vary on the detail but basically, after this, they all go for a walk and a variety of betrayals and miracles unfold, resulting in the Crucifixion and subsequent Resurrection of Christ.

It's powerful stuff, but in culinary terms it's very basic. Not a lot of detail, not much spectacle, and the food is barely mentioned. Our view of the event is often subsumed by Leonardo da Vinci's 1498 painting of the Last Supper in the refectory of the Convent of Santa Maria delle Grazie, Milan, one of the most famous paintings of all time. I'd imagine that for the vast majority of us, when we think of the Last Supper, it's Leonardo's version that springs to mind—but it isn't the only interpretation. Another sits in Cusco Cathedral, central Peru, and features Jesus about to tuck into a roasted guinea pig (more about that on page 219). Much better on many levels, if the truth be told.

Postsupper analysis

What happened here was a simple combination of well-chosen guests, a key historical moment, a twist (in this case, a betrayal), and the perspicacity to get Leonardo to paint a great picture for everyone to remember it by.

Christ made sure that his actions during the meal had resounding effects—the food wasn't that important, no one remembers the napkin rings, and there's not a canapé to be seen, thank the lord (no, really: thank the Lord). He even made a virtue out of the tragedy that was about to befall him. He invited twelve other diners that night, and ever since, tables of thirteen have been seen as terribly unlucky. (At the Savoy Hotel in London, if your table numbers thirteen they will set an extra place and produce Kaspar, a wooden cat, as the fourteenth diner.)

Now do it yourself

Staged with care and tenderness, your own re-creation of the Last Supper needn't be heretical or blasphemous. People have been doing it since the Middle Ages. Indeed, the Mystery Plays reigned supreme from the thirteenth to the sixteenth centuries (and in subsequent revivals in the 1980s—when Brian Glover as God with a broad Yorkshire accent entered the stage on a forklift truck at the English National Theatre, it was the coolest thing I'd ever seen), and they got away with biblical re-enactments from the Creation to the Ascension. The trick is to avoid making exaggerated claims: Saying that you're the Son of God won't wash, for starters.

The Last Supper is constantly re-created across the world in the form of Holy Communion, the most controversial and difficult tenet of Christianity and easily the most extraordinary eating experience of all time. The exact spiritual interpretation depends on your ecumenical stance. For some communicants it's purely symbolic, but others believe that they are actually *eating Christ's flesh and drinking his blood*. This sounds spectacular. Cannibalistic even. But as with most spiritual experiences, it's much, much more complicated than that, so I needed someone who could explain. I needed a priest.

Enter Father Evan Jones. Here is a man who exudes love. You can almost smell it wafting from him as he strides past on his way to church. He's my trusted guide on all matters Christian—he's calm, frank, and funny, and is comfortable talking about everything from sex to food. The last time he was in my house was after he'd christened my daughter, Daisy, and we'd got him terribly drunk by failing to mention that the tomatoes he thought were canapés were actually soused in vodka and hence highly alcoholic. Heh heh.

He describes giving communion as an act of love, "a meal with friends," a natural high giving him a "heightened awareness of who and what we are," the "awakening of a consciousness of the Creator," and a sensation of "feeding on the living God." This sounds amazing and I'm genuinely envious that I've never been able to experience this. I deflected enquiries into my, frankly, parlous spiritual state by asking whether or not consecrated wine tasted better than unconsecrated wine. Father Evan said that in its unspiritual state, communion wine tastes like Madeira. There's nothing wrong with drinking it for dinner and there's nothing sacred about it until it's been consecrated. During communion, however, the concept of taste is overridden by an intense spiritual focus. He added that he once took a bottle of communion wine to a party, and it was the last bottle to be drunk.

So how do you use the key elements of the Last Supper in the modern domestic environment? Well, to re-create the actual meal alone would be missing a transubstantiatory trick, but here is the basic Passover format, which you can embellish with whatever Da Vinci Code interpretation you fancy. (I read Dan Brown's *The Da Vinci Code* in the course of my research: great first half, but the author throws it all away by making his key villain a half-wit, posh twat.)

To start with, you'll need to have a massive spring-cleaning to clear out anything in your house related to leavened food—basically anything other than wine (luckily enough) that's fermented. This is symbolic of the fact that when the Jews fled their homes in Egypt, they left their bread unleavened. The meal itself is made up of:

Unleavened bread: Usually matzos made with unfermented wheat.

Wine: These days it's usually Manischewitz, a kosher wine of varying types. It can be an acquired taste.

Lamb: Served with artichokes.

Seder tray: A collection of dishes with ritual significance:

maror: Horseradish (or another bitter food) as a reminder of the bitterness of slavery.

karpas: A green veg dipped in brine as a reminder of the tears of captives.

zeroa: Lamb representing the paschal sacrifice on the eve of the Exodus.

betza: A roasted egg representing the sacrifice offered in the Temple.

haroset: A mixture of fruit and nuts the same color as the mud used to build the pharaoh's pyramids.

That's the food sorted. Now you need to engineer a spiritual crisis. Although you may not see yourself as the Son of Man, you could invite another living deity or cult leader along. Try asking Danny Wallace, who started his own cult called "Join Me" one day when he was bored. These days, however, he's a busy man; so if he's not free perhaps you should start your own cult with yourself as the leader. If that's aiming a bit high, but you still need to raise the level of spirituality around the table, you could just get yourself ordained as a member of the clergy. I got myself ordained online with the Spiritual Humanist Church—it takes about a minute—and I'm available for weddings, christenings, and blessings (sorry, Father Evan).

Another top tip from the Last Supper is to keep the focus off the table decorations and on the controversy. In fact, invite an enemy, in the way that Jesus invited his betrayer—an ex-girlfriend or boyfriend, perhaps—then all you can do is set the events in motion and hope for some sort of divine spectacle to unfold. If it does, you'll need to bear the following in mind: Make sure you only set your table on one side in the classic sitcom style—because you'll need a picture, and you don't want a shot of everyone's backs. A real artist of Michelangelo's standard would be useful but, to be fair, a photo would be grand.

Of course, the Lord's masterstroke was to get a great write-up in the Bible. He knew the value of faith mixed with a clever bit of PR, and this launched a highly successful religion and combined sales of over six billion Bibles. (In case you're interested, the second bestselling book of all time is generally accepted to be Mao Tse-tung's *Quotations from Chairman Mao*. It was published as recently as 1966 but has already racked up 900 million copies sold.)

Cracking this last bit is the tough one. Obviously you need to have lived a spectacular life of good works and adventure that's worth writing about. Changing the course of humanity would be useful, as would a fair smattering of miracles. Being the Lamb of God would help. That would make you a very special person indeed, but if you think you fit the bill, I'm sure we could get the story in *Food & Beverage* magazine at the very least. I'd be happy to cook you supper and write it up as best I can. Just don't expect anything fancy to eat.

MUSIC SUGGESTIONS

Aretha Franklin's *Amazing Grace* gospel album, Elvis's gospel album *Ultimate Gospel*, with twenty-four tub-thumping tracks, *Jesus Christ Superstar*—the 1996 double-disc version. Best musical ever.

How To Stage a Bacchanalian Orgy
In the comfort of your own home

For gastronomic thrill seekers and social whirligigs alike, bacchanalian orgies are surely the pinnacle of exhibitionist entertaining. They are the ultimate in transcendental eating experiences: hallucinatory cocktails of decadent arcana and bizarre food. And, as anyone who's thrown one knows all too well, they can be a bitch to pull off. Too *soigné*, and they feel like an elaborate funeral to celebrate the death of taste. Too relaxed, and before you know it you're in Delta House circa 1977 with John Belushi drinking a flagon of his own pee. But deftly staged, a truly great BO should leave the discerning guests feeling like they've been on a fleeting visit to hospitality heaven.

The modern BO is essentially a Renaissance construct—classical Greece lends order and harmony, an obsession with washing, ritual, and poetry, while late imperial Rome is plundered for its "strap-on-a-large-one," ABBA Forever, *fin de siècle* abandonment. So we'll be creating a mixture of a Greek symposium and a Roman *convivium*. And just to be absolutely clear, the "orgy" bit is primarily about the orgiastic sense of sensual enlightenment. Optional bolt-ons, such as wife-swapping and other fornication-based fun, are really a matter best dealt with by the individual host and his conscience.

Why Bacchus? Why orgy?

The modern BO has little to do with the torrid, bloodthirsty, cross-dressing rites of ancient times (not the least for legal reasons) but let's indulge in a brief history lesson nonetheless. The Bacchanalia were originally religious rites performed in honor of Bacchus, who is not only the god of wine but also is largely interchangeable with Dionysus, god of fertility. Most rites were relatively tame, but there were a fair few that involved the tearing apart of live bulls, cross-dressing, licentiousness, and jiggery-pokery of both the straight and the gay variety. The Greek playwright Euripides (480–406 BC) wrote of infanticide and hordes of cow-tipping women in his seminal text on the matter, *The Bacchae*. (Cow-tipping is a game played by rural troublemakers that involves pushing over sleeping cows.)

But what was it all for? The worship of Bacchus/Dionysus was intended to enhance your afterlife, and this was enormously important to believers. The crazed rites and the accompanying musical cacophony were also intended to drive the worshipper out of her wits and, in this ecstasy, transcend her earthly bounds. At around 500 BC the cult was uniquely female, but, as you can imagine, when the boys saw what fun was to be had, they wanted in on the party, and BOs soon became a general excuse for drunken, licentious excess, until they were finally forbidden by Roman law in 186 BC.

But, of course, when the Romans took over, the feasting gave rise to many more exciting tales of excess. Dancing girls, transvestites, dwarves, and clowns weren't the half of it: Caligula enjoyed dining while prisoners were tortured and killed, Lucius Verus watched gladiators fighting, P. Vedius Pollio held a feast during which a cupbearer broke a goblet and had his hands cut off and hung around his neck as punishment. If the food was wrongly or badly cooked, the chef was stripped and beaten. There was a fair amount of sex, too, if that's your bag. A banquet that Tigellinus threw for Nero in AD 64 was renowned for having pleasure pavilions and brothels beside the floating banquet table. The guests would visit them to have sex with the women therein, who weren't ordinary prostitutes, but "the most beautiful and distinguished [women] in the city" according to the historian Dio Cassius.

So, with an official history of over three hundred of your classical years, it's rather hard to draw up the definitive authentic version of a BO. Luckily, they left us with some guidebooks, including the only reliable classical cookbook—Apicius's *De Re Coquinaria*, from the first century—as well as Trimalchio's feast from Petronius's *Satyricon*.

The food

The exact menu depends on your budget and bravery, but you'll need three basic courses with a spread of entirely separate dishes. The first course is called *gustatio*, and is generally a selection of hors d'oeuvres or *amuses bouches*, accompanied by a spiced, honeyed wine. Then we have the main section of the meal, the *cena*, and this is itself broken down into a minimum of three courses—*prima*, *secunda*, and *tertia*. This is followed, finally, by the *mensae secundae*, including succulent fruits, such as figs and grapes, nuts, and sometimes more shellfish.

The types of food we're looking for are flights of fancy and marvels of sybaritic indulgence, such as those provided by the Roman Elagabalus, whose guests ate camels' feet, the combs from live chickens, peacocks' tongues, flamingos' brains, and nightingales' tongues. These are hard to find in your local supermarket, but a good butcher will supply offal, game, and a variety of small animals. Apicius's *De Re Coquinaria* is full of unlikely-sounding combinations and lord knows how many recipes for sauces. There's a translation and reinterpretation by John Edwards called *The Roman Cookery of Apicius*. It's got tripe with fennel, fried testicles, and peas with sausage and calf brains.

A good scattering of oysters, quails, and snails would work, along with any other small animals you can lay your hands on—pigeon, rabbit, dormice (outlawed in 115 BC, but hey). Then try out some insects (see page 47)—you can buy deep-fried insects in cans—pigs' trotters with salsa verde, testicles (see page 166), pressed ears (see page 171), seaweed or laver bread (see page 111), *Mock Turtle Soup* (see page 152) and *Rhinoceros Soup* (see page 167). Then you need a central dish to give focus to the meal—I'd push the boat out a bit by investing in a suckling pig (see page 194), or perhaps suckling kid goat (in season around Easter).

The menu for Trimalchio's feast is a glorious, if hideously expensive, guide. Many of the ingredients are hard to come by, so I've added my suggestions for alternatives in square brackets.

Sensual manipulation

Much of the BO is about using the physical environment to control the senses. So how to set up your dining room? A conventional dining table will be useless as it's too food-focused and confrontational. The Roman-style *triclinium* was not just for dining in—it acted as an arena, a theater, and a place of worship as well. Tricky in modern urban flats.

MENU FOR TRIMALCHIO'S FEAST

Gustatio
(hors d'oeuvres)

Olives • Dormice sprinkled with honey and poppy seeds
[if you can't catch any dormice, quails will have to do]
Grilled sausages • Damsons and pomegranate seeds
Fig-peckers in spiced egg yolk [again, use quails]
Muslum (honeyed wine)

Cena
(main meal in three sections: ferculum, secunda, and tertia)

Chick peas [whip up a salad] • Beef [carpaccio] • Kidneys [try devilled]
Myrtle [use juniper and bayberries—perhaps to make a jelly]
Figs • A sterile sow's womb
[crikey—maybe a tripe dish or some French sausages, such as andouillettes]
Tarts and honey cakes
Scorpion fish [use baked gurnard if you can't find any]
An eyefish
[lordy—perhaps giant catfish, the eyes of which are a delicacy for Laotians]
Lobster, goose, red mullet—two of each, all served with bread
Roast fattened fowls • Sow bellies [again, it's tripe time] • Hare
Roast whole wild boar with dates, stuffed with live thrushes
[quails again], and piglets made of cakes [Yorkshire pudding]
Boiled whole pig stuffed with sausage and black puddings

secundae Mensae

Fruits • Cakes • Goose eggs
Boned, fattened chickens • Pastries stuffed with raisins and nuts
Quinces and pork dressed up as birds and fish
Oysters and scallops • Snails

So unless you can fit three full-sized sofas and a table in your front room, we're looking at the floor. Use your biggest room and clear as much furniture and junk out as is feasible. Create a luxurious sense of abandon with scatter cushions and pillows around the edges of the room, with specific places for your guests laid out in a U-shape. If you have them, a patchwork of rugs can be nice. Make sure you leave a stage area where guests can perform.

In front of each guest, you'll need some sort of table. It'll need to fit glasses and plates, bowls for hand washing, a *salinium* (salt cellar) and an *acetabulum* (bottle of vinegar). Remember to leave enough room for feet washing.

It's best to keep the lighting low—a liberal scattering of candles should do the trick. The room should be perfumed with expensive aromatic oils heated in a censer (or failing that, a smelly candle from the Body Shop). Appropriate perfumes are frankincense, sandalwood, and patchouli, but make sure they aren't too strong, otherwise your guests may feel a bit queasy.

A good scattering of decoration can help—the Romans were rightly fond of flower petals spread over the floor or falling from above the diners while they ate. I'd also decorate the table with branches and creeping ivy, and a few large plants borrowed from the garden are useful. We're trying to build a sense of sensual abandon here.

A note on *vomitoria*: In theory your guests should overeat, throw up to make space for more, then start all over again. In practice I've found it intensely difficult to affect this level of abandon, but if you manage it, they could always use the bathroom.

Your guests

The French gastronome Anthelme Brillat-Savarin (1755–1826), who knew a thing or two about throwing a party, reckoned twelve to be the perfect number of dinner guests. The collective term for a group of *maenads* (the original bacchanalian orgiasts) was generally a "frenzied horde," and hence exact numbers are hard to define. The Romans were much clearer, suggesting three couches, each holding three diners. I tend to agree with the latter. As to whom you should invite, it's always good to get a few *bon viveurs*, renowned epicures, and feted poets, but it doesn't really matter if your friends are neither famous nor witty, because chatting won't be a major feature of the evening. They'll have too much to do, what with all the listening, eating, performing, and washing that's planned.

A note on slaves

Tricky one, this. While feasts in the Greek and Roman empires were often civilized and refined, they were, as the art historian Sir Roy Strong puts it in his book *Feast*, "underpinned by a vast substructure of slavery, which was in turn based upon brutality, violence and every form of cruel subjection." Nonetheless, the thorny question of appropriate staff must be dealt with. Someone needs to welcome the guests, wash their hands and feet at various intervals, as well as ferry plates of food around—all this while singing constantly.

Slaves used to be treated abominably by their owners and were ritually humiliated for any perceived fault. So, unsurprisingly, good ones are getting harder to come by. A call to any extras agency shows you that for a relatively bargain sum of 50 bucks (more for a dwarf) an out-of-work actor is willing to come around to carry out menial tasks for an evening; but once it's a cash arrangement, it's really not the same. You could try employing your own offspring to carry out these tasks in return for favors, though perhaps it's better that they don't see you and your friends in the sort of state you've got planned.

Performance

The evening should be broken up by regular bouts of poetry reading, political debate, foot washing, singing, drinking games, and dancing. If you have the resources, a troupe of dancing girls from Cadiz would be marvelous, but otherwise the only recourse is the guests themselves. Hence, you should try to include on your guest list at least one person who can hold a tune, crack off an adequate samba on a toy xylophone, or at least strum "Mrs. Robinson" on the guitar.

You should try to fill the room with visual diversions, too. I have a Super 8mm projector and a collection of classic '60s soft porn on celluloid that I could lend you, but they can give people the wrong idea. Try playing silent or nondialogue movies such as *Koyaanisqatsi* and *Powaqqatsi*. (See page 45 for music suggestions.)

It is essential that your party has frequent artistic performances to keep building up that sensual head of steam. If all else fails, you can pick up a karaoke machine for a few bucks these days and they aren't to be sniffed at.

The running order of the symposium

So what actually happens during a bacchanalian orgy? Here's a template to work from:

Before arrival

All guests should bathe before arriving. You want them cleansed of both grit and worries, with their minds clean and ready to perform.

On arrival

Guests should be greeted with a song and be given a gift, preferably an enigmatic one that acts as a statement about what you think of them.

Feet washing #1

Guests should remove their shoes when they arrive and swiftly afterward they should have their feet washed. Although the Romans wouldn't have agreed, in our version the host will have to do this for each guest at least the first time around. They should then go straight to the *triclinium*. Heavenly yet esoteric music should be played on arrival—perhaps a soundtrack of birdsong or whale noises.

Taking assembly

When all the guests have arrived, the symposiarch (the person who's running the orgy) sets the subjects for debate and decides on the proportion of water that should be mixed with the wine. I suspect that for most symposiarchs, a happy balance is likely to be no water and lots of wine. It would be useful to introduce everyone at this stage, preferably with a short poem explaining a little about them.

Anointment

Guests should anoint themselves with perfume. Not Calvin Klein Eternity, but a dab of sandalwood or similar.

Hand washing #1

Hands should be washed before *every* course.

Music

Musicians serenade the guests. If you don't have any musicians, it's probably too early for karaoke, so try playing some CDs of ancient music (see page 45).

Gustatio *(hors d'oeuvres)*

Served while someone reads out loud from their works.

Hand/Feet washing #2

Remove the plates while singing. More washing of hands and feet. A brief round of political debate should be introduced.

Cena *(entrées)*

The main courses are served, broken up into three sections (*prima, secunda,* and *tertia*). If you have some dancing girls, now's their big moment. Otherwise, encourage your guests to take the floor. Chaotic revelry should ensue, possibly including fights and inappropriate outrages.

Hand/Feet washing #3

Remove the plates while singing. More washing of hands and feet.

Secundae mensae *(dessert)*

The final course is served to more music, and the games should begin. I recommend starting with simple classics like Jenga and the Name Game, and moving on to vicious drinking games as you see fit. Making balloon animals would be useful here (I'm actually rather good at this).

> **A footnote on decadence:** While it is a gastronaut's duty to venture forth into the culinary unknown, we should also learn a lesson from the Romans: It can all go too far. From 182 BC onward they realized that this level of indulgence couldn't continue without undermining a civilization built on austerity, so they introduced laws on how many guests could be entertained at once, what could be eaten, and how much could be spent on food. Of course, it didn't work, and the tales of excess continued. But let's remember how the more decadent rulers ended their days: Murder and treachery, and finally the Empire crumbled and fell apart in AD 476. You be careful out there.

Decline

At some point, your guests should start passing out—this is a good sign, and shouldn't be taken as an insult. Visits to the *vomitorium* are appropriate from now on. What you're after is a scene of thorough devastation in the morning, featuring a guest or two who forgot to return home.

MUSIC SUGGESTIONS

Classical: the Kronos Quartet's *Early Music* is useful. Henry Purcell is good stuff, too. You could also try Arvo Pärt's *Tabula Rasa*.

You'll need to stop for poetry and philosophy readings during the evening, but if your friends just don't cut it in the poetry department, there's an amazing CD called *The Spoken Word—Poets*, available online. This features some of the greatest poets of all time reciting their work and it includes a remarkable (if a bit scratchy) 1890 recording of Tennyson himself reading from "The Charge of the Light Brigade." There are also readings by Browning, W. B. Yeats, T. S. Eliot, and Robert Graves, but, sadly, both Shakespeare and Chaucer are missing. You can also get *Voices of History*, featuring clips of Gladstone, Gandhi, Trotsky, and Florence Nightingale, as well as Edward VIII's abdication speech in its entirety.

Why Not Eat Insects?

In 1885 a chap by the name of Vincent M. Holt wrote a pamphlet entitled *Why Not Eat Insects?* Vince was, of course, writing in the noble tradition of the dotty English amateur botanist with nothing better to do, and his little ninety-nine-page beauty set the world to rights, solving the dual ills of world hunger and crop infestation in a flash. Eat the bugs that damage the plants, so his theory went, and the farmer will see his harvest increase and the poor need never go hungry again. While rather optimistic, Vince's theory wasn't entirely without merit. If the toffs would only set a good example to the peasantry, we'd all be scarfing *Potage aux Limaces à la Chinois* (slug soup) like it was going out of fashion.

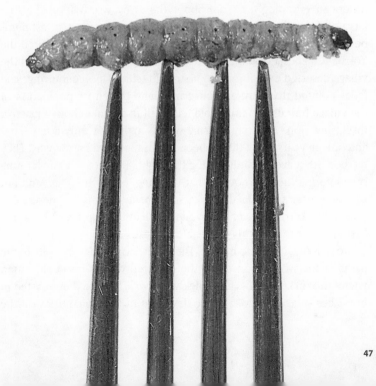

I'm not kidding myself that any great number of you have the slight-est intention of eating insects, but consider this: Thousands of tons of insect secretions are eaten every year by the English alone in the form of honey. Is it really that much of a jump? And you probably eat a huge amount of insects anyway—the U.S. Food and Drug Administration permits 205 insect fragments per pound in wheat flour. Insects are numerous, cheap, and readily available. They have been described as the most successful class of living organisms, so it seems perverse *not* to eat them. (Incidentally, the total weight of insects eaten every year by spiders is more than the total weight of humans in the world.)

Of course, I'd be remiss if I didn't admit that collecting insects is a young man's game. It's all very easy catching ants and worms, but the real delicacies are grasshoppers, which are a bitch to lay your hands on in any great numbers. Indeed, I've just bought a can of pre-prepared grasshoppers from a Thai Web site. It's a bargain until you have to add up the postage and handling. If you're on a more slender budget, however, a bit of hedgerow foraging should do nicely for an interesting supper.

Sometimes it's feast or famine with insects. Samuel Barrett, an American ethnologist, wrote about the army worm (probably the larva of the cotton moth), which would suddenly appear in vast num-bers every few years. On the morning of May 15, 1904, he visited the Yokaia Rancheria of the Pomo tribe of American Indians, to find the village deserted except for two hoary old fellas. Upon enquiring, said fellas pointed thataway, and our Sam found the entire population of the village (minus two hoary old fellas) all in a lather about a massive insect invasion. Apparently, army worms arrive for only a few days, and only in years when there's been lots of fog—lord knows why. They feed on ash leaves, mainly during the night, and move at an alarming speed during the afternoons. That morning, out of the blue, and not having written or phoned for years, the army worms had descended on the Pomo tribe's river. Everyone had had to drop everything in a flash in order to reap this unreliable harvest.

Not a moment was to be lost. The tribespeople dug large pits in the paths of the worms and threw the captured worms into cold water, where in Sam's words, "They quickly drown. They are then roasted in hot ashes or are boiled, and are devoured in large quantities on the spot. When everyone has satisfied his appetite, the cooked worms are spread out in the sun to dry for winter use." However, if you fancy getting your grubby mitts on some of them thar army worms, you'll definitely need to be wearing your lucky pants. Sam's friends hadn't seen the worms for nigh on six years, and they stuck around for only a few days. However, that May the Pomo Indians went home with about 110 pounds of the little fellas.

I've given a few everyday recipes that shouldn't require such a stroke of good fortune (see pages 160–162). Happy hunting.

How Britain Lost Its Culinary Edge

What do the following have in common: *Fitless Cock, Clapshot, The Dean's Cream, Wet Nelly, Aberdeen Nips, Girdle Sponges, Flummery, Hunters' Buns, Lancashire Nuts,* and *Slot?* They are all bloody silly names given to perfectly good foods.

The recent renaissance in British cuisine was a long time coming. The theory is that way back in the mists of time we used to have a rich culinary tradition, and the peasantry had a symbiotic relationship with the land. Then, around the time of the Industrial Revolution (1750 to you, squire), it all went pear-shaped. The masses were forced from the land that used to support and feed them, and into cities, causing a "dislocation in the food supply" (according to Dorothy Hartley's *Food in England*) and a culinary decline.

The general theory is that before the Industrial Revolution the peasantry, although mired in grinding poverty, *droit de seigneur*, and all that, generally managed a healthy and ample diet because they were given a generous patch of land to farm; they kept chickens and a pig, and had all the time in the world to make oatcakes, cheese, and milk puddings.

The trouble is that linking culinary decline with the Industrial Revolution never quite rings true. The Industrial Revolution made its way to France (I hear they even make cars these days), yet they never lost their culinary élan.

No. There's a better reason for our culinary decline: bad marketing. When the French created foods, they were wise to the customer, so created wonderful, memorable names such as *Vol-au-Vent* ("flying in the wind"), *Châtelaine, Bouillabaisse, Mirepoix, Tartiflette* and *Millefeuille.* They aren't necessarily the best foods in the world (I'd rather boil my own head than make a *Vol-au-Vent*) but you have to admit that they *sound* great.

So what do the Brits do? We decide, quite rightly, that our strongest national characteristic is a good sense of humor and then, quite wrongly, that this humor should be the basis for our national cuisine. And so we came up with *Inky-Pinky, Flummery, Cullen Skink, Beef Cecils* and *Buckinghamshire Bacon Badger*. Must have been funny at the time, watching all that culinary potential being laughed down the drain.

Many of the names of our ancient foods are so silly that you wonder if the name was invented before the dish. Take a look at these:

Fitless Cock: Oatmeal pudding made roughly chicken-shaped

Clapshot: Equal quantities of mashed potatoes and turnips with a sprinkling of chives and lard, very delicious (see page 130)

The Dean's Cream: Fool (a mixture of fruit and whipped cream) made with sponge cake, jam, and sherry, invented in Cambridge

Wet Nelly: A suet-based pudding (like roly-poly) made with bread crusts and spices

Aberdeen Nips: Left-over smoked haddock on toast

Girdle Sponges: Sponge cakes made in a frying pan

Flummery: A molded pudding using lemons, egg yolks, and rather a lot of brandy (see page 141)

Hunters' Buns: Spicy oatmeal biscuits

Lancashire Nuts: Custard cream–like biscuits with a sweet butter filling

Hasty Pudding: A gloopy mixture of butter, flour, milk, eggs, and sugar (see page 139)

Slot: Cod roe dumplings

Inky-Pinky: A kind of slurry made up of left-over beef and stock

Whim-Wham: A fool with sponge fingers and redcurrant jelly

Beef Cecils: Rather exotic meatballs

Priddy Oggies: Pork and cheese pasty

Buckinghamshire Bacon Badger: A steamed suet pudding made with bacon and potato (but no badger, see page 118)

Huffkins: Milk-based bread rolls

Glasgow Magistrates: Stuffed, baked herrings

Wow-Wow Sauce: Pickled walnut gravy

Brotherly Love: Buns made in Suffolk

Singing Hinnies: Currant cakes

Love in Disguise: Stuffed, baked calves' hearts

This list barely scratches the surface—take a look at Lizzie Boyd's *British Cookery* for thousands more. It's all very funny, but the trouble is that when culinary history was being laid down hundreds of years ago, fashion was dictated by the nobility, and presumably nobles don't eat *Girdle Sponges*. In 1816 the Prince Regent famously dragged Antonin Carême across the Channel to be his chef. Why did he choose a Frenchman? Because British chefs made *Priddy Oggies*, while Frenchmen made *Petits Vol-au-Vents à la Nesle*. See? It's all in the marketing.

Of course, these days the marketing *chaussure* is firmly on the other *pied*. (Have you watched French TV ads? Oh, *mon Dieu!*) British cheese making is undergoing a renaissance, London is regularly cited as the restaurant capital of the world (OK, most cities seem to make this claim), French food is, at least in my experience, in the doldrums and—get this—they're even watching our very own Jamie Oliver in translation.

> **Incidentally:** If ornate French food terminology is your thing, you'll love Louis Saulnier's *Le Repertoire de la Cuisine*, which offers 7,000 French culinary terms, each with a rudimentary recipe. For sole alone it lists 345 different ways of cooking it. If you're desperate to know your *Côtelettes d'Artois* from your *Côtelettes Pojarsky*, or you run a small-town vanity restaurant (and there's nothing wrong with that), you need this book.

I like to think that our current ascendancy is due to an enlightened, less snobbish approach to food—we no longer see French food as the culinary zenith. (I always snigger when I see a British menu scattered with French words—it always seems a little old-fashioned.) It would make Brillat-Savarin turn in his grave, but I like the idea that British food comes served with a slice of humor. Even more so when it's a bit juvenile and toilet-based. I love the fact that, as a nation, we choose names for our food that are true to our national characteristics of naughtiness and mischief making. But perhaps that's just me.

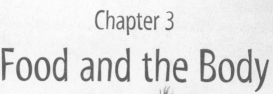

Chapter 3
Food and the Body

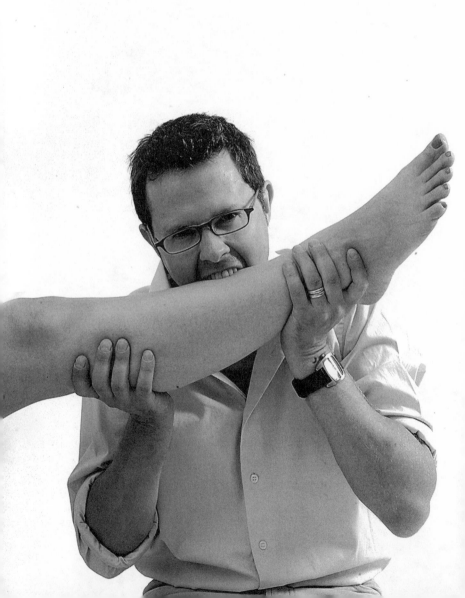

Our Secret Cannibal Desires

Anthropophagy is a rum old game. I'd love to say that it has a long and noble history, but sadly a few bad eggs (namely Dahmer, Shawcross, Kemper, and Gecht) have ruined cannibalism as a popular branch of gastronomy for the rest of us. Far be it from me to dictate what constitutes a nutritious, balanced, yet varied diet, but you should be aware that there are delicate moral issues regarding the consumption of human flesh. Moral outrage is no good indicator of legality, and the recent case of the engineer-munching Armin Meiwes has done nothing to clarify the situation.

Gastronautical Survey Result	
Are you tasty?	
Tasty	54%
Not tasty	28%
Don't know	18%

A lot of hysterical nonsense has been written about cannibalism, so let's get the basics out of the way so that we can proceed straight to the fun:

🔊 Reports about cannibalism are invariably secondhand. A liberal sprinkling of cannibalism was often deployed to help strengthen racist polemics, often without a shred of substantiation, whenever a hint of savagery was useful (especially by nineteenth-century missionaries needing to drum up funds). Conversely, the explorer David Livingstone, in his 1865 *Zambesi*, declared that "Nearly all blacks believe the whites to be cannibals."

🔊 My old and rather smelly *Shorter Oxford English Dictionary* lists cannibalism as "the practice of eating one's kind."

🔊 The earliest evidence of cannibalism is claimed to be on a 600,000-year-old skull found in Ethiopia. Peking Man (who lived about 500,000 ago) is also suspected of it.

🖝 Some say that human flesh tastes like pork, with a minority (albeit a more believable minority) claiming beef. These sources are rarely firsthand.

🖝 In China, during the Ming and Ch'ing dynasties (1368–1912), it was not uncommon for a daughter whose parent was mortally ill to cut a slice of flesh from her own thigh and make a broth out of it for the parent to drink.

🖝 The Roman emperor Nero spread the rumor that the Last Supper was a form of cannibalism. In the Bible John (6:55–56) quotes Jesus as saying "For my flesh is meat indeed, and my blood is drink indeed . . . He that eateth my flesh, and drinketh my blood, dwelleth in me, and I in him." He did have a point.

🖝 During World War II, Britain's Minister of Food (Lord Woolton) rejected a serious suggestion from his scientific advisers to ease the effects of rationing by using the surplus of blood donated by the enthusiastic public to make black puddings.

🖝 Kuru is a CJD-like disease that was controversially identified in Papua New Guinea as a result of the ritualized eating of brains of recently deceased tribal members. The practice stopped in 1957.

🖝 The movie *Alive* is the true story of a Uruguayan rugby team whose plane crashed in the Andes in 1972; they reluctantly resorted to eating each other after ten days. However, the best bit of the movie is the midair explosion.

Gastronautical Survey Result	
If you were a cannibal, which famous person would you most like to eat?	
Brad Pitt	5%
Kylie Minogue	3.5%
Nigella Lawson	3%
Ainsley Harriott	3%
Wouldn't eat a famous person	3%
Cameron Diaz	2.5%
Delia Smith	2.5%
Britney Spears	2.5%
George Clooney	2%
George W. Bush	2%

The remaining 71 percent offered no clear favorites but included Dawn French, Lisa Riley, the Reverend Iain Paisley, Vanessa Feltz, Luciano Pavarotti, Napoleon Bonaparte, Chris Tarrant ("if I can kill him first"), Roseanne Barr, the Rock, and Hattie Jacques.

Gastronautical Survey Result	
If you were a cannibal, which body part would you most like to eat?	
Thigh	17%
Buttock/rump/bottom	15%
Breast	6%
Cheeks	5%
Ear	4.5%
Leg	4.5%
Arm	4%
Liver	4%
Baby's bottom	3%
Testicles	2%

The remaining 35 percent offered no clear preference.

✑ Famine and war have resulted in widespread reports of cannibalism in most countries at one time or another, including England and Ireland between AD 695 and 700.

My wife has a fondness for biting my chin. I don't know why—it's not particularly attractive. I, for my part, am rather partial to biting her arse. But when I give her a playful bite, I'm occasionally overcome by the urge to lock those jaws and rip off a chunk. I thought it might be nascent psychosis, but the Gastronautical Survey revealed that we've all wondered what others would taste like and which bit would be the most tasty.

A Personal Journey Into Cannibalism

O n a rainy spring morning I decided to discover whether or not cannibalism is legal. I contacted the UK's Home Office, examined the Crown Prosecution Service's Web site and called the Citizens Advice Bureau. I looked through all the Web sites hosted by Adviceguide, the Law Commission, the Metropolitan Police, and even an online guide to legal terms. Not a sausage. Either no one could tell me and didn't know who else might be able to help, or no one was qualified to tell me, or they thought I was joking.

It transpires that you can't necessarily find out if something you are planning to do is illegal. I always thought that the government—someone—would have a big crime-identifying search engine that you can type your planned transgression into and find out a) if it's illegal and b) what the penalty is likely to be if you go ahead and do it anyway. There was only one thing for it: Ask the local fuzz.

The following morning I visited the Islington police station in north London. The place was quiet; empty except for a lingering sense of human tragedy and a few people waiting quietly on plastic chairs. I began to wonder if my quest was a flippant waste of police time, but remembering how much the Met had just added to my council tax, I approached the little window with my head held high. I was a customer.

The policeman looked young and friendly, so I came straight out with it: "Is cannibalism illegal?" He raised his unamused policeman's eyebrow, delivered his unamused policeman's pause, and suddenly I felt very small and very stupid. I explained that I was trying to find out a question of law, I'd looked through all the Home Office literature and every legal Web site I could find, but no one could help me. Where do you go to find out if something's illegal or not? After another long pause he said, "Books." "Which books?" I said. "I don't know," he said. "Have you tried Borders?" I laughed. On the one hand, no, I had not tried Borders. But on the other hand, this bloke was a flatfoot, a copper. He was in charge of the law; surely he must be able to give me an answer. Was there anyone else he could ask? He grudgingly left his place at the window and went into the station room behind him. I was expecting to hear the place roar with laughter, but there was nothing. He'd probably gone to make a cup of tea. Two minutes later he reappeared, shaking his head. "We're *pretty* sure it's illegal, but we're not *completely* sure. Is that any help?" Well, no, not really, but thanks all the same. "Funny, isn't it, that you can't find out if something's illegal?" I said. He clearly didn't think so, so I left him to do something more important.

Three minutes later I was in Borders, which has a large and, to the prospective cannibal, unhelpful legal section. I flicked through every book on the shelves to no avail. I did, however, find a book called *Medical Law* by Messrs. Kennedy and Grubb, in which I learned that a corpse falls under a "no property" rule, and cannot therefore be owned by anyone. Excellent. Also, in a book called *The Control of Living Body Material* by B. M. Dickens, I discovered that if you are still alive, you can "assert [a] right of ownership . . . for good reason or for no good reason, over such things as excrement, fluid waste, secretions, hair, fingernails, toenails, blood." Interesting but not, strictly speaking, helpful.

So in the end all roads led, as they inevitably do, to a lawyer. In this case, my friend John (his real name), who explained that a lot of law, particularly common law, is not written down in statutes. Rather, the legal system relies on case law, the concept of precedent and interpretation. Basically, what this means is that if someone was found guilty (or not) of a similar charge in the past, then the same should apply to you, though it's all open to interpretation. So what you need is not a book of laws, it is . . . a lawyer, who will not be able to tell you anything definite, but will be able to give you an *opinion*. Funny, that. Another big-shot lawyer called Richard (his real name) couldn't establish that cannibalism of itself is illegal, but warned that the sourcing of the flesh was the gray area—was somebody murdered? Was it cut from a living person? If so, it's grievous bodily harm irrespective of whether they consented. Right—there's an answer of sorts.

My conclusion was that if I wanted a definitive answer to any of these questions, I had to go out, commit my protocrime and then invite prosecution. So it's not so much the cannibalism that's illegal, as the steps you've taken to get there. Like killing somebody. This is bad and should be avoided at all costs. And if you want to share a lump of your own arm with your mates? The only way to find out the consequences is to give it a go.

Cannibal Recipes

'll readily admit that I am fascinated (and slightly scared) by the idea of eating human flesh. However, other than little snippets of my personal jetsam (I am an inveterate biter of my own cuticles), I haven't yet had the opportunity. I think that we should taste everything we possibly can and that wasting food, especially meat, is a tragedy. I've made complex moral justifications for being an omnivore and it seems wrong that these shouldn't be extended to eating humans. I know that there are other moral issues, but I'm just not sure if they wash. It's not a question of disrespect for humanity: In many cannibal cultures the act of eating someone after their death is the ultimate tribute.

I've eaten horse, donkey, and all sorts of animals that might be seen as pets; and it's impossible to escape the fact that some people think this is wrong because an emotional connection has been made with the species, but I just can't agree that this translates into moral absolutes. I'm eating *a* rabbit, not *your* rabbit. Would I eat my pet rabbit if he died? No. I would bury him in my garden so that I could remember the joy he gave me. But did I enjoy the roast wild rabbit we ate last week? You bet I did, and I don't feel guilty. A rabbit is cute, but so is a cow, and although I'm grateful that I can eat meat, I'm never gleeful that an animal has died for my meal. I have the utmost respect for it and I hope it lived a happy life and had an unanticipated death.

So eating human flesh is a tricky thought—I probably wouldn't eat my own leg because I'd be too upset about having lost it. But someone else's? If I could sort out the emotional turmoil, I think I've got the moral bit cracked.

One of the few calm and thoughtful, purportedly firsthand accounts of eating human flesh is William Bueler Seabrook's *Jungle Ways*. He lived with the African Gueru tribe and observed them eating a man who had been killed in battle. Their reaction on being asked why they ate human flesh was, "Why shouldn't we eat it?" They reckoned the loin cuts, ribs, and rump steak were the best for solid meat, but the tribesmen were too suspicious to allow William to eat any—they knew that the practice was frowned on by the authorities.

Seabrook wasn't able to eat human flesh in Africa, but apparently managed to find some in France, where he went to write about his experiences. A hospital intern at the Sorbonne got hold of a loin and a steak for him from someone killed in an accident. The flesh resembled good beef but was slightly less red, with faintly yellow solid fat. The loin was spit-roasted and the steak grilled. When roasted, the meat turned grayish, as lamb does, rather than reddish like beef. Seabrook said it tasted good, like mature veal, but not quite the same as beef. So the long-held belief that human flesh tastes like pork (the "long pig" myth) is nonsense, it would seem.

> I've just listened to BBC Radio 4's *Food Programme,* and a Tory MP claimed that the British people **without exception** do not want to eat horsemeat. I'd have begged to differ if I hadn't just fallen off my chair.

And so it is with a bowed head that I offer recipes I haven't yet tested. As is common with ancient recipes, the authors left a lot of detail out, but these are genuine recipes from relatively reliable sources. The recipes of famous modern cannibals are of little consequence as they are clearly the result of fevered minds, not of the gourmet kind. Incidentally, after Meiwes was convicted (of manslaughter) there were numerous press reports that he was going to publish the recipes, together with an autobiography, at a later date. And one last thing: Don't go killing someone to try these out. I know who'll get in trouble for it. Me.

Boiled Prisoner

The causes of cannibalism in ancient China were manifold: war, famine, hatred, natural disaster, or filial piety. In Yuan and Ming times (1279–1644) minced human was popular, and there are references to steamed dumplings made with minced man.

During the Sung dynasty (960–1279), Chuang Ch'o notes that enemies were either grilled over the fire, boiled in hot water, or had boiling water poured over them while their hands and feet were tied. Afterward, the skin of the boiled or steamed bodies was peeled and the human flesh without the skin was put into a cauldron to stew. When completely cooked, it was ready for eating. Usually a man's two thighs and a woman's two breasts were carved out first and eaten.

Voodoo Stew

Writing in 1884, Sir Spenser St. John (1825–1910), a British consul in Haiti, recalled the following account of cannibalism, described during a trial noted for confessions extracted by torture, in his notorious book *Hayti, or the Black Republic*. After flaying, the flesh is cut from the bones and placed in a wooden dish, and the entrails and skin are buried nearby. The flesh is cooked "with Congo beans, small and rather bitter" and the head is put "into a pot with yams to make some soup."

Pickled Chinaman

As Key Ray Chong explains in his book *Cannibalism in China*, pickling was very popular in ancient China. When prisoners were taken in times of war, they were frequently chopped up and pickled in wine, salt (*ts'o*), sauce, vinegar, and the like. This practice was designed not only to punish enemies, but also to scare off potential enemies. Having been pickled or sauced for one hundred days, the human meat was usually distributed to those who might challenge the power of the victor.

Roasted Placenta Loaf

Makes 1–6 pounds

1/2 to 6 pounds fresh placenta (up to 3 days old)

1 onion, chopped

1 green or red pepper, chopped

1 cup chopped tomatoes

It is to my eternal shame that my daughter's placenta was doggy-bagged for me but got left behind at the hospital in the excitement. I am reliably informed, however, that this recipe should work. (Placentas generally weigh about 15–20 percent of a baby's weight.)

⌀ Preheat the oven to 350°F. Prepare the placenta like liver, cutting the main membranes away with a sharp knife. Discard them and chop the placenta

1/2 cup breadcrumbs

4 bay leaves

1 teaspoon each of
ground black and
white pepper

1 clove of garlic,
roasted and minced

into large chunks. Add it to the rest of the ingredients, transfer to a large bread tin and bake for ninety minutes, occasionally pouring off excess liquid if necessary.

Human Sauce

The Confucian scholar Cheng Hsuan (d. AD 200) gives this recipe:

"Dry the meat, then cut it up, blend with moldy millet, salt, add good wine, and place it in a jar. The sauce is ready in a hundred days."

This meat sauce was often used as an ingredient in a hot dish or soup in antiquity.

Marinated Criminal

This description comes from *The Divine Origin of the Craft of the Herbalist* by E. A. Wallis Budge: "Select a cadaver of a red, uninjured, fresh unspotted malefactor, twenty-four years old, and killed by hanging, broken on the wheel, or impaled, upon which the moon and the sun have shone once: cut it in pieces, sprinkle with myrrh and aloes, then marinate it for a few days, and pour on spirits."

The Human Harvest

Anyone who knows me can testify that I am blessed with luxuriant, sprouting ear hair. Although it lacks volume at my tender age—a learned trichologist would probably call it "bum-fluff"—I hope that one day it will be as dense and tufty as that belonging to my late grandfather Wilfred. Even he, however, could not compete with Mr. Tyagi of Bhopal, India, who in 2002 was the proud owner of the world's longest ear hair—a whopping four inches—and was awarded an official Guinness World Record certificate. But it is to my continuing annoyance that I can't find a way to make it edible.

Thankfully, this is not the case with the rest of our corporeal form, which can be readily harvested to provide a small but interesting range of foodstuffs that are staple fare for young children, but scorned out of hand by most grown-ups. Let's not be shy—we all know the substances in question: breast milk, snot, scabs, urine, sperm, fingernails, toenails, skin, hair, ear wax, blood, sweat, pus, and feces. My survey of the nation's secret eating habits threw up some surprising results about what goes on behind closed doors—I was pleasantly surprised to find that almost every one of you is, to varying degrees, an autocannibal.

It has been a struggle getting reliable dietary information about these, but I've done my best.

Gastronautical Survey Result	
Have you ever eaten or drunk . . . ?	
Nails	53%
Boogers	44%
Scabs	36%
Breast milk (as an adult)	35%
Ear wax	10%
Urine	6%
Semen	4%
Hair	3%
Feces	2%
Any of the above belonging to someone else?	5%

Nails

Apparently there's little to fear from eating your fingernails as long as they're clean. One dietitian was mildly concerned about damage to the esophagus when eating sharp substances, but didn't see much cause for concern. It's one of those things I've never really gotten into, so I've always felt like a nail-eating outsider. I decided to conquer this small area of gastronomic interest by making a batch of fingernail cakes, and I hoped that by eating them I'd feel more worldly. I'll admit right now that it was one of the most stupid things I've ever done.

I started collecting nail clippings three years ago, aiming to amass enough to make a cake. My wife has found it consistently disgusting, so I tend to do it in private, which adds a gratifying seediness to the whole operation. I started by collecting the nails in tiny little sealable plastic bags bought specifically for the purpose, but it looked like I had little bags of drugs lying around my office, so I had to change over to a matchbox. My stash of nails grew very slowly, despite the fact that I have abnormally large fingernails (I'll show them to you sometime), and the whole operation was dealt a terrible blow when we moved a year ago and the matchbox and all its contents were lost.

I persevered, and a few months ago, I had re-amassed a quarter of a matchbox of nails and I could bear to wait no longer. I washed them and dried them out in an oven set low so they could be ground into a powder, but it wasn't much use. The small quantity made it impossible to grind them in a food processor or blender, and they were so hard that my wooden mortar and pestle didn't do the trick. Finally my stone mortar worked. With difficulty I pounded the nails into a gritty powder. I then made up the dough, mixed my nails into it, and baked several small cakes.

I didn't know what to expect, but a fleeting sense of transcendence, excitement, or achievement would have been nice. The reality: nothing. Not a sausage. There was a flicker of disgust at crunching on some of the larger bits of nail and a vague taste of fairy cake, but other than that, the experiment was a total waste of time. I recommend that you don't bother.

Boogers

Commonly known as *snot* in the liquid form, mucus also has a lightly desiccated incarnation: the popular and eminently more flickable *booger*. But what is it? Well, it's a substance produced by cells lining the respiratory tract as a defense mechanism to trap airborne dust, bacteria, and pollen. Mucus is moved toward the back of the throat by tiny hairs called *cilia*, which means that we are constantly swallowing snot. Basically, the lungs are delicate organs needing protection from pathogens (germs), while the stomach is a ferocious, caustic environment designed for destruction. As a result, all those particles extracted from the air are much better off being processed in the stomach. Incidentally, the *Oxford English Dictionary* defines a booger rather unromantically as "a piece of dried nasal mucus."

But is it unhealthy to eat boogers? No, no, no. Though commonly reviled by prissy parents, booger-eating has been hailed for its positive medicinal effects by Innsbruck-based lung specialist Dr. Friedrich Bischinger, who says: "Medically it makes great sense and is a perfectly natural thing to do. The nose is a filter in which a great deal of bacteria are collected, and when this mixture arrives in the intestines it works like a medicine."

Basically, it's a variation on the idea that kids brought up on farms develop resistance to disease because their immune systems are well exercised by dealing with so much muck and manure. The quote doesn't necessarily stand up to intense medical scrutiny, but dietitians seem to concur nonetheless: There's no harm from eating boogers, but they should be extracted with clean fingers, neat and short fingernails, and not shared with friends. Friedrich is clearly on message, if you ask me. What he fails to point out is that if we didn't pick it out of our noses and eat it, we'd probably be swallowing all of that mucus anyway due to the incessant motion of our cilia. Our body has been *built* to consume snot.

But the question you're all asking is: "Why is snot green or yellow?" I've had conflicting stories from the medical profession on this one. It's either due to the antimicrobial agent peroxidase—the same enzyme that makes wasabi green—or, if the UK's *Guardian* newspaper's "Notes and Queries" column is to be believed, it comes from the green-tinged iron used by the body's immune system to destroy nasal bacteria. It begins to turn yellow when the bacteria have been in the nose for some time, and other cells move in and die.

It may well be revolting to eat boogers—that's a value judgment to which you must bring your own prejudice, but you should keep an open mind because standards of polite behavior, like table manners, are liable to change at a moment's notice and from one culture to another. My gastronautical survey shows that 44 percent of everyone I questioned has eaten their own boogers as an adult, though only 2 percent admitted to ever having eaten someone else's. For my part, I am happy to consume the stuff from my own nose, but shun everyone else's, even my wife's, on grounds of flavor.

Scabs

Picking and eating scabs is quite common—36 percent of people have tried them—and anecdotal evidence points to a high popularity with children. The temptation is strong, and it can become an obsessive/compulsive disorder, but dietitians see little harm in dietary terms.

According to Stedman's medical dictionary, scabs are a "crust formed by coagulation of blood, pus, serum, or a combination of these on the surface of an ulcer, erosion, or other type of wound." It really isn't very clever to pick scabs as the body produces them for a specific purpose, namely to cover wounds as a barrier to infection and to encourage healing. Pulling off a scab may result in a secondary wound, infection, or irritation. But, in terms of eating them, the stomach is such a reliably caustic environment that it will kill off pretty much anything. Incidentally, the powerful acids in there tend to slaughter the bacteria in those pointless "friendly bacteria" fermented milk products way before they reach the lower intestine, where they might have actually been of some use. With this in mind, you might be better sticking them up your bottom.

Breast Milk

Magical stuff, this, averaging eighty-three calories per half a cup and supplying everything required to keep a baby alive. I love the fact that up to the age of four months, my daughter was made entirely of breast milk and love, before I began to ween her on sugar and spice and all things nice. Breast milk contains lactoferrin, a protein that provides protection against intestinal and respiratory infections, and it's very different from cow's milk—it's more watery (in fact, it's 87.2 percent water) and sweeter, and contains less fat and protein, allowing humans to grow more slowly. I have made cheese from spare breast milk, but it didn't work particularly well, probably because the amount I used was too small. The chap I spoke to from the Dairy Council reckoned that it could be done. Incidentally, I've heard of camel's-milk cheese, but it ought to be possible to make cheese from all sorts of milk—cat's milk, dog's milk, etc.

Incidentally, some men (and male goats) can lactate. It's relatively rare, but not by any means abnormal—if a man lets a baby suckle his nipple for long enough, he may produce milk, and similarly the mother of an adopted child doesn't have to give birth to lactate. In 2002 a Sri Lankan man developed this ability after his wife died in childbirth. Men have the same physical structure for the task, but our milk glands are smaller.

Ear Wax

Otherwise known as *cerumen*, ear wax is a substance secreted by special glands in the outer ear canal. It contains chemicals that fight infection and it helps trap dust and dirt that shouldn't get into the eardrum. It's safe to eat (although no one could give me a nutritional breakdown for it) but extremely dangerous to harvest as the eardrum is extremely delicate. My doctor insists that the smallest thing you should put in your ear is your elbow.

Urine

Urine therapy is enormously popular in many countries, although figures are generally supplied by devotees and may be unreliable. Apparently five million Germans regularly drink it, as do more than three million Chinese (according to the official Xinhua news agency) in the belief it is good for their health. Jim Morrison, John Lennon, and Mahatma Gandhi were advocates. Boy George drank his own urine for six months and enjoyed shocking his friends by doing it in public. He reckoned his tasted like Bovril.

We produce four to ten cups of urine a day, although the average is six cups. It is 95 percent water and 2.5 percent urea, with the remaining 2.5 percent made up of salt and other minerals, vitamins and other substances. Advocates claim that it's a panacea, treating a spectacular list of ailments from birthmarks to Kaposi's sarcoma, but, funnily enough, the medical establishment doesn't seem to agree.

Although urine isn't generally toxic, and when you're stranded in the desert you can drink it without too much bother, that doesn't mean it's good for you. It's a fluid excreted through the kidneys that helps the body get rid of waste products, especially acids. If you drink it, you are recycling those waste products and they can accumulate as if your kidneys weren't functioning properly. Doctors generally don't recommend it.

There is, however, widespread anecdotal evidence that it cures a multitude of complaints, and alternative therapists claim that doctors are conspiring against a natural cure so cheap that it would destroy the pharmaceuticals industry. Urine does, indeed, contain minerals, vitamins, proteins, amino acids, and hormones, but that doesn't necessarily mean it's good for you. It's true to say that urokinase, an enzyme extracted from human urine, is used to treat victims of heart attacks, but it takes around twenty million gallons of pee to make five pounds of urokinase. Still, if pee excites you, try reading Dr. Beatrice Bartnett's *Urine-Therapy: It May Save Your Life*.

Semen

You're probably already curling your lips, but hold on—this stuff is fascinating. Semen and sperm refer to two separate things: Sperm are the swimming cells that can fertilize a woman's egg, whereas semen is a combination of about 1 percent sperm and 99 percent liquids provided by the prostate and other glands. It's made up of 90 percent water, together with proteins, carbohydrates, sugars, fats, and a few minerals. It breaks down into lots of substances, including ascorbic acid, calcium, chlorine, fructose, cholestrol, vitamin B12, phosphorus, nitrogen, and zinc. The full ingredients list is enormous and sounds like the recipe for margarine. It is usually slightly alkaline.

Taste can, according to nutritionists, vary depending on the producer's diet, with meat and fish producing slightly meaty or buttery-tasting semen, and asparagus having the same effect that it does on urine (a strong, acrid smell). Nonacidic fruits and alcohol, on the other hand, can lead to a sweeter taste.

Semen doesn't offer great nutritional benefits, truth be told, with around twelve to fifteen calories per ejaculation, coming mainly from the fructose. It is not considered wise to share your semen with others due to the risk of HIV infection, but there's absolutely no danger in cooking with your own.

Hair and Feces

Stop right there: Hair is indigestible and feces is extremely dangerous to eat.

Aphrodisiacs

A Lothario cuisine

Good news. I have discovered which foods are best for achieving sexual congress with a partner of your choice. Bad news. None of these foods is an aphrodisiac.

Mankind is forever searching, and the more elusive the prize the more obsessive the exploration. As the French novelist Gustave Flaubert said, "Anticipation is the most reliable emotion." The search is the thing, not the discovery. Consider the searches for the Holy Grail, Atlantis, alien life, the meaning of life, the uphill struggle of alchemy. All very noble in their ways, but imagine if one day, by chance, you stumbled across the answer to all of those searches, but just as you were about to pick up the phone to the Nobel Institute, you also invented the world's first aphrodisiac—a magical elixir that would ensure your success in the sack with women/men/goats? I know what I'd do: Forget about the Nobel Prize, for starters, and instead call Downing Street and the White House to inform them that I would shortly be taking over the world.

Of course, most foods have at some time been proclaimed as sexual stimulants, including the following:

potatoes	ginseng	walnuts	marrows
eagles' livers	mandrake	almonds	carrots
lentils	foie gras	pistachios	spinach
menstrual blood	sparrows' tongues	coffee	radishes
oysters	orchids	chocolate	broad beans
nail parings	pine nuts	chickpeas	peppers
velvet from the horns of young stags	mushrooms	beets	bamboo shoots
	truffles	cabbage	watercress
frogs' bones	asparagus	pumpkin	celery

artichokes	seaweed	parsley	pomegranate
avocados	garlic	fennel	apples
camel's milk	goat	chervil	peaches
prawns	venison	sage	figs
caviar	hare	cinnamon	pears
anchovies	sparrows	nutmeg	strawberries
lobster	liver	ginger	grapes
crabs	snails	cloves	and, of course, partridge brains
elvers	honey	saffron	
octopus	mint	chili	
sea urchins	thyme	dates	

By rights, if you made a meal out of all these ingredients, your pants ought to explode. But it's all poppycock.

Sorry everyone, but as yet there's no such thing as an aphrodisiac. All the items on the previous page are listed by holistic nutritionists from Pliny the Elder to Dr. Gillian McKeith, but none has convincing proof of their increasing sexual potency. An American company called Erox has done some exciting work in human pheromones, producing two active compounds (ER-670 for women and ER-830 for men) that our pheromone receptors respond to. Erox's claim is pretty modest, though—apparently the compounds make female subjects feel warmer and male subjects more confident and assured. Woo.

No, no one has *ever* discovered a real aphrodisiac—a substance that reliably stimulates sexual desire where it isn't strictly deserved—though there have been hundreds of snake-oil-style pretenders. Even David Berliner, a former professor of anatomy now working for Erox agrees. "Everybody is looking for an aphrodisiac," he says. "But I have said it a million times: Such a thing doesn't exist."

There have been some crazy theories about food and sex, but just because they're nonsense doesn't mean they aren't worth telling you about. Roman peasants believed that onions, leeks, and fennel increased semen production, and that carrots, celery, mushrooms, nutmeg, cinnamon, and lettuce all aided sexual excitement (which seems like an underhanded way to get your husband to eat his greens).

Vanilla was once championed simply due to the vaginal shape of its pod.

In Germany men used to hide their pubic hair in a hole in a tree by the light of a new moon, and Bavarian peasants made amulets of the penis bones (my research failed to discover what a penis bone might be) of the pine marten and the polecat to bring them sexual luck.

Gastronautical Survey Result	
Which meal, if any, is most likely to end in sexual congress?	
Meal with lots of alcohol	11%
Takeout meal	7%
Chocolate	5%
Expensive meal	4.5%
Breakfast	4%
Oysters	3%
Fish (various)	2%
A light meal	1.5%
Cooked by male partner	1%
None/no response/ expression of outrage	18%

Other items that cropped up more than once included: lobster, sushi, crispy duck, champagne, strawberries, fruit, lunch, quick meals.

But what about Viagra? Well, Viagra isn't an aphrodisiac—it's an aid to penile erection that ensures the flow of blood to the penis is increased *following* sexual stimulation. In case you're interested, Viagra is essentially a British invention, its development shrouded in the mists of press releases by Pfizer. What seems clear is that Viagra was developed around 1998 by a group of chaps in Kent, who were looking at chemicals used for treating heart problems. They invented a substance that increases blood flow to the penis when activated by nitric oxide—a chemical that enters the bloodstream in response to sexual stimulation.

And what about Spanish fly, the stimulant that the Marquis de Sade was wont to slip into the bonbons he fed to prostitutes and friends? It's the powdered remains of a beetle found in southern Europe that specifically irritates the urogenital tract, causing your genitals to burn, swell, and itch (which I suppose you could mistake for arousal). It also encourages better blood flow, so, in combination, these symptoms could lead to powerful erections for both penis and clitoris. However, Spanish fly can also lead to damaged kidneys, nausea, pain, and, in extreme cases, death.

But that's enough about what doesn't work: How about what does? In the gastronautical survey I asked a lot of people the simple question: Which meal, if any, is most likely to end in sexual congress?

My lovely survey respondents confessed that the following float their boats:

Meal with lots of alcohol	Chocolate	Oysters	Cooked by male partner
Takeout meal	Expensive meal	Fish (various)	
	Breakfast	A light meal	

These statistics belie the fact that obscure and enigmatic answers were the norm, such as "urgent," "Thursday night, lots of drink," "legs," "Lady wrapped in bacon," "dinner," "meals tend to start an argument," and "I'd be lucky." The answer "bottle of wine and a joint" seemed pretty clear, though, as did my friend Ewan's unprintable and, may I suggest, fanciful suggestion.

There was loads of advice in fluffy *conceptual* terms, but it was irritatingly conflicting, and defied all attempts to establish a pattern. Here are some of the main ones:

⊄ Make sure that alcohol is involved.

⊄ Spend lots of money. Expensive meals or ingredients seem to be pretty reliable.

⊄ Conversely, don't spend lots of money. Get takeout (although simply cooking with cheap ingredients was never mentioned). Indian food topped the list pretty clearly, and my friend Danny swears by chips and curry sauce. Thai food and pizza were also mentioned several times.

⊄ Make the food light and the meal long.

⊄ Various expensive seafood was popular.

⊄ And whatever you do, don't forget the alcohol.

It's not really my place to offer any scientific diagnosis of these results but it does seem that there's no quick-fix ingredient, which is a crushing shame.

But I sniff a conspiracy. Imagine a world where an aphrodisiac does exist—let's assume for these purposes that the banana is a potent aphrodisiac. What would people spend all their time doing? Eating bananas and making love. And when they finished making love, they'd make love some more. At that point they'd maybe eat some bananas and then, my guess is, they'd get back to the lovemaking. Call me old-fashioned, but I know I would. The whole point about a potent aphrodisiac is that it would be, to some extent, irresistible. And because sex is so great, someone would always pop round with a banana, and off you go again, dancing the merry dance of love.

This is all rather lovely, exciting, and good for the heart, but powerful aphrodisiacs come with a built-in civilization-busting flaw: Nothing would ever get done. No one would drive the trains, no one would build the houses, and no one would write the food books, that's for sure. The only people who would do a stroke of work would be the banana farmers, and then only so that they could eat more bananas and have more sex.

I reckon that at some point someone *has* discovered or invented a real aphrodisiac, but they've either been assassinated or paid off by some shadowy Bilderbergian Christian fundamentalist businessman or the U.S. government—anyone who wanted to keep the masses in their uneroticized place and ensure that the wheels of industry keep turning. In many ways they'd be right to do so; with the world overrun by aphrodisiacs, the human race would be extinct within a few generations, slain by banana poisoning and exhaustion. But what a way to go.

Flatulence

How to maximize your wind power

We all produce gas throughout the normal day, but do you know the scale of the operation? According to Glenn Gibson, professor of food microbial sciences at Reading University, we each produce 1.1 to 1.3 gallons of gas, via twenty-four to thirty farts, *per day*. The gas expelled by our bodies is made mainly of odorless vapors: carbon dioxide, oxygen, nitrogen, hydrogen, and sometimes methane, but farts often smell due to sulfurous gases released by bacteria in the colon—the very last bit of tubing that food passes through, way past the stomach, liver, and small intestines. Basically, as your food sits there for the last day or two of its passage, these bacteria work on anything that hasn't been properly digested at an earlier stage (due to an absence of appropriate enzymes). The foods that cause gas are usually carbohydrates, but the effects vary from person to person, so I carried out a small survey of my acquaintances to try to get the measure of the elusive wind. Interestingly, fats and proteins rarely cause flatulence, but sugars, starches, and fiber often do.

I'll come clean: I'm rather fond of the odd *coup de vent*, yet there's a stigma attached to this perfectly innocent bodily function. It wasn't always thus. Chaucer

Gastronautical Survey Result	
What food is most likely to make you fart?	
Beans	29%
Cruciferous vegetables and asparagus	11%
Jerusalem artichoke	9%
Curry	5%
Onion and garlic	5%
Potatoes/corn/noodles/ wheat	5%
Fruit	4%
Cheese	1%

The remaining 31 percent showed no clear preference, were statistically irrelevent, or just plain stupid.

knew that there's nothing funnier than a well-timed "frap" to enliven a ribald tale, and there's a generous scattering of them in the *Canterbury Tales*, and Shakespeare, Joyce, and Swift all happily drew on the fart as a comic device. And then there are the Germans, who are renowned scatologists and who devour tons of pumpernickel bread every day. (It is said that in some areas of Germany *pumpern* means "to fart" and nickel is the devil—the bread is so hard to digest that it is said it would make even the devil fart.)

But in the modern world, the use of farts as a narrative intensifier has fallen into disrepute, and today they are rarely heard around the dining table. I think this is a shame, and I've often served well-roasted Jerusalem artichokes to an unsuspecting table of guests, only to delight in their malodorous discomfort and symphonic trumpeting later in the evening. I've found the Jerusalem artichoke to be the most reliable flatulence brewer—as far back as 1621 the English botanist John Goodyer wrote that it causes a "filthy and loathsome stinking wind" (although most modern cookbooks archly fail to warn the reader).

I was initiated into the rarefied world of the fart at an early age by my sister, who enjoyed expelling her spare wind on my pillow and occasionally my head. This happened mainly when I was ten years old and she was thirteen. In adulthood she now refrains from farting, in public at least, but the damage was done and I am now an active enthusiast.

So, I have toiled at two tasks. Firstly, analyzing why different foods make us fart and stink, using both scientific record and firsthand observation. Secondly, I decided to perform an experiment on myself by spending an entire day eating Jerusalem artichokes, beans, brussels sprouts, and roast onions—the fartiest foodstuffs I could find—and keeping track of my nether weather for the benefit of science.

CULPRIT	**Beans**
SURVEY	29%
WHAT ARE THEY?	Pulses—foods that are effectively seeds from pods. Mild by comparison to other foodstuffs, but powerful when consumed in sheer numbers. These must be responsible for millions of tons of methane every year.
WHY?	Raffinose—an indigestible sugar and soluble fiber that can only be dealt with by suphurous gas-producing bacteria in the colon.

CULPRIT	**Cruciferous vegetables and asparagus**
SURVEY	11%
WHAT ARE THEY?	Cruciferous vegetables include cabbage, brussels sprouts, broccoli, and cauliflower. Asparagus is from the lily family (and makes your pee smell). They are all powerful wind generators.
WHY?	Raffinose again.
CULPRIT	**Jerusalem artichoke**
SURVEY	9%
WHAT IS IT?	Neither artichoke, nor from Jerusalem, it's actually a relative of the sunflower, and it originated in Canada. Without a doubt, my personal number-one rectal troublemaker. This baby can be peeled or not, then eaten raw or made into salads (ouch), or boiled and mashed, mixed with potatoes, or roasted (my personal favorite). It really does the trick and demonstrates possibly the most clear and direct connection between a food and a fart.
WHY?	Inulin—a largely indigestible carbohydrate that's left to the bacteria in the colon to pounce on.
CULPRIT	**Curry, ice cream, and some processed foods**
SURVEY	5%
WHAT ARE THEY?	You might wonder what curry and ice cream have in common. The answer is lactose—the sugar found in milk.
WHY?	Lactose can be hard to digest—you need the enzyme lactase to break it down, and the older you get, the less lactase you produce.
CULPRIT	**Onion and garlic**
SURVEY	5%
WHAT ARE THEY?	Ah, the allium. Interestingly, its heady aroma is produced when it's cut or crushed, allowing an enzyme called allinase to combine with the precursor/substrate alliin to form allicin . . . if that makes any sense.
WHY?	Not always problematic, but when it is (especially in roasted form), Lord have mercy! Fructose to blame here, bizarrely.
CULPRIT	**Potatoes, corn, noodles, and wheat**
SURVEY	5%
WHAT ARE THEY?	Starch-rich foods.
WHY?	Starch is a complex carbohydrate that is broken down and absorbed in the small bowel. However these foods will also contain nonstarch

polysaccharides, which basically form the fiber in our diet. Fiber passes straight through the small bowel into the large bowel (the colon). The small bowel has relatively few bacteria, but the colon contains billions of them. A little bit of starch may escape small-bowel digestion, and certainly most of the fiber will, and when this all reaches the colonic bacteria, they ferment it, producing gas. Although high levels of fiber are usually recommended for a healthy diet, people with irritable-bowel type symptoms reduce the amounts of these types of foods in their diets because up to 50 percent of those people get more bloated and uncomfortable on a high-fiber diet.

CULPRIT	**Fruit, especially apples, pears, prunes, and peaches**
SURVEY	4%
WHAT ARE THEY?	All rich in sugars.
WHY?	Sorbitol, another indigestible sugar. Personally, I've never made the farty connection with apples but prunes have certainly been an aid to movements.

CULPRIT	**Cheese**
SURVEY	1%
WHAT IS IT?	A dairy product accused of causing both dreams and flatulence.
WHY?	Lactose/lactase again.

This list is obviously intended as a guide to help you build up a good head of steam around the table. If, however, you have imbibed an excess of these ingredients and need deflating, you should drink an infusion of lemon balm and chamomile at regular intervals until achieving sweet relief. Other flatulence relievers are dill, fennel, and anise, though you may find it easier to pop a Gas-X from your local pharmacist.

A Personal Journey Into Extreme Flatulence

For reasons that I can't entirely remember, but they must have been good at the time, I thought I would carry out an experiment to find out how flatulent I could get. My plan was simple: Eat as much as I could of the things I knew caused me wind over a twenty-four-hour period and record my thoughts and experiences. I tried, with varying degrees of success, to make it less of a stag-party escapade and more of a scientific research project. It was certainly a fascinating journey for me, but possibly less so for those in the immediate vicinity. Here's what happened.

TIME:	**7:30 AM Breakfast (1)**
SUBSTANCE:	**Prunes in yogurt, two apples, and a cup of tea.**
THOUGHT:	All is well, though feeling quite anxious. It's a bit too early to start on the hard stuff.

TIME:	**9 AM Breakfast (2)**
SUBSTANCE:	**Cup of tea. Beans on toast.**
THOUGHT:	The experiment begins. Can't entirely remember why I'm doing this, but push ahead anyway.

TIME:	**11 AM**
SUBSTANCE:	**Another apple. Large latté.**
THOUGHT:	Dismay—nothing to report except for an enthusiastic bowel movement. Finding it hard to concentrate on work, mainly because I'm too excited.

TIME:	**1 PM Lunch**
SUBSTANCE:	**Jerusalem artichoke salad with roasted garlic, salad of broccoli, artichokes, cannellini beans, and asparagus.**
THOUGHT:	This should break my duck.

TIME:	**2 PM Lunch finished.**
THOUGHT:	Still nothing. Feel a little deflated, emotionally.
TIME:	**2:30 PM Continue working.**
THOUGHT:	Oh, crikey, first few rumblings. A bit bloated now.
TIME:	**2:50 PM Still working.**
THOUGHT:	Here we go: one enormous, but silent fart. God, that stinks.
TIME:	**3:30 PM Tea break (1)**
SUBSTANCE:	**Cup of tea.**
THOUGHT:	Okay. Getting a good head of steam now: regular pumping at intervals of thirty-five minutes or so. Wife distressed by olfactory experience and not enormously amused on hearing of experiment. Perhaps I should have run it by her in advance? Too late now—must crack on.
TIME:	**5 PM Tea break (2)**
SUBSTANCE:	**Cup of tea.**
THOUGHT:	Still regularly pumping. While happy that the experiment appears to be yielding results, I'm actually feeling a bit bilious now.
TIME:	**6:30 PM Start cooking supper.**
THOUGHT:	Feeling deep anxiety about my physical state. What can I gain from doing this? Resolve to persevere.
TIME:	**7:30 PM Still cooking supper.**
THOUGHT:	Slight let up, but still feeling deep discomfort.
TIME:	**8 PM Supper**
SUBSTANCE:	**Roast lamb, more Jerusalem artichokes, brussels sprouts, roast potatoes.**
THOUGHT:	Christ alive. This just feels wrong, like driving down the freeway on the wrong side. I'm already pumping regularly, producing quite a stench. Wife is frankly appalled.
TIME:	**9 PM**
SUBSTANCE:	**Wine.**
THOUGHT:	Okay, this isn't right. They're coming thick and strong now. Feels almost hallucinatory. Don't know how much more of this I can take.

TIME:	**11 PM Snack**
SUBSTANCE:	**Cheese plate.**
THOUGHT:	No letup for the last seven-and-a-half hours and feeling quite beaten around. My butt hole stings like a grazed knee in lime juice.
TIME:	**11:45 PM Go to bed.**
THOUGHT:	With a very disgruntled wife. Manage to ignore her pleas to sleep in spare room. Still appear to be passing silent but powerful gusts. Decide that amorous advances may not be viewed sympathetically and fall asleep.
TIME:	**7 PM Wake up.**
THOUGHT:	No dreams that I can remember, though a merry, hefty fug pollutes the bedroom. Wife and daughters both deeply unimpressed by my scientific endeavors for the good of mankind. Tired but happy, I ponder my lack of dreams. Will try again in a few days.

Interestingly, although she ate most of the same food as I did, I haven't noticed my wife experiencing any of the same. Why?

During the experiment, one thought cropped up again and again: Could you capture farts in a jar—perhaps some classic, souvenir-quality wind that should be collected for posterity? Who knows what it will be worth in years to come? I asked several dietitians this tricky question but no one could give me a clear answer. If anyone thinks that they can answer this, please send me your suggestions.

MUSIC SUGGESTION

Should you wish to re-create this experiment, don't be tempted by the obvious route for musical accompaniment, Ivor Biggun's "I've Farted." It's cheap and not very funny. Instead, accept the fact early on that your inner turmoil needs to be ameliorated by aural tranquillity. Try *Officium*, a beautiful and haunting collaboration between Norwegian saxophonist Jan Garbarek and the glorious Hilliard Ensemble, a vocal chamber group.

Physiological Fun

The stranger effects of food

The gastronautical survey threw up lots of delightful and strange symptoms that respondents experience after eating certain foods. These included:

- Apples make my legs itch.
- I get nightmares after eating potatoes.
- Blue cheese gives me an instant headache.
- Golden syrup makes me cough.
- Glacé cherries dramatically change my metabolic rate (an iodine/thyroid link, apparently).
- Omelettes give me diarrhea.
- Nuts make me itchy.
- Chocolate makes me itchy.
- Chili gives me hiccups.
- Cashews make me sneeze.
- Cheese makes me vomit.
- Curry gives me smelly sweat.

The link between cheese and dreams was especially strong. Many talked of particularly vivid, scary, and violent dreams.

I put these and a spread of other strange symptoms to a couple of dietitians to try to find out

Gastronautical Survey Result	
What food makes your pee smell?	
Asparagus	51%
Sugar Puffs	6%
Curry	5%
Alcohol	4%
Artichokes	3%

why people might have these reactions, but many were difficult to identify. Apparently, although there has been a great deal of evidence of certain symptoms, there has actually been little research to match it. Here's what we do know.

FOOD:	**Asparagus**
EFFECTS:	Can make your urine smell. Some people are lucky enough to experience this, but not others.
REASON:	There's a great deal of disagreement on exactly what causes the smell, but probably sulfur-containing thioesters. When your digestive system breaks down mercaptan, strange-smelling by-products are created. Another theory points to asparagines-amino-succinic-acid monoamide derived from the amino acid asparagines. The process happens very quickly—your urine can develop the smell within fifteen to thirty minutes.
FOOD:	**Sugar Puffs**
EFFECTS:	Make your urine smell malty—or like Sugar Puffs.
REASON:	No research available, but the process is assumed to be similar to that of asparagus.
FOOD:	**Artichoke**
EFFECTS:	After eating it, water tastes sweet on the tongue.
REASON:	Cynarine alters the performance of taste receptors.
FOOD:	**Beets**
EFFECTS:	Turns urine and feces a fetching purply red.
REASON:	Natural (and harmless) pigments not broken down in the gut.
FOOD:	**Cheese**
EFFECTS:	In my survey group 34 percent experienced dreams after eating cheese. They were variously described as "erotic," "action-thrillers," "violent," "weird," or "cheese-based" adventures. One person dreamt that he was "driving a cheap car" after eating cheese.
REASON:	Various theories. One is that when you eat food that's difficult to digest (e.g. hard cheese) before bed it causes gastric distension, which will disturb your sleep. Another theory points to tyramine in aged cheese. This is an amino acid that can cause serotonin to be released, leading to constricted blood flow. This can lead to headaches if you're awake and vivid dreams if you're asleep. Tyramine can interact with monoamine

transmitters (such as 5HT), and this may affect sleep. If you enjoy this effect, try other tyramine-rich foods, such as alcoholic drinks, liver, salami, aged game, pickled herrings, and commercial gravy.

FOOD: **Nutmeg**

EFFECTS: Hallucinogenic, sometimes with erotic consequences, if eaten in vast quantities.

REASON: No definite answers as to what causes this, though generally accepted to be true.

FOOD: **Carrots**

EFFECTS: Can cause hypercarotenemia—a yellow-orange coloring of the skin if eaten in excess. This is not jaundice.

REASON: The beta-carotene pigment found in carrots.

FOOD: **Rhubarb leaves**

EFFECTS: Poisonous, should never be eaten, especially by people subject to urinary irritation. Interestingly, rhubarb leaves have sometimes been used to make fake cigarettes.

REASON: Oxalic acid.

FOOD: **Turkey**

EFFECTS: Makes you sleepy.

REASON: Several possible reasons. It is true that turkey contains a lot of the amino acid L-tryptophan, which the brain changes into serotonin, which

---

A note on hiccups: Not strictly a physiological effect of food, but fascinating nonetheless. We know what hiccups are, but medical science still hasn't got to the bottom of what their function is or how to cure them.

A hiccup is a sudden contraction of the diaphragm that forces air into the lungs. At the same time the glottis (a flap of tissue at the top of the windpipe) snaps shut, blocking off the same sudden flow of air and causing the slight snapping noise.

Severe cases of hiccupping are treated with antispasmodics, such as Baclofen, but if that doesn't work, the phrenic nerve in the diaphragm and the vagus nerve in the glottis (which are believed to be the culprits) can be crushed or even severed. There is no reliable cure, as one Mr. Charles Osborne discovered: he suffered from nonstop hiccups for sixty-five years.

calms and aids sleep. But turkey also tends to be eaten as part of an enormous meal with large amounts of carbohydrates, and this causes increased blood flow to the stomach and less to the brain, making the eater sleepy. On Christmas Day we usually consume three times as many calories as normal—6,000 or more.

FOOD:	**Toothpaste**
EFFECTS:	After brushing our teeth, orange juice tastes sour.
REASON:	Toothpaste strips our tastebuds of phospholipids, then the residual chemicals it leaves behind, e.g. formaldehyde and chalk, mix with the acids in orange juice to create a sour taste.

A note on vitamin and mineral supplements

Many people take vitamin supplements, making them a huge industry, but few people seem to realize that they can be dangerous if the recommended daily amount (RDA) is exceeded, especially if this happens over a long period of time. The manufacturers seem reluctant to tell people this, and many supplements offer doses that are many times over the RDA and, by inference, encourage the user to exceed advised doses, so here are a few pointers from the FDA. Supplements can occasionally be useful, but you should be aware that there are potential negative aspects, which were assembled using the *FSA Expert Group on Vitamins and Minerals* (May 2003) and the *Nutritional Desk Reference*.

VITAMIN/MINERAL:	**Vitamin A**
RDA:	750 μcg
POTENTIALLY DANGEROUS DOSE:	8,450 μcg and over
POTENTIAL SYMPTOMS:	Headache, nausea, potential for birth defects if high levels of retinol are consumed

VITAMIN/MINERAL:	**Vitamin C**
RDA:	60 mg
POTENTIALLY DANGEROUS DOSE:	1,000–5,000 mg
POTENTIAL SYMPTOMS:	Gastrointestinal problems, kidney stones, withdrawal symptoms

VITAMIN/MINERAL:	**Calcium**
RDA:	800 mg
POTENTIALLY DANGEROUS DOSE:	Maximum dose should be 1,500 mg (but most people get 1,400 mg from their food and water anyway)
POTENTIAL SYMPTOMS:	Milk-alkali syndrome, resulting in hypercalcemia, alkalosis, and renal impairment (progressive lethargy, headaches, renal stone formation can result)

VITAMIN/MINERAL:	**Iron**
RDA:	10 mg
POTENTIALLY DANGEROUS DOSE:	18 mg and over (100 mg is approximately lethal dose)
POTENTIAL SYMPTOMS	Severe gastrointestinal damage, hemorrhagic gastroenteritis

VITAMIN/MINERAL:	**Zinc**
RDA:	15 mg
POTENTIALLY DANGEROUS DOSE:	50 mg and over
POTENTIAL SYMPTOMS:	Gastrointestinal problems, including cramps and nausea, secondary copper deficiency, especially in diabetics and sufferers of hemochromatosis

CHAPTER 4
Exhibitionism for the Romantic

Cooking with Aftershave

The way we men choose aftershave reveals nothing of our true nature, but everything about the brooding depth, sexual magnetism, and general unputdownability we'd like to project. That's not astringent antiseptic we're slathering on—it's *jus d'amour*. Personally, I use Issey Miyake: slightly spicy, subtly exquisite, understatedly sophisticated, expensive, and above all, unique—a set of adjectives that couldn't be further from your mind when you actually met me.

Airy fairiness aside, what we buy in aftershave is a package of flavors, premixed to perfection, which is just what a chef attempts with every dish he makes. Think about it: If Brillat-Savarin had been able to lay his hands on some Calvin Klein Eternity, would he have bothered going to the expense of truffling so many turkeys? I think not. So what better substance to use for cooking? A combination of spices suspended in alcohol—all common ingredients in good food. It can't be that bad for you.

Except, of course, it can. The Material Safety Data Sheet drawn up by the makers of Old Spice (Proctor & Gamble) warns that it poses a health hazard with "Low order of acute toxicity. Acute ingestion may cause transient alcohol intoxication. Chronic ingestion may cause same health hazards as chronic alcoholism, e.g. liver dysfunction, mental impairment."

Nothing to really put you off, though. Since when did transient alcohol intoxication become a bad thing? And I'm not planning on chronic ingestion—all I need is a drizzle of the stuff. I thought I'd double-check though, so I called up the people at Chanel, who were gloriously haughty on the phone and refused even to comment. P & G on the other hand was very helpful. They refused to endorse my efforts and would only say "that's not what Old Spice was made for." And that's despite the life I was generously trying to breathe into their frankly rather elderly brand.

Undeterred, I drew up some shocking stereotypes of who buys what aftershave and then made some wild assumptions about the type of foods these people might eat. I think you'll agree that the following makes sense:

◖ Herrings soused in Old Spice

◖ Periwinkles marinated in Aramis

◖ Ravioli with Versace and mascarpone stuffing

◖ Lobster poached in Hugo Boss

◖ Lagerfeld lamb kibbeh

I tried a few of these, but by far the best was a simple dish created using my favorite brand (something to do with that understated sophistication, I guess). By making a ceviche, nothing is cooked, so you don't burn off any of that delicious flavor (and in case you're not fa-miliar with the technique, it's about marinating fish or vegetables in citrus fruits full of citric acid to denature the proteins—a chemical process similar to that which it undergoes when cooked using heat).

Disastrously, the aftershave leaves a bitter taste in the mouth that works against the sourness from the limes. I did also feel a slight sense of nausea. I reluctantly came to the conclusion that cooking with af-tershave is not a good idea after all.

Salmon and Issey Miyake Ceviche

For reference only—best NOT to try this at home

Serves 4 as a starter

zest of half a lime

juice of 1 lime

freshly ground black pepper

2 teaspoons Issey Miyake aftershave

1 pound of salmon fillet, skinned, boned, and sliced as thinly as you can

1 teaspoon fresh parsley, chopped

1 teaspoon fresh chives, chopped

1/2 teaspoon red chilli, finely chopped

olive oil

⊘ Zest your lime before juicing it (much easier this way). Combine the zest, juice, pepper, and aftershave in a small bowl. Lay your salmon in a dish, pour over the juice and cover with plastic wrap. Refrigerate for thirty minutes max.

⊘ Mix the parsley, chives, and chili with the olive oil. Remove the salmon and arrange on plates. Dress with this oil mixture and serve with some nice fresh bread.

MUSIC SUGGESTIONS

Bryan Ferry's 1973 solo album *These Foolish Things*, Andy Williams's compilation album *The Best of the '70s*.

Fanny Sandwich

I've never been much of a fan of Fanny Cradock's TV shows, but her writing was sublime. She's just as snotty and overbearing on the page as on TV, but somehow the self-serving, name-dropping snobbery reads like irony. Her most endearing feature was her membership in a small but dedicated culinary subgroup known as fanny-cookers. These are people who believe that a good pair of warm fleshy buttocks can be put to work as an excellent low-temperature oven.

Fanny's fanny generally stuck to currant buns. This is from Fanny and Johnnie Cradock's *Time to Remember*: "Fanny always sat on currant buns . . . sitting on it squished the currants which made the flattened bun taste far nicer." I've tried it and she's dead right—the slightly clammy warmth given off by one's posterior softens the buns up nicely. It's best to butter them before slipping them under, but beware: Put them in a plastic bag, otherwise you'll stain your knickers.

On a grander scale, there's a lovely tale told by Mark Kurlansky in his book *Choice Cuts* about the legendary food writer M. F. K. Fisher, who made a French bread sandwich, wrapped it in cling wrap, and instructed her guest to sit on it for an hour. This also has echoes of the French *pain bagnat*, which is a kind of salad niçoise in a baguette, slathered in vinaigrette, wrapped tightly, and left for a couple of hours to soak.

Intrigued, I carried out extensive experiments and became rather obsessed with the technique. Basically, you sit on a well-wrapped sandwich and squash all the ingredients together with the aid of your constant 98.6°F body temperature and the downward pressure of your torso—like a human sandwich toaster. Incidentally, kids seem to love it. I've tested currant buns, sourdough, and a variety of fillings, all of which were glorious. It always pays to use a few aromatic ingredients, such as herbs, pesto, or Moroccan *charmoula*, whose flavors will seep through the sandwich during the long, slow process. For best results you should procure the posterior of a pregnant woman—at the time of writing, my wife is with child and she works perfectly.

Here's the technique:

Serves 1

bread—crusty French bread or sourdough are perfect, but anything will do

butter

fillings—choose two from ham, good cheese, chicken, avocado, etc.

mustard (or pesto, *charmoula, taramasalata, salsa verde,* etc.)

mayonnaise

fresh herbs if you have them— parsley, thyme, and rosemary are all good, as long as they go with your filling ingredients

watercress or arugula

Cut your bread thickly and butter it lavishly. Make your sandwich with generous amounts of filling and, most crucially, spread on the pesto, mayonnaise, herbs, and watercress (or arugula). Wrap the sandwich securely in a generous quantity of cling wrap—this will protect your clothes from greasy ingredients, and the sandwich from any noxious escapes.

Instruct your guests to sit on the sandwich for as long as possible—an hour is ideal.

Unwrap the sandwich and cut into finger-thick strips. Serve with cornichons and perhaps a glass of cider.

The Venus Sandwich

This is another fanny-cooked classic and reputedly an aphrodisiac (isn't everything?). Take a French loaf and extract its doughy white innards. Drizzle with olive oil, then stuff with anchovies, stoned olives, capers, chopped tomatoes, and artichoke hearts. Wrap it tightly in cling wrap and sit on it. Again, an hour should do it just fine. Spend as much of that hour thinking lascivious thoughts, then eat it in the sack. With someone else, mind.

MUSIC SUGGESTIONS

Ash's "Girl from Mars," Belle and Sebastian's "Simple Things" and "If She Wants Me," the Clash's "Train in Vain," Queen's "Fat Bottomed Girls."

Red and White Soup

This is simply two very hearty soups that are served together on either side of the same bowl. It's always a joy to see your friends baffled as they wonder whether to try to keep the soups separate or to mix them together in pretty patterns. The trick to getting it right is to make your soups nice and thick and to pour them into a bowl with the care of a barman crafting an Irish coffee.

Seeing as you're doubling the workload by making two entire recipes, it's only reasonable to give you a couple of easy soups to make. You can, of course, do this with any soups you want, but remember that they will inevitably mix together, so I'd avoid pairing gazpacho with blue cheese and broccoli.

Making the Beet Soup

Serves 8

1-1/4 pounds of fresh beets

splash of olive oil

1 red onion, chopped

butter

1 quart vegetable stock

salt and pepper

⌒ If you have the time, first roast the beets for forty-five minutes in a splash of oil in the oven at 375°F. This will give a real intensity to the flavor. If not, don't worry.

⌒ Fry the onion gently in the butter until translucent. While it's frying, peel the beets (whether raw or roasted) and slice into thick chunks. Place the fried onion, beets, and vegetable stock in a saucepan and simmer for about forty-five minutes (five minutes if you roasted the beets first). Allow it to cool for a few minutes, check the seasoning, then blend in a food processor. Cover and keep warm until the other soup is also ready.

Making the Celeriac Soup

SERVES 8

12 ounces celeriac, peeled and roughly chopped

5 ounces potatoes, peeled and roughly chopped

butter

1 quart vegetable stock

juice of half a lemon

2/3 cup milk

salt and pepper

Throw the chopped celeriac and potatoes into a large pan with the butter and fry gently for five minutes. Pour in the stock and lemon juice. Bring to boil and simmer gently for fifteen minutes or so until the vegetables are tender. Allow to cool for a few minutes, then add the milk and seasoning and blend in a food processor.

To serve

This is a group task, to be carried out at the table. You need to transfer the soups into separate jugs, or similar vessels that are good for pouring, then find a guest with a steady hand to help you. Simultaneously, after a brief countdown, pour the soups into each bowl from either side so that they meet in the center (use the flatter type of soup bowls if you've got them, as they make the presentation easier and more striking). You'll screw up the first few, but by the last bowl, you'll have gotten the hang of it, and you'll want to start making yin and yang shapes. Save that until next time.

MUSIC SUGGESTIONS

The White Stripes' crashing *Elephant* and *White Blood Cells* albums, and the Smashing Pumpkins' album *Machina/The Machines of God*.

Mumbled Mushrooms

My *Shorter Oxford English Dictionary* explains the etymology of the word "mumble" with a quote: "And Gums unarm'd to mumble Meat in vain." It's jumbled, but basically "mumbled" means a dish that's suitable for toothless gums or precarious dentures. This old English recipe for mumbled eggs is basically scrambled eggs with extra cream, and believe me, it's certainly not going to trouble your PoliGrip. Which is why I've added a life-threatening, daredevil twist to it.

This recipe is for when you've managed to lay your hands on some posh mushrooms and you want to show them off—ceps, chanterelles, or *pieds de mouton* are ideal. It's also got a lovely element of danger—that's a raw egg you're serving to your guests. But the twist here is that you serve the dish nice and hot with the raw egg yolk ready to be broken onto the mushrooms by the guests themselves and thereby shift the blame for any food poisoning fairly and squarely onto their shoulders. I like that in a recipe.

Of course, according to the chair of the Food Standards Agency, "Food-borne illness probably accounts for about five hundred deaths per year," which sounds pretty tiny to me and hence weakens the sense of drama. On the flip side, deaths from the dietary elements of cardio-vascular disease and cancer alone "kill more than a hundred thousand people a year." So, scanning the ingredients of this dish (yup, that's a ¾ cup of oil) you should be able to nail your guests either way.

Serves 4

4 egg yolks, with half of each shell reserved for serving. Buy the best, free-est of range eggs you can afford. Chuck the whites away—you'll never use them.

🍂 If your eggs are in the fridge, get them out and allow them to warm up to room temperature, otherwise they'll make everything cold and clammy when they are broken over the mushrooms. Also warm your plates.

🍂 In a large frying pan, heat your olive oil until it's just smoking. If you've only got small pans, use

3/4 cup extra virgin olive oil (sounds like a lot, I know)

1 pound mushrooms (the posher the better, though any will do), brushed free of dirt and chopped. If you've bought ceps, remove their heads and chop the stalks into large chunks.

salt and pepper

4–5 cloves of garlic, roughly chopped

a bunch of flat-leafed parsley, chopped

two separate ones, otherwise you won't be able to get the temperature high enough and your mushrooms will poach. Drop the mushrooms into the oil. Keep the temperature high and don't cover the pan. When the mushrooms have browned on one side (about two minutes), turn them over and season with salt and pepper.

⌒ Add the garlic and parsley and fry for a further three to five minutes.

⌒ Put a pile of mushrooms on each plate (more on your own, especially if you bought posh mushrooms) and nestle the egg yolk, still in its shell, on top. When serving, tell your guests that a) they are supposed to break the egg yolk over the mushrooms and b) that they aren't supposed to eat the shell.

Variations

To push the boat out, you could give everyone three or four quail egg yolks as they really do have a silkier texture. The shells are a bitch to break, though. Use a knife and be prepared to screw a few up.

For an even more unctuous touch, you could add a few drops of truffle oil. It then becomes an incredibly rich little dish. If you bought those posh mushrooms, you might be covering up a bit of their flavor and hence doing them a disservice. Great for the cheaper ones, though.

MUSIC SUGGESTIONS
Frank Sinatra's *Rare Sinatra*, Kings of Leon's *Youth and Young Manhood*, *Murmur* by REM and "Murder" by New Order.

Homemade Gravlax

This is a deeply satisfying project—completely delicious and rather beautiful to look at. It's annoyingly easy to make this, but luckily it has a three-day curing time to test your patience.

Serves 12

4-1/2 pounds fresh salmon cut from the middle of a large fish—split in half (it's essential that you have two matching halves), cleaned, filleted, and scaled (all of which your fishmonger should happily do for you)

1 large bunch of dill

2 ounces coarse salt

2 ounces caster sugar

2 tablespoons white pepper, coarsely ground (black will do, if you really can't find any white)

⌒Remove the pinbones (the small lateral bones) from the salmon using fish tweezers (see page 113) or a clean pair of pliers.

⌒Wash and dry the dill, then roughly chop it. Place half the fish skin-side down on a small dish (glass or stainless steel) or in a casserole and spread the dill on top. Combine the salt, sugar, and pepper in a bowl, then spread evenly on top of the dill. Place the other salmon piece on top, skin-side up, to make a salmon and dill sandwich. Cover it with foil and put a dish on top, weighing it down with something heavy. Put in the fridge for two to three days, turning it over every twelve hours or so and basting each half with the juices that are released.

⌒After your two to three days have elapsed, scrape the dill and seasoning away (otherwise it's difficult to cut) and pat dry. Slice the salmon diagonally very thinly, discarding the skin, and serve with hot buttered toast and a cucumber salad.

MUSIC SUGGESTIONS

Anything by the Wannadies, especially the singles "Shorty" or "You and Me Song," or anything by the Hives, Soundtrack of Our Lives, or ABBA.

Smug Homemaker Iced Pea and Lemon Grass Soup

It pains me to say it, but this soup is simple, quick, easy, unshowy, and absurdly delicious—everything (other than the delicious bit) that I hate in a recipe. It's even cheap, for crying out loud, yet I urge you in the strongest possible terms to try it. I know, I know: There are a hundred "quick and easy" recipes published every week, and I despise every last one of them for their smug Martha Stewart slickness and the clean, bright, "lifestyle-y," short focal–length photos that illustrate them. But this really is delicious, and you must make it.

How I ever came up with "pea soup with a fusion twist" is a shameful mystery—that's not cooking, that's marketing. Where's the guilt and redemption of adventurous cooking? Where's the decadence, the alchemy, the sex, and the power? In mitigation, can I just say that I invented it (if you can ever invent a recipe) as an apology to a pregnant vegetarian friend called Ruth who I'd invited over when I was cooking suckling pig?

To raise the stakes a bit, the best way to serve this is in a bowl cast from thick ice. That should add a bit of unnecessary spectacle. The only slight complication is that the soup needs to be made early

enough before your meal to allow it to chill in the fridge—anywhere from three to six hours, but hey. You can, of course, just put it in a normal bowl, but that would be missing a trick.

Look, I'm sorry, okay? Cook suckling pig for your main course and you won't need to hang your head in gastronautical shame.

Serves 8

a splash of olive oil

a bunch of spring onions or baby leeks, finely chopped

2 cloves of garlic, sliced or crushed

5 cups vegetable stock—cubes or paste are fine

2 pounds frozen peas

lettuce, chopped

2 handfuls of cilantro leaves and roots, chopped

a bundle of lemon grass—say, 6 stems

6–8 lime leaves, if you can find them—it's no tragedy if you can't

juice and zest of 2 limes

salt and pepper

crème fraîche, to serve

Peel the outer layers of the lemon grass away and tie them up together with a piece of string. Chop the tender white centers and put aside.

In a large saucepan, heat the olive oil and gently sweat the spring onions (or leeks) and garlic. Add the stock and bring to a gentle boil. Add the peas and bring back to boil. Add the lettuce. When the peas are tender, turn off the heat.

Add the cilantro, lemon grass, lime leaves (if you've got them), and juice and zest of the limes. Cover and put somewhere to cool.

When it's cool, take out and reserve the lime leaves and lemon grass bundle and whiz the rest in a food processor.

Transfer the liquid to a large serving bowl, put the lime leaves and lemon grass back to steep in the soup and leave in the fridge to chill for three to six hours.

To serve, check the seasoning (cold soups generally need more salt), ladle into bowls, add a spoonful of crème fraîche to enrich it, tuck in and feel the guilty pleasure. I'm sorry. Did I say that already?

MUSIC SUGGESTIONS

Something to eliminate smuggery: the Jesus and Mary Chain compilation *21 Singles* or the John Spencer Blues Explosion's *Extra Width*.

King Edward's Chippenham Cheese Savory

Chippenham is a town near Bath. King Edward VIII gave up the throne of England for love (with governorship of the Bahamas thrown in, which isn't such a bad gig, truth be told). What the two have in common has eluded me, but allegedly this was one of his favorite dishes. It's great for a light supper or big afternoon snack, so I recommend you go for a big walk after lunch and come back to a serving of this to fill the gap. In nature, it's a kind of fondue-on-toast, but much nicer than any fondue I've ever tasted. (Other than *Toffee Fondue*, but that's a whole different bag—see page 144.)

Serves 4 as a small snack (multiply according to greed)

1 egg yolk

1 egg

a wineglass of heavy cream

2 tablespoons milk

hot toast

5 ounces Parmesan, grated

salt and pepper

Separate the egg yolk and then add it to the whole egg in a saucepan together with the cream and milk and beat them all together. Make the toast, and meanwhile add the cheese to the pan and put it on a gentle heat. Keep stirring until the mixture is thick and creamy, then test and add salt and pepper if you think it needs it. Put the whole saucepan on the table and advise each guest to pour a spoonful of the cheese mixture onto their slice of toast.

MUSIC SUGGESTION
Elgar's "Pomp and Circumstance."

Chicken-foot Stew

Chicken feet deep fry wonderfully—they puff up like prawn crackers. They should then be marinated for twenty-four hours before being steamed. However, the marinade ingredients are quite hard to find, so I thought it best to settle for this stew instead. Feet are available from lots of butchers—if yours is posh, you will need to order them, but if it isn't, they'll often be in stock. You can choose to make just a strained broth for wimpier guests, but if you are dining with more adventurous types, leave some chicken feet in the soup.

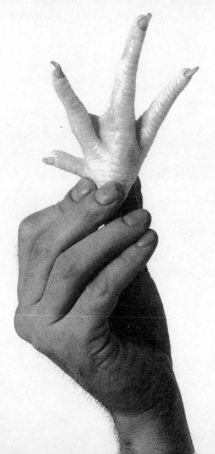

Serves 6

2 pounds of chicken feet (the bigger the better)

a knob of butter

1 pound of potatoes, thickly diced

2 onions, chopped

3 carrots, sliced

a handful of green beans

4 bay leaves

1 clove of garlic, chopped

2 quarts water

Wash the chicken feet and chop the nails off—with poultry shears, if you have them, scissors or wire cutters if you don't. Set aside.

Heat the butter in a large saucepan and add the potatoes, onions, carrots, beans, bay leaves and garlic. Fry gently for five to ten minutes, then add the water and chicken feet and turn up the heat. Simmer gently for thirty to forty-five minutes.

Either strain the stew and reduce it for ten minutes to serve as a broth, or, if your guests are brave, serve as is.

MUSIC SUGGESTIONS

Funky, swampy music from the Meters—*Best of the Meters* even has their "Chicken Strut" track. Also Little Milton's "Grits Ain't Groceries."

Laver Bread

Alongside leeks and mead, laver bread has always been referred to as a Welsh cultural curiosity and has never been given the love it deserves. To be honest, no traditional Welsh food has been given the love it deserves, possibly because the Welsh themselves haven't enormously appreciated it. But all this is changing. One of my current favorite-cheeses-in-the-world-ever comes from Wales (Gorwydd Caerphilly, and I'm a man who normally hates Caerphilly). Passion abounds in the higher culinary echelons of Welsh restaurateurs and food producers, and there seems to be a noticeable rediscovery and reinvention of traditional cuisine. For this last fickle reason alone, it's worth jumping on the bandwagon.

Laver bread has nothing to do with volcanoes (that would be lava bread). It is made from the purple-fronded seaweed *Porphyra umbilicaulis* (the same stuff that the Japanese use to make nori for sushi) that is commonly found on the Welsh coast and is traditionally served for breakfast with bacon, eggs, and cockles. The taste is hard to explain: It doesn't taste fishy, but it does have something of the sea. It reminds me of a sludgy spinach (in a good way), and it has a slight tartness to it—if "zinc-y" was a flavor adjective, it would be right.

Like spinach, laver is used as a side dish or as an addition to fish or vegetable pies, pasta, and risottos. It can be added just as it is, but if you're looking for a spinach consistency, it needs to be cooked for a long, long time before use. I prefer it for brunch.

If you're too far from the sea to lay your hands on the raw ingredient, or don't have six hours spare to cook it, you'll be relieved to know that it also comes in cans.

🖙 If you're using fresh laver bread, wash it thoroughly to remove all the sand, then place it in a thick-bottomed pan and cover with water. Bring to a boil, then cover tightly and simmer very, very gently for four to six hours, stirring it occasionally to stop it from sticking. Top up the water when necessary, but allow the liquid to evaporate at the end of cooking for that spinachy consistency.

𝒪 Add it to scrambled eggs as they are almost cooked. If you can handle cockles in the morning, put some hot laver bread in an ovenproof pan, scatter cockles on top, and sprinkle with breadcrumbs, cheese, a few shavings of garlic and a knob of butter before grilling it for three minutes.

MUSIC SUGGESTION
The Super Furry Animals' album *Out Spaced* (with explicit lyrics).

Mackerel Tartare

The French word *maquereau* means both the oily fish and "pimp." I can't vouch for the taste of fresh pimp (though if anyone can, please contact me at the usual address), but mackerel is one of the great undervalued gems of the sea: stunningly beautiful, delicious, and cheap. As long as they are fresh, they are delicious when eaten raw. Mackerel sushi, for instance, is even better than salmon, but it's nowhere near as popular, which has always been a mystery to me. Perhaps it's because mackerel is so cheap and looks so much like fish, whereas most raw salmon looks like boiled sweets.

At this point, I should mention fish tweezers. Sounds ridiculous, I know, but they make boning fish so quick and easy that it's possible to whip up a spread of sashimi in less time than it takes to make fish fingers and peas. The ones made by Global are my current favorites, if you don't mind spending a twenty on something that sounds so pretentious. No one need ever know.

Like all members of the tuna family, mackerel is a particularly powerful fish, carnivorous and active, and migratory. They are pelagic, traveling in shoals, and because of their high oil content, they spoil quickly, so eat 'em fast. Best to have this as a starter—a full-size plate will make heavy going. The Jerusalem artichokes are a nice base for the tartare, and as well as ensuring a lively evening in the lower intestines, they ensure that the dish isn't too rich. As with all major ingredients, start by naming your fish.

Serves 4 as a starter

1 pound Jerusalem artichokes, peeled

2 very fresh whole mackerel or 4 mackerel fillets

↪ Put the peeled Jerusalem artichokes in a saucepan of cold, salted water and bring it to a gentle boil. Cook them until tender—ten to twenty minutes, depending on their size.

↪ While they are cooking, look to your fish: remove all the bones from the mackerel, including

juice of half a lemon

salt and pepper

a splash of olive oil

For the dressing

1 egg yolk

1 teaspoon Dijon mustard

1/4 cup groundnut oil or peanut oil

1/4 cup olive oil

a smidge of lemon juice

a splash of water

a small handful of herbs, such as dill, chervil, tarragon, and chives, finely chopped

1 pack of lamb's lettuce

the pinbones, then skin it (a decent fishmonger will do this for you if you lack the dexterity). Dice it finely, then put it into a bowl with the lemon juice and season with salt and pepper. Cover and keep this in the fridge for the moment.

↻ When the 'chokes are ready, drain and leave to cool with a small splash of olive oil. Once cool, chop them finely to the same texture as the mackerel, and slip them into the fridge, too.

↻ Now for your dressing: Make a mayonnaise base by putting the egg yolk and mustard into a mixing bowl, then add the groundnut oil (or peanut oil) and olive oil drop by drop, stirring constantly with a wooden spoon. Add a smidge of lemon juice, then some water to loosen the mixture (we're after a dressing rather than a whippy mayo). Fold in the chopped herbs.

↻ Place a cookie cutter or upturned glass on a plate and arrange a base of artichokes around it. Cover that with a layer of the mackerel and top it with lamb's lettuce. Remove the cookie cutter, leaving a nice timbale shape. Drizzle the dressing over the top and serve.

MUSIC SUGGESTION

Try Nick Drake's delicious *Bryter Layter* album. A testament to the fact that miserable people can make beautiful music.

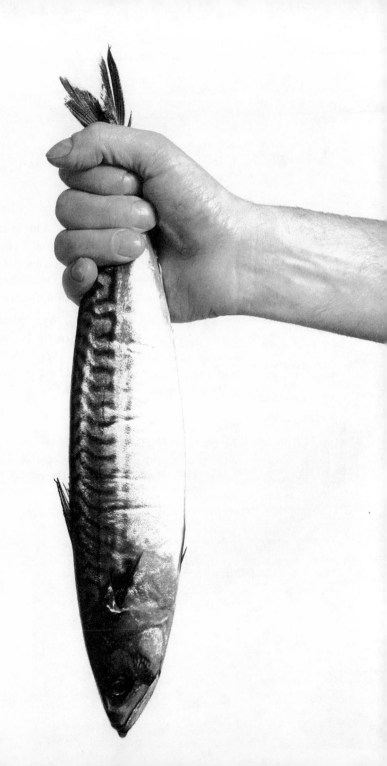

Heartbreaker
Elvis's Fried Peanut Butter and Banana Sandwich

There's no suggestion that Elvis died directly as a result of eating these, but it wouldn't have been a bad way to go. In his later years he would frequently request this heartbusting confection from his cook, so he was clearly a man who knew that his days were numbered. There's just *so* much fat in these babies, you could always cut out the middle man and staple them straight to your bottom.

Serves 1

1 small ripe banana

2 ounces peanut butter

2 slices white bread

3-1/2 ounces butter

In a bowl, mash the banana with the peanut butter. Spread the resulting goo on the bread and sandwich together. In a small frying pan, melt the butter until it's foaming, then add the sandwich and fry on each side until golden brown.

MUSIC SUGGESTIONS
No question: Elvis's version of "Suspicious Minds"— quite possibly the greatest song ever. Carry on and listen to the whole *Elvis Recorded Live on Stage in Memphis* album.

Lumpydick

For historical purposes, this one—it's far too similar to *Hasty Pudding* (see page 139) to be of real use. That said, the childishly amusing name makes it almost worth the effort. This is a dish championed by the Mormons (read from that what you will) but it actually has English ancestry. The word "dick" was used for boiled puddings (like spotted dick) and this was invariably lumpy. What's surprising is that it is, indeed, quick, cheap and easy. Tasty it isn't, but hey.

Serves 4

2 cups milk

3-1/2 ounces plain flour

pinch of salt

3 tablespoons molasses or treacle

a handful of sultanas

Warm the milk without boiling it. Slowly add the flour, stirring constantly as it turns into a mushy pea consistency. Add the remaining ingredients and serve. Good luck.

MUSIC SUGGESTION

Napalm Death's "Scum"—very quick but very horrid.

Buckinghamshire Bacon Badger

This is a meat suet pudding. It's from Buckinghamshire. Incidentally, "pudding" was a word for "entrails" in the fifteenth and sixteenth centuries, and other types of suet pudding include *Wet Nelly*, all sorts of roly-polys, *Plum Duff* and *Spotted Dog*. You'll need a cloth to steam this in, but don't let that put you off. You can use a clean dish towel, or even one of those muslins you use to wipe baby sick off your suit, if you have been blessed with progeny.

Bear in mind that the badger will need boiling (or steaming) for up to three hours, but you will be making one of those fantastically comforting suet puddings, encased in a deliciously soft pastry. It really is worth the effort. The good folk of Buckinghamshire tell me that there's also something called a *Buckinghamshire Clanger*, with meat at one end and apples or plums at the other, which the farm workers used to eat in the fields in times of yore.

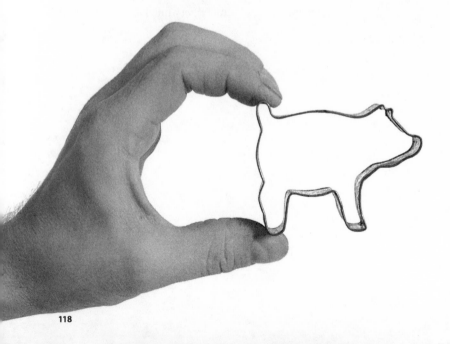

Sadly, this recipe doesn't involve a real badger. However, if you are fortunate enough to have one in the fridge, you could deal with it in the traditional Irish way, treating it as if it's pork to be cured for bacon. It has an ample layer of fat, by all accounts. Lay the legs and shoulders in a brine solution overnight and then spit-roast them. If you have no badger, try this for a party of four.

Serves 4

For the suet pastry

7 ounces self-raising flour

black pepper

3 ounces shredded beef suet

cold water

For the filling

14 ounces back bacon, sliced

1 medium onion, chopped

1 teaspoon sage, chopped

1 teaspoon fresh parsley, chopped

black pepper

3-1/2 ounces potatoes, diced

First, make your suet pastry: Sift the flour into a mixing bowl and grind in some black pepper, then add the suet and mix together using a knife. Add water drip by drip, mixing all the time until you have a nice gluey dough. Now use your hands to work it, binding it together into a smooth, elastic dough.

Lightly flour a work surface and roll the pastry out into an even rectangle about ten inches wide and as long as you can manage without the pastry getting too thin. Spread the bacon slices over the pastry, leaving a one-inch border around the edges. Cover the bacon with the chopped onion, sage, and parsley. Season with black pepper (no salt) and spread the diced potato along the middle. Roll the whole thing up, sealing the edges by pressing them together.

Wrap the roll tightly in your muslin or dish towel to keep its shape and boil gently in a large pan of water for three hours. Unwrap it and carve into large slabs. Serve with a salad and English mustard.

MUSIC SUGGESTIONS

Fairport Convention's *Unhalfbricking* album. Failing that, the Clash's *London Calling*.

Nettle Soup and Nettle Haggis

The noble art of hedgerow cookery is all very well if you have ready access to bucolic plenty, but less practical if you live in town.

One ingredient, however, is readily available, even in the city: nettles, which are found pretty much everywhere. In the spring and summer they'll grow almost anywhere there's a handful of soil. Believe it or not, nettles have a grassy, summery, rather optimistic taste.

Serves 6

For the soup

nettles—one small bag full

butter

salt and pepper

1 medium onion, chopped

1 medium potato, diced

1-3/4 cups vegetable stock

3/4 cup milk

3/4 cup crème fraîche (optional)

✍ Pick through your nettles, removing any coarse leaves and stalks and bugs. Wash them in water and then, without draining them too much, put them straight into a large saucepan. Boil very gently for about fifteen minutes. Strain the water off, then add a large knob of butter and seasoning. Set aside.

✍ Gently fry the onion and potato in butter in another pan until soft, then add the vegetable stock and the milk. Simmer for five minutes, then combine with the nettles and purée in a food processor.

✍ Serve with hot bread and butter and a floating knob of crème fraîche in every bowl.

MUSIC SUGGESTIONS

Anything by Ben Folds or the Ben Folds Five, especially the albums *The Unauthorized Biography of Reinhold Messner*, *Rockin' the Suburbs* and the tracks that Mr. Folds has recorded with William Shatner of *Star Trek*.

For the haggis

nettles—one small bag full

2 large knobs of butter

salt and pepper

7 ounces oatmeal, barley or rice

7 ounces leeks, chopped

7 ounces cabbage, chopped

6 bacon slices

As with the soup, pick through your nettles, removing any coarse leaves and bugs. Wash them in water and then, without draining them too much, put them straight into a large saucepan. Boil very gently for about fifteen minutes. Strain the water off, then add a large knob of butter and seasoning. Set aside.

Partially cook the oatmeal (or barley or rice) by boiling it in water for half of the cooking time stated on the packet. Gently fry the leeks, cabbage, and bacon in butter. When they are well sweated, mix well with the partially cooked oatmeal and the nettle mixture, wrap it in a dish towel or (preferably) a muslin cloth and simmer gently in a pan of water for one hour.

Serve with a nice gravy of your choice.

This really isn't a daredevil dish—Samuel Pepys himself enjoyed a nettle porridge in 1661. Formic acid is the stinging nettle's weapon but it's easily destroyed by cooking. You really need to pick nettles when they're young—spring and early summer—otherwise they become coarse, slightly bitter, and a tad . . . ahem . . . laxative. June is often the cutoff point, but it depends on the weather. When you're out gathering, wear rubber gloves and just pick the tops—the first four leaves are the best. And whatever you do, don't pick budding nettles. I did this recently when pressed for time, and I had to ditch a whole batch of soup. It won't take long to fill your bag.

Rabbit Pie

In the scheme of things, this isn't really exceptional, but it is still surprisingly uncommon. Why so many people can't eat a bunny wabbit but are happy to tuck into a cute little chicken is bizarre. Rabbit is usually something you eat in restaurants or on holiday rather than at a friend's house, which is a great shame. It's a lovely meat, similar to chicken, but with a nice depth to the flavor and pretty cheap. Samuel Pepys thought very highly of it and, frankly, that's enough for me.

It's a good exercise in anatomy to skin and prepare the rabbit yourself. Pulling the skin off is pretty easy, but it's an undeniably gruesome task (you start wondering if you could skin a human, and what your own body might look like with no skin) and even more so if you need to skin a wild hare. Bizarrely, the worst bit is having to push the last contents of its bowels out through its bottom. Pathetic, I know. For full instructions on skinning a rabbit yourself, Hugh Fearnley-Whittingstall's *The River Cottage Meat Book* is very clear.

But let's be honest about the rabbit: It has more bones in it than chicken, which makes it slightly fiddly to eat, and because people are unfamiliar with it and don't know where to find the flesh, it can seem light on meat. Rabbit also carries very little fat, and if cooked without love and affection, it can be dry. This can be avoided if you cook it with a good fatty accompaniment, such as bacon or pancetta, or lots of butter. You just need to remember not to overdo it or it will be squeaky on the teeth like overcooked chicken.

You will need more than one rabbit if you want to feed four people, unless they are on a diet (the people, not the rabbits). Check with your butcher if you're unsure. This pie will give you a hands-on meal—literally—because fingers are essential to aid stripping the rabbits of their flesh. If you or your guests really can't cope with this, you could take the flesh off the bones in advance, but it's a tricky task for the uninitiated to perform with an uncooked carcass.

Serves 6

2 young rabbits
(You might want to
ask your butcher to
joint them for you if
the idea scares you.
Wuss.)

a knob of butter

salt and pepper

7 ounces dried fruit,
roughly chopped;
prunes would be
great, but figs,
sultanas, or dates are
also good

a large handful
of fresh parsley,
chopped

11 ounces bacon or
pancetta, thinly
sliced

1 glass of white
wine (a nice floral
Gewürztraminer
would be good)

2 cups chicken stock

flour

14 ounces puff pastry
(ready-made is fine)

1 egg yolk, beaten

✎ Name your rabbits.

✎ Preheat the oven to 350°F. Chop the rabbits into small joints (if the butcher hasn't already done this for you) and lightly brown them in a pan with a little butter.

✎ Choose a pie dish that looks as if it will fit your ingredients and place a layer of rabbit in the bottom. Season, place a few pieces of dried fruit on the meat, scatter a little parsley on top, and cover with a layer of bacon (or pancetta). Continue with these layers until you have used up all the ingredients. Add the glass of wine and enough stock to cover the rabbit with a little to spare. Cover the dish and place it in the oven for forty minutes or until the meat is tender. Add a teaspoon of flour if you like your gravy thicker.

✎ Remove the dish and roll out a lid of pastry. Very carefully (so as not to burn your hands) place the pastry on top. Brush this with the egg yolk and return to the oven for forty minutes or until the pastry is a good golden hue.

MUSIC SUGGESTION
Anything by Belle and Sebastian.

Gruel

I always used to wonder what gruel was. I imagined a thin broth tasting of brackish water thickened with dust or wood chippings. From reading my Dickens it seems that it must have been a cruel culinary torture aimed at maintaining the social order. I was upset to find that it's actually quite pleasant. It's a kind of sweetly spicy porridgy mess. I've used a splash of brandy, sugar, and a piece of orange peel, all of which would presumably have been reserved for the evil beadle back in the workhouse, but were common in recipes of the day. If I were broke, I'd definitely be happy to tuck into a bowl of gruel, especially after tilling the land all day. My two-year-old daughter was very happy eating it, but hard as I tried, I couldn't get her to look me rebelliously in the eye and say, "Please Sir, I want some more."

You wouldn't choose to eat gruel every day, but nonetheless, I thought the recipe for it might come in useful. You might want to play Victorian house, or, more importantly, you might have some unruly progeny, friends, or neighbors who need to be put in their place. Well, remove the last four ingredients from the recipe opposite and this baby is bound to ensure a merry equilibrium of misery and wipe out any upstart ambitions from their minds. Not only is it a grim affair, but it's specifically designed to firm up relaxed bowels. Heh heh.

Serves 8

9 ounces rice (you could substitute barley or wheat)

a length of orange peel

a stick of cinnamon

6 cups cold water

2 ounces brown sugar or golden syrup

a splash of brandy

◔ Put the rice, orange peel, cinnamon stick, and water in a saucepan and cover with a lid. Bring to a boil, then simmer gently for one hour until the rice has disintegrated, stirring occasionally and adding more water if it dries out (you're looking for a porridgy consistency). Add the sugar and brandy and serve.

MUSIC SUGGESTIONS

Here's one of the loveliest songs ever recorded, wrapped up in the hopes and dreams of children, to ameliorate the grim history of this dish and its association with Oliver Twist. It is Chet Baker's rendition of "Over the Rainbow" from the album *White Blues*. Melting. Also, try the Langley Schools Music Project—a children's choir that sings classic '60s pop—sounds goofy but it is actually very, very cool. If you're re-creating a bit of Victoriana for fun, the original cast recording of *Oliver!* has some cracking tunes that you've long forgotten.

Monkey Gland Steak

This recipe was popularized in South Africa in the last century, but its roots go back to Victorian times. This recipe is completely faux—which is handy, because it's a nightmare laying your hands on monkey glands. What we have here is a sweet, piquant sauce that goes with steak and is mildly amusing to tell your guests about.

Incidentally, that whole thing about the Chinese lopping off the skull of a live monkey and then poking it up through a hole in the table to allow diners to spoon out the brains is a myth perpetuated by movies like *Indiana Jones and the Temple of Doom*. There are hundreds of secondhand or apocryphal stories, but no reliable firsthand accounts. Maybe it's one of those mythical recipes born of fear and ignorance.

Anyway, as I said, this recipe is also an imitation—it may well taste in some way of monkey glands, but I have no way of confirming this (if you can corroborate, do tell). There seem to be hundreds of recipes for it, but whether these were born of humor, distaste, or the Victorian love of mock recipes (see *Mock Turtle Soup* on page 152), I know not.

Serves 4

2 tablespoons olive oil

1 pound thin sirloin steak

2 ounces butter (or drippings if you have some)

1 medium onion, chopped

a handful of fresh parsley, chopped

salt and pepper

a splodge of tomato ketchup

✐ Heat the oil in a sauté pan, then sear the steak very quickly on a high heat. Depending on the thickness of the meat, you'll need different cooking times, but beware: This should be very lightly seared or it will become tough. Remove and keep on a warm plate (not in a hot oven or it will overcook).

✐ Let the pan cool, then add the butter and gently fry the onions with the parsley until translucent. Add the seasoning and the sauces (for God's sake, don't overdo it with any of the sauces as it's the combination that's important) and enough water to give it a loose gravy consistency. Simmer for two minutes.

a splodge of HP
brown sauce

a shake of
Worcestershire sauce

water

✐ Add the meat and cook for another two
minutes. Serve with *Clapshot* (see page 130) to mop
up the juices.

(see page 130)

MUSIC SUGGESTIONS
Captain Beefheart and His Magic Band: *Safe as Milk* or
Trout Mask Replica albums—strange and slightly scary
types of twisted blues, with insane, surreal lyrics.
When your guests are already slightly worried about
the nature of their supper, this will add nicely to the
paranoia.

Carpetbagger Steaks

Americans might think these were served in the South after the Civil War, but these little fellas actually grew up in Australia—traditionally not the best hunting ground for gastronautical flights of fancy, but by all accounts a lovely place for a holiday. This unlikely food combination probably has its roots in the traditional beef and oyster stew taken over by the original English émigrés. Oysters used to be cheap peasant fare, but fillet certainly never was. It's safe to say that this is now a bloody expensive dish, and you can only really justify it by comparing it to the amount that a party of four might spend in a restaurant. Actually, that's no comfort at all, is it?

Serves 4

8 oysters

2 pounds fillet of beef in one piece, cut from the thin end of the fillet

salt and pepper

2-1/2 ounces butter

a splash of olive oil

watercress for garnish

✑ Open the oysters and drain their juices in a colander for a minute or two. Cut a long pocket deep into and along the fillet and stuff the oysters into it. Bind the fillet up carefully with string, or, if you have the means, sew up the slit.

✑ Season the fillet all over. Heat the butter and oil in a thick-bottomed frying pan or sauté pan. When the butter begins to froth, add the seasoned steak and sear for five minutes on each side, making sure to sear the uncooked edges.

✑ Cut the steak into four and try to manhandle two oysters into each portion. Garnish with watercress and serve to great acclaim.

MUSIC SUGGESTION

Kylie's duet with Nick Cave, "Where the Wild Roses Grow."

Clapshot

A wonderful mash of turnips and potatoes that originated in Scotland. It's a classic accompaniment to haggis but is also great with other strong flavors, such as sausages or cod, or as a bed for scallops and black pudding. The good people of Orkney in Scotland lay claim to this dish, and as they seem to eat a frightening amount of the stuff, it seems churlish to argue.

Serves 4

1 pound of potatoes, peeled and cut into largish chunks

1 pound of turnips, peeled and cut into largish chunks

1 tablespoon chopped chives or 1 small onion, finely chopped

3-1/2 ounces lard or butter

salt and pepper

🍥 Boil the potatoes and turnips until soft. Drain and add the chives (or onions), lard (or butter), salt, and pepper, and mash the bejesus out of everything.

🍥 Incidentally, I often add a raw egg to my mash for an extra luxurious touch, though you should under no circumstances do the same.

🍥 For a spectacularly simple meal, fry some black pudding until just cooked (don't fry it to a crisp whatever you do) then mix it in with some warm clapshot, breaking it up as you go. Rather good with brown sauce, i'faith.

MUSIC SUGGESTIONS

Meatloaf's album *Bat Out of Hell*. *Dead Ringer* would do, if you've got that. Not Scottish, but brilliant.

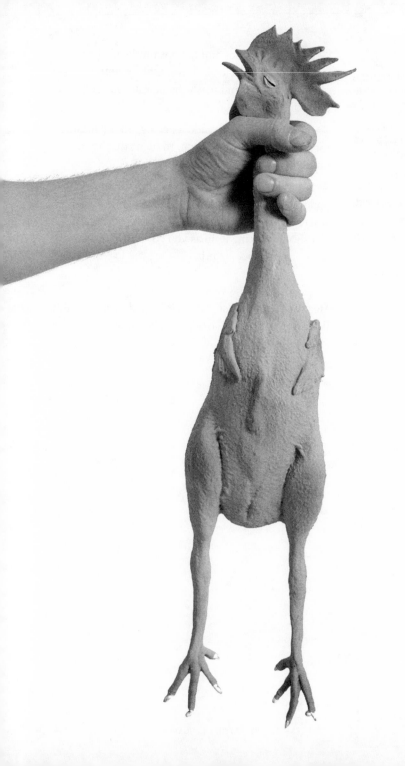

Picasso's Poussin

Poussins are young chickens. Some say that they haven't developed enough flavor to be truly great, but I urge you to ignore these crazy fools. They're the sort of people who claim you should never cook an oyster. When you calculate the surface-area to body-mass ratio of a poussin, you realize what all the fuss is about. They have a spectacularly high proportion of delicious skin, and the smaller the bird, the higher that proportion gets. That's why quails are so delicious—who cares about the lack of meat when there's so much of that delicious crispy skin to tear off?

Anyway, I have it on good authority that Picasso would always eat this when he visited the bistro *Chèz Camille Renault* in Paris. The man was no fool. Mad as a bag of frogs, sure, but foolish, *not*.

Serves 2 greedy people as a large main course

2 poussins

olive oil

salt and pepper

4 very ripe plum tomatoes (or similar)

20 pitted green olives

20 pitted black olives

2 ounces butter

✐ Preheat your oven to 425°F. Split the chickens along the back (i.e., not the breast side—the other side) and spatchcock them (spear them with two wooden skewers to keep them spread out). Splash olive oil all over them, season them with salt and pepper, and lay them breast down in a roasting pan. Cook for twenty minutes, turning them over after the first ten minutes.

✐ While they're roasting, boil a pan of water and drop the tomatoes into it for ten seconds, then peel, quarter, and seed them. Put the tomatoes in a bowl with the olives.

✐ When the poussins are done, remove them from the roasting pan, spread the butter over them, and cover them with foil to keep warm. Place the tomatoes and olives in the empty dish and put into the oven for five to six minutes.

When the tomatoes are just getting soft, remove from the oven, add the poussins and butter to the pan to slosh around in the juice and then serve the lot. To experience the full effect, eat with your fingers rather than knives and forks.

MUSIC SUGGESTION
Django Reinhardt's *Djangology.*

Interactive Pizza Engineering

There's nothing interesting about making pizzas unless you own a successful Pizza Hut franchise. However, pizzas are the perfect way to eat good ingredients, so why not get your guests to build their own? It's very amusing, and I thoroughly recommend it. If you've screwed up an otherwise pleasant supper by inviting a bunch of people who clearly have nothing in common, you can still salvage the evening by getting your guests to build their own pizzas at the table. It's a great icebreaker, and the happy chaos distracts everyone from your appalling lack of judgement. Needless to say, children love making their own pizzas. Witness with joy the dismay on their parents' faces when you actively encourage kids to play with their food.

You do have to make dough, but trust me, it's dead easy. It's also a good way to get rid of any weird cans of anchovies, squid, figs, prunes, etc., that you've got knocking about the cupboard and can't, for the life of you, think what to do with them.

Warning: Throwing lots of different ingredients on the pizzas will generally make them taste the same. Restraint here is everything. To maximize the fun, encourage your friends to build a series of small pizzas rather than a single large one.

Making the dough

Serves 6

For the dough

1 pound, 2 ounces of flour (00 Italian flour if possible) plus a bit for dusting

salt and sugar

1 sachet dried yeast

1-1/3 cups lukewarm water

◌ Start this bit at least forty-five minutes before you plan to eat. Put your flour and salt into a big bowl. In a separate bowl, dissolve the yeast in the warm water and add the sugar, then slowly add this mixture to the flour, stirring as best you can until it forms a good, firm dough (you may need slightly more or slightly less water, depending on your flour). Shape the dough into a ball and leave it to rest for five minutes. Knead it gently for eight minutes, then split it in half and shape it into a couple of balls. Sprinkle a dish towel with flour and put the dough on it. Dampen another towel and lay it over the top. Leave the dough to rise for thirty minutes or so and start sorting your toppings.

Making the toppings

For the toppings

2 14-ounce cans of chopped tomatoes

salt and pepper

fresh herbs such as basil, rosemary, oregano, marjoram, or thyme—chopped

1 pound, 5 ounces of red peppers, zucchini, eggplant, fennel, red onions, etc.

olive oil

Parmesan

a small tin or jar of anchovies

olives

ham—Parma or Bayonne—torn into strips

chorizo, sliced

arugula

whatever else is knocking around: sardine fillets, mushrooms, figs, apricots, canned octopus, etc.

3 mozzarella balls, sliced

These should all be tackled well before supper— the day before, even. Pour off the juice from your tomatoes and place the chopped bits in a bowl. Add seasoning and any herbs from the list you can lay your hands on.

Chop your vegetables into strips (do the aubergines at the last minute else they'll turn brown). Pour a few splashes of olive oil into a ridged griddle pan and put it over a high heat. (Alternatively, oil your broiler and use the oven.) When the oven starts to smoke, slap the exhaust fan on and add the vegetables (you'll need to do a couple of batches, but try to keep the different vegetables separate). After four to five minutes they'll have those pretty grill marks on them and you can turn them over. They'll spit at you now. Give them a few more minutes and then do the same with the eggplant. Purists may say that you should salt the eggplant and zucchini, but it isn't strictly necessary. Once everything is done, throw some herbs and seasoning on the vegetables, slosh some more olive oil over them, and cover. They will become a little sloppy, but that's all for the best.

Making the pizzas

✐ Preheat the oven to 475°F, or as high as your oven will go. Put all your toppings into separate bowls and spread them around the table. Chuck a small hunk of dough at each of your guests and pair them up to share a baking tray. They should lightly flour their tray first, then squish their dough—thin for flavor, thick for hunger. Tell them to start with a splash of tomato and olive oil, then go crazy. Save the mozzarella to the end, then pour more olive oil on top.

✐ Once everyone's ready, pour another splash of olive oil over the top of the pizzas and season. Slip them into the oven for seven to ten minutes, checking that the dough has baked. Serve, remembering that the pizzas will be volcanically hot for a couple of minutes.

Eggplant, as you may well know, is a fruit, not a vegetable. It has a warm, fleshy womb in which pretty little seeds are nurtured. You may not be aware, however, that The Priest Fainted is the most renowned eggplant dish in the whole of Arabia. It consists of a scooped-out eggplant filled with a mixture of garlic, onions, tomatoes, currants, parsley, herbs and loads of olive oil, which is then boiled or braised and served at room temperature.

Among the various ridiculous and unalluring names appended to this poor fruit is "apple of madness" (Greek from the Latin). And why you Yanks turned our perfectly good "aubergine" into "eggplant" I'll never know. The very thought of this, I'm sure, brings tears to the most modest chicken's eyes.

MUSIC SUGGESTIONS

Raucous opera: Mozart's *Così fan tutte*, *The Marriage of Figaro*, and *Don Giovanni*, or Rossini's *The Barber of Seville* should do the trick.

Andy Warhol's Chocolate Balls

I n 1959 Warhol and his friend Suzie Frankfurt made the world's best cookbook, called *Wild Raspberries*. Be warned that it's also the world's most useless, as the recipe quoted below shows.

Chocolate Balls à la Chambord

"Decorate a ten-inch-round silver platter with maraschino cherries, fresh mint, and almond fillets, then call up the Royal Pastry Shop and have them deliver a pound of half-inch chocolate balls. Serve with no-cal ginger ale to very thin people only."

MUSIC SUGGESTIONS
Obviously, Lou Reed's *Transformer* and anything by Frank Zappa.

Hasty Pudding

D espite the popularity and rich history of this British classic (whose pedigree can be traced back to the Middle Ages), it is possibly one of the worst dishes I have ever had the privilege to cook. After experimenting with several different versions, I served it just yesterday to a tablesworth of my closest friends and they all hated it without exception. One of them, a lad who we'll call Ewan (mainly because that's his name) proclaimed it "****ing disgusting." It pains me to admit this because, heaven knows, I love tinkering with ancient dishes and am happy to endure many an iffy meal if the sense of adventure makes up for the food. But there are lines to be drawn, and mine is drawn at *Hasty Pudding*.

Normally I wouldn't bother wasting your time telling you about dreadful food, but since you're an intrepid soul who might be tempted by the recipe's provenance, I feel it's only my duty to warn you.

The clue's in the name of this dish—it's about rustling something up quickly out of the sorts of food you'll have lying around the house. Namely sugar, flour, milk, and some stale spices. Variations include butter, raisins, nuts, and apples, but the overall effect is the same every time: a dull, gloopy custard made out of flour rather than eggs. The question is: Why not just make nice custardy custard?

Of course, if you have a version of this that you swear actually tastes good, I'm reluctantly interested. After all, you can't believe anything Ewan says—the lad doesn't eat cheese, for Christ's sake. **Under NO circumstances should you bother to make this.**

Serves none

4-1/4 cups warm milk

5 ounces butter

2-1/2 ounces plain flour

3-1/2 ounces powdered sugar

2 teaspoons ground, stale cinnamon or nutmeg

a pinch of mace or 1 bay leaf

✎ Don't warm the milk in a saucepan and don't boil it. Don't set it aside. Don't melt half the butter in another pan or stir in the flour. Don't add the warm milk little by little, stirring all the time until the mixture is smooth. Don't add the sugar, cinnamon (or nutmeg), and mace (or bay leaf), and don't simmer for a few minutes. Don't cool it and above all, don't bother to serve.

MUSIC SUGGESTION

Punk Rock Baby—a collection of punk classics reworked as lullabies for nascent hooligans. I'd put this on and have a nap instead of making the Hasty Pudding.

Flummery

This is essentially jellied booze. No bad thing really.

Flummery started life as a porridge-derived jelly, mentioned in fifteenth-century Scottish manuscripts. It can be flavored with honey, rose water, or alcohol, and in the seventeenth century it evolved into a sweet jelly made with cream or almonds. Mrs. Beeton, the legendary English food writer, gives a recipe for Dutch Flummery in her Book of Household Management, but it's not enormously practical— she seems to have been more of a compiler than a cook. Don't worry, though: I've screwed up several of these so that you don't have to.

Serves 6

rind of 1 lemon

2 cups water

9 ounces sugar

gelatine—enough for 6 cups (see packet for instructions)

8 egg yolks

juice of 4 lemons

2 cups sherry or Madeira or good white wine

a small shot of brandy

◌ Lightly oil a six-cup jelly mold. Mix the lemon rind, water, and sugar in a pan and simmer gently for ten minutes. Turn off the heat, add the gelatine and stir until dissolved. Beat the egg yolks well, then add them to the pan with the lemon juice and sherry (or the Madeira or wine). I know it sounds like a huge amount, but hey.

◌ Heat very gently to thicken it—around fifteen minutes should do—stirring all the time so it doesn't curdle or boil. If you've got a bain-marie, that would be ideal to use. Otherwise, just take care.

◌ Add the brandy at the last minute, then turn into the lightly oiled jelly mold. Leave to set, preferably overnight. Be careful serving to kids as it will still be alcoholic.

MUSIC SUGGESTION
Lemon Jelly's album Lost Horizons.

Deep-fried Mars Bar

Serves 1

1 Mars bar

3-1/2 ounces plain flour

2 ounces cornstarch

a pinch of bicarbonate of soda (baking soda)

3/4 cup (approx) beer—bitter or ale

8–12 cups groundnut oil or sunflower oil for frying

ice cream, to serve

⟲ Chill the Mars bar in the freezer for at least thirty minutes.

⟲ To make the batter, put the flour, cornstarch, and bicarbonate of soda (baking soda) together in a bowl, then slowly pour in the beer, mixing it in until it has the texture of double cream.

⟲ Heat your deep-fat fryer to maximum (if it's electric) or until a shred of bread will brown within a few seconds. It shouldn't be so hot that it smokes, though. Take the Mars bar out of the wrapper and coat it in the batter. Drop it into the hot oil and fry until the batter is golden brown.

⟲ Serve with ice cream.

Variations

Try the mini-Mars bars or dabble with healthier options, such as deep-fried battered satsuma portions, bananas, grapes, or olives. But beware: they are wont to explode.

MUSIC SUGGESTION
Ian Brown's *Music of the Spheres*.

Toffee Fondue

Possibly the naughtiest food I've ever had the privilege to eat, this was standard fare at my parents' dinner parties. My sister and I would invariably wake early the following morning to find the table in a completely slutty state, with half the toffee fondue abandoned in the middle, possibly because their guests all had spontaneous heart attacks soon after eating it.

You can force a minor level of sophistication into this by using foods that contrast with the heft of the toffee—cold grapes and strawberries are good. You'll find, however, that your friends are inexorably drawn to the gloopier combinations using jellybeans, marshmallows, almonds, or, heaven forbid, hunks of chocolate.

Serves 6

1 pound of your
favorite toffees

3/4 cup heavy cream

For dipping

pieces of apple
and pear, grapes,
pineapple cubes,
figs, strawberries,
etc., preferably
chilled

marshmallows,
Jellybelly jelly beans,
hunks of chocolate

◇Unwrap your toffees and put them with the cream in a thick-bottomed saucepan (or fondue pan if you have one). Put the pan on a very low heat and stir continuously as the toffees slowly melt.

◇Put all your dipping fruit and sweets on the table, together with some forks or wooden kebab sticks (proper fondue forks are obviously best). Place the pan in the middle of the table . . . and dive in. Make sure you leave some in the pan for small people to steal in the morning.

MUSIC SUGGESTIONS

Mullet rock, such as Manfred Mann's *"Blinded by the Light,"* Starship's *"We Built This City,"* Foreigner's *"I Want to Know What Love Is,"* Van Halen's *"Jump"* and Peter Frampton's *"Show Me the Way."*

Frumenty

I t's a slightly laughable name, but back in the Middle Ages this was all the rage. A staple food, *Frumenty* was the medieval version of chips, as Nichola Fletcher describes it in *Charlemagne's Tablecloth*. It's basically a porridge made from wheat or oats, and was even eaten by Henry IV for his wedding feast on the occasion of his marriage to Joan of Navarre. They ate "porpoise with frumenty," which sounds interesting, if hard to re-create.

After its heyday, *Frumenty* was transformed into a sweeter affair, eaten in the north of England as a Christmas dish. This is a recipe for a sweet version—the wheat porridge version is, frankly, pretty dreadful—and it's a good accompaniment to venison.

Serves 4

3-1/2 ounces whole kibbled wheat (e.g., bulgar wheat)

1-2/3 cups whole milk

2 cinnamon sticks

2 tablespoons sultanas or raisins

1 egg yolk

1 tablespoon honey

a pinch of salt

✏ Put the wheat in a pan and cover with lots of water. Leave it overnight at room temperature to soak and expand. In the morning drain it, then add it to a pan with the milk and cinnamon sticks, bring to a boil and simmer gently for twenty minutes. Add the sultanas (or raisins) and continue simmering for forty-five minutes. Beat the egg yolk with the honey and stir it into the mixture. It should be rather glutinous, with soft grains. Add the salt. If the mixture gets too dry, loosen it up with extra milk.

MUSIC SUGGESTION

Christopher Hogwood records lots of early music, playing all sorts of wheezeboxes, clavichords, and sackbuts. You could also try Vaughan Williams's *Fantasia on Greensleeves* (the original was allegedly written by Henry VIII), or Brian Eno's album *Ambient I: Music for Airports*.

Chapter 5
Adventures for the Bold and the Brave

Sea Urchin Gonads

Sounds odd, I know, but that's what the edible bits of sea urchins are. Just as the roe of a scallop contains both the sexual organs of male and female (the orange section is the ovum, and the adjacent white section is the testis), so the sea urchin has five orange or pink ovaries (yellowish in the males), which can be eaten raw with a touch of lemon or, if you really feel that you have to cook them, made into an omelette. Always good to eat for your bacchanalian orgy, though they are quite hard to lay your hands on.

> If you're having trouble finding sea urchins, you could visit St. John restaurant on St. John Street, London EC1, where they and a host of other exciting culinary journeys await you. I recommend their ox heart, which is delicious and surprisingly tender. If you can't afford the airfare, try Asian food markets or fancy seafood markets in the U.S.

That's it. No recipe, no ingredients list. Just find your urchin (lots in the Mediterranean, but some do crop up around the coast in Britain and the U.S.), cut open horizontally (and carefully), squeeze lemon over it, and eat. If you can keep the salty liquor in the bowl of the urchin's carapace, you'll find this exquisite to spoon into your mouth with a little bread—salty and sweet at the same time. It's quite rich, though, and I find it best to have just a few teaspoonfuls with each urchin.

MUSIC SUGGESTION

If you manage to find sea urchins in their natural habitat, chances are you're lying on an air mattress, bobbing around off the coast somewhere in the Mediterranean. Paolo Conte's smooth—nay, oleaginous—collection, *The Best of Paolo Conte*, is therefore a perfect accompaniment.

Cow-heel Soup

I t's rare to spot footless cows in the field and it's relatively hard to find cows' feet in the shops. They can, luckily, be ordered from the butcher's or found in markets that specialize in West Indian or African produce (this dish is particularly popular in Trinidad and Tobago). With their high gelatine content, cows' feet are great for making broths. I find them mesmerizing.

In 1861 Charles Elme Francatelli (Queen Victoria's chief cook) published *A Plain Cookery Book for the Working Classes* with the stated intention of helping the poor to obtain "the greatest amount of nourishment at the least possible expense." His concept of expense appears to be a bit cloudy, with his recipes for goose and suckling pig admirably optimistic, even for the middle classes, but he did include a few cheaper recipes, including one for cow-heel broth, which he mixed with rice. It's a bit murky, though, so here's a slightly nicer one. It's a simple yet hearty affair, in the vein of *Mock Turtle Soup* (see page 152). "Unctuous" is the word.

Bear in mind that although it's very simple, it will need to simmer for four hours, and if you don't already have some stock it will take another three hours. But don't be deterred because, in Francatelli's words, "you will thus provide a savoury meal at small cost."

Serves 6

1 cow's foot— cleaned and sawn into pieces (there's not a chance in hell that you'll be able to do this yourself, so ask the butcher to do it)

1 beef shin— cleaned and sawn into pieces

✑ Put all the first seven ingredients in a pan. The stock should cover everything amply—if not, add more water or stock. Bring to a boil and simmer very gently for four hours, then add the glass of sherry (or Madeira).

✑ Melt the butter in a separate pan and stir in the flour. When it's a good paste, add a few splashes of the beef liquid to dilute it and add to the large pan. Simmer for another ten minutes, then serve with lots of lovely fresh bread.

15 black peppercorns

a pinch of mace

a large handful
of fresh parsley,
chopped

salt and pepper

10-1/2 cups light
beef stock (not stock
cubes, though—
sorry)

1/2 cup sherry or
Madeira

2 ounces butter

2 ounces flour

For simple beef stock, just roast three pounds of beef bones (your butcher will probably slip you some for free) at 425°F for an hour or so until nicely browned but not burnt. Tip the bones into a large pan with a quartered onion, two carrots, a celery stalk, a leek (all roughly chopped), a sprig of fresh parsley and thyme, and a few bay leaves. Cover with lots and lots of cold water (at least four quarts), bring to a boil and simmer very gently for two hours. (Normally you'd simmer for four to six hours, but for cow-heel soup you need to have quite a light stock.) Skim off the scum as it floats to the surface and top up with more water if necessary. Cool and strain.

MUSIC SUGGESTION
Trinidad Tropicana Steel Band's *Music of Trinidad.*

Pigeon Pie

I t may or may not come as a shock to you that pigeon pie traditionally contains as much beef as pigeon.

Serves 8

1/2 pound streaky bacon or pancetta

1-1/2 pounds rump steak or other good stewing beef

4 pigeons (or 8 pigeon breasts)

1 medium onion

2 medium carrots

7 ounces celeriac or celery

2 cloves of garlic

splash of olive oil

1 tablespoon plain flour

1 cup red wine

1 cup chicken stock

palmful of fresh thyme

salt and pepper

1 pound puff pastry

1 egg, beaten

⌀ Preheat your oven to 400°F. Meanwhile, prepare your ingredients: Roughly chop the bacon (any shape that takes your fancy, but not too small), and chop the steak into cubes. If you have whole pigeons, joint them into four pieces each— two breast joints and two scrawny leg joints. If you have only breasts, leave them whole. Roughly chop all your vegetables and the garlic.

⌀ Heat the oil in a frying pan, then fry the bacon until nicely crispy. Put this into a lidded casserole dish. In the frying pan, quickly sear the pigeon and beef a handful at a time, and add to the casserole. Fry the vegetables and garlic in any remaining fat (add more if you need to) and throw them into the casserole dish too. Stir in the flour to coat everything, then add the rest of the ingredients except the puff pastry and egg. Put the lid on and cook in the oven for two hours, checking occasionally to make sure it isn't drying out. Add water if necessary.

⌀ If you're a pigeon pie connoisseur, let the meats go cold before baking into a pie, otherwise put the contents of the casserole into a pie dish that will hold everything snugly. Cover this with a nice slab of puff pastry and brush the beaten egg over it. Bake this for twenty minutes at 400°F

Mock Turtle Soup

O f all the classic recipes that have gone the way of the deviled dodo, *Mock Turtle Soup* is surely the most deserving of recognition. As a dish, it's got it all—a mention in *Alice in Wonderland*, a bumptious pedigree rooted in colonial spoils, yet the humility to admit to the fake that it undoubtedly is. I like that in a dish.

Mock Turtle Soup was immensely popular from the 1750s until quite recently. To understand why, we must look at its posh sister, *real Turtle Soup*. Turtles used to be imported into Britain from the West Indies. They have always been seen as luxury ingredients (and had to be slaughtered in a rather gruesome manner involving spikes), so it was not long before chefs began to look around for an easier and less expensive substitute.

A turtle contains large amounts of green fat, which lends a silky texture to soup. The cheaper option is to use a calf's head, which, when cooked, releases huge amounts of gelatin, thereby creating a similar texture. With a touch of culinary humor that was unusual in Victorian hotel kitchens, a creative chef somewhere started to make mock turtles' eggs out of veal forcemeat balls to go in the

> **Incidentally:** Here is a selection of other mock foods: Poor Man's Goose (potatoes, onions, and lamb's liver); Fitless Cock (an oatmeal pudding); Mock Goose (pork fillet stuffed with apples and prunes); Toad in the Hole (no toad).

Mock Turtle Soup, so ironically the dish ended up as a rather luxurious item on the menu in its own right.

In the 1747 edition of her book *The Art of Cookery Made Plain and Easy*, Hannah Glasse includes a recipe for *Turtle Soup*, and by 1758 a mock turtle version was knocking around. Mrs. Beeton has two recipes for the mock version and a long, drawn-out one for the real deal.

Mock Turtle Soup is essentially a clean, clear, yet intensely rich broth made with veal stock, veal gelatin, and . . . well . . . bits of veal. The huge quantity of natural gelatin you get from these ingredients makes it velvety on the tongue. It also tastes very healthy—the sort of soup you'd give to a convalescent, or a whining, wheelchair-bound aunt.

You'll need to find a good butcher (he won't necessarily have to be a posh one) who'll supply you with loads of bones and slightly unusual cuts of meat. These days, calves' heads are a bitch to find—according to Chris at the famous north London butchershop Frank Godfrey, anything near the spine of a cow is just too fraught with regulatory hassle to be worth selling. So we came up with a workable alternative: A couple of calves' feet (sawn into pieces), some veal knuckle, and some stewing veal. A calf's foot is full of the glorious gelatinous goo that the head would have provided, and the stewing veal has the strength of character to withstand the hours of cooking required.

You need to start this recipe the day before you want to eat it, as the consommé can't be rushed. And go slowly, enjoying the fact that you're indulging a glorious part of British culinary heritage.

DAY 1

Making the Mock Turtle Soup

Serves 8

For the soup

2 calves' feet, sawn into 4, plus any veal bits the butcher might otherwise throw out

3 ounces pan drippings, lard, or butter

7 ounces of ham or 4 unsmoked bacon slices

1 pound stewing veal (shoulder, knuckle, etc.)

1 pound shin of beef

a stick of celery

2 each of carrots, onions, and turnips, quartered

⌒ Preheat the oven to 425°F.

⌒ Give your main ingredient a name to engender a mutual respect. In this case your main ingredient is a calf, so a name like Flora will ensure bovine familiarity. Do your *mise en place* (i.e., gather and prepare your ingredients) for the soup.

⌒ Lay the bones flat in an oven tray and roast them in the oven until they're nicely browned— usually about twenty minutes.

⌒ Heat the pan drippings, lard, or butter in the largest pan that you have and fry the ham (or bacon), the veal, and half the beef until it all begins to brown, then add the vegetables. Fry them for another five minutes or so.

⌒ Add the herbs, peppercorns, salt, and water. Bring the whole lot slowly to a boil, and skim off the oomskah that rises to the top.

a bouquet garni of fresh parsley, thyme, marjoram, and a bay leaf, tied with string

6 black peppercorns

salt

2–3 quarts water

a glass of Marsala or sherry

2 egg whites

⌀ Add the browned feet and other bones. Bring the mixture back to a boil, skimming again, then simmer on a gentle shudder for three to four hours.

⌀ Strain the liquid—this will be your clear soup— into a bowl to cool, and refrigerate it overnight. Reserve the most gooey and gelatinous parts of the calves' feet and chuck the rest of the foul mess away.

DAY 2

⌀ When you take the soup out of the fridge you should find that your stock is a rock-solid gelatinous block. Skim off any fat from the top and put it in a pan with the rest of the beef (this will help the soup clarify).

⌀ Next you need to clarify the soup with egg to remove the impurities that make it cloudy. It's quite fun to do, and should take you about twenty minutes, so whip the two egg whites to a froth in a bowl and then add them to the soup. Whisk the entire soup until a crust forms (this should take four to six minutes). Transfer to a pan, add the Marsala, heat it through, and let the whole thing simmer for ten minutes. When it's done, leave it to cool again, then gently pour off the liquid through a sieve (preferably covered with a muslin, too) into a clean bowl.

Making the forcemeat quenelles

For the forcemeat quenelles

3 shallots, chopped

4 ounces butter

9 ounces lean minced veal (from fillet or

⌀ Gently fry the shallots in half the butter until soft, then mix them together in a bowl with the minced veal and bacon (or ham or pork).

⌀ Squeeze as much milk out of the bread as you can, then add it to the meat, mixing thoroughly. Add all the remaining ingredients (make sure you

escalopes—the
butcher will mince it
for you)

7 ounces lean bacon
or ham or pork,
minced (again, ask
the butcher)

7 ounces stale white
bread, soaked in milk
for 30 minutes

7 ounces mushrooms,
finely chopped

a handful of fresh
parsley

salt and pepper

cayenne pepper

a pinch of mace (or
nutmeg, if you don't
have any mace)

1 egg, beaten

beat the egg), and when it's all nice and stiff,
separate into small egg-shaped dumplings for
poaching.

⌒ Heat a shallow saucepan of salted water and
poach each meatball for about four minutes,
depending on their size.

⌒ Take the remains of the calves' feet that you set
aside after making the soup and cut them into
small squares. You will use these bits of gelatinous
oomskah as a garnish.

⌒ To serve, reheat the soup, then pour it into
bowls with the forcemeat "turtles' eggs" and
scatter the diced calves' feet liberally over the top.
Serve, with some nice bread, to rapturous
applause.

MUSIC SUGGESTION

Victorian Britain was a musical desert, which is
fine because it allows me to mention an album that
the Victorians would surely have been appalled by:
Goran Bregovic's *Tales and Songs from Weddings and
Funerals*, a gypsy classic.

Fish Sperm on Toast

I always wondered how naughty it would feel to feed your guests something—only to shock them with its true nature afterward. The trouble is, if my friends refused to eat my food because they didn't trust me, it would be a disaster, so it's best to be honest, but to force your friends to eat what's offered using a two-pronged approach:

❈ Make sure they understand that they'll be mercilessly taunted and humiliated if they fail to eat what you serve.

❈ Make sure there's nothing else edible in the house, thereby narrowing their options.

Fish sperm is one of those scary-sounding ideas, although the reality is much more approachable. It is simply the soft roes of fish—often called milt—and the best come from carp, herring, or mackerel.

Serves 2

1 bay leaf

juice of half a lemon

a handful of soft herring roes, washed and cleaned of any membranes

1/2 cup dry white vermouth (Noilly Prat if you have it)

1 shallot, chopped

1 cup heavy cream

salt and pepper

✍ Heat a small saucepan of salted water to a boil, then turn down to a simmer. Add the bay leaf and lemon juice, then poach the sperm for four minutes, drain, and set aside. In another pan, heat the vermouth and simmer the shallot in it until the liquid has reduced by half. Stir in the cream, season, and heat until it's nearly boiling. Add the sperm and turn off the heat. Let it cool, then chill in the fridge.

✍ Serve with toast and a cucumber salad.

MUSIC SUGGESTION
Anything by the Tigerlilies.

The World's Oldest Recipes

There's no getting around it: The re-enactment of ancient recipes is a fool's game. I know this because I have frequently re-enacted them for my utterly unimpressed friends, and while food history has always fascinated me, it's never really caught the imagination of the public on a large scale. There are difficulties, too: It's hard to re-create historical dishes when the original ingredients are often impossible to find, and so many early recipes are impractical and elliptical for the modern cook. But let's persevere. It's such an extraordinary voyage of discovery to eat the way our ancestors did, and I love making the process of eating into something more than a fuel stop.

The earliest surviving cookbook is the ancient Roman Apicius's *De Re Coquinaria* from the first half of the first century AD. When Apicius discovered that he'd lost his fortune he ordered the most luxurious banquet Rome could provide, and after indulging himself alone, swallowed poison and died at the head of his table. His book lists 470 recipes, including this one.

Stuffed Dormouse

Gut your dormice (one per person) and stuff them with a mixture of pork, dormouse trimmings, pepper, nuts, stock, and laser (a fennel-like spice), all pounded together. Sew them up, place in a clay pot, and roast in an oven or boil in a larger pot.

All very gruesomely entertaining, but although *De Re Coquinaria* is the oldest cookbook, it doesn't have the oldest recipes. Oh no. These were discovered among the vast Babylonian collection of battered clay tablets at Yale University that displayed cuneiform (wedge-shaped) indentations made with reeds, dating back 3,700 years. They came from the birthplace of civilization, generally agreed to be the plains between the rivers Euphrates and Tigris—an area we currently know as Iraq. For years no one could translate the obscure text until the eminent French Assyriologist Jean Bottero spent several years deciphering three tablets and discovered thirty-five recipes, some of them remarkably complex, revealing a rich, sophisticated Mesopotamian cuisine. His book *The Oldest Cuisine in the World* is fascinating if a little impractical. Here are a couple of recipes to try—I reckon the pigeon broth is more achievable than the kid stew.

Kid Stew

"Singe the head, legs, and tail. Other meat [in addition to kid] is used. Prepare water; add fat; onion; samidu [probably a plant from the onion family]; leek and garlic, bound with blood and mashed. Then a corresponding amount of raw suhutinnu [probably another onion-related plant]."

Amursanu-pigeon Broth

"Split the pigeon in two; [other] meat is also used. Prepare water; add fat; salt, to taste; breadcrumbs; [something else]; onion; samidu [that onion family plant again]; leek and garlic. Before using, soak these herbs in milk. It is ready to serve."

MUSIC SUGGESTION
As luck would have it, the Babylonians also left us a selection of cuneiform tablets on music and music theory, which reveal a refined understanding of the art. It's relatively hard to find examples of this on CD, but there is one release that covers a whole slew of ancient cultures called *Music from the Earliest Times* on the label Harmonia Mundi Musique d'Abord.

Cooking with Insects
Grasshoppers, locusts, and crickets

These can be a bugger to catch, so while hunting, you'll need a steely demeanor, strength of purpose, and a big jar. The bugs have to know who's boss. Grasshoppers, locusts, and crickets are all members of the insect orders Hemiptera Orthoptera (characterized by large hind legs adapted for jumping), and they have a noble history as food, endorsed by the Bible no less: "Even these of them ye may eat: the locust after his kind . . . and the beetle after his kind, and the grasshopper after his kind" (Leviticus 11:22). Of course, Leviticus said a lot of stuff that wasn't worth the papyrus it was written on ("an eye for an eye" was one of his). But the point is that these little beauties are considered a delicacy across the known world—other than the Western world, where we tend not to value food if it's cheap and plentiful. As many a farmer will attest, grasshoppers create havoc with crops, so everyone's a winner when you cook them. Except the grasshoppers themselves.

Serves 2

20 assorted grasshoppers, locusts, cicadas, crickets, etc.

2 ounces butter

4 tablespoons (approx) olive oil

a splash of cider vinegar

a handful of fresh parsley, chopped

salt and pepper

↪ Pluck the heads and wings off your grasshoppers, etc., and boil them in salted water for thirty minutes, or until they're soft. Drain thoroughly.

↪ Heat your butter together with the oil in a frying pan until gently foaming. Add your grasshoppers, etc., and fry on a high heat until nice and crispy. Remove them from the oil and place on paper towels to drain. Transfer them to a warm bowl and sprinkle with the cider vinegar, chopped parsley, and salt and pepper. Dig in.

Woodlice (*Oniscus muriarius*)

If you don't have a ready supply in your house, take a trip to the nearest park or wood. Woodlice are often to be found lurking under the bark of rotten trees. Collect as many as you can—a full jam jar's worth is recommended to make the exercise worthwhile. These little critters have a habit of crawling out of your jar as it gets full, but don't worry—they don't go very fast. They taste similar to shrimp, which makes sense if you think about it.

Serves 4

1 full jam jar of common woodlice

4 ounces butter

1 teaspoon plain flour

1/2 cup water

1/4 cup milk

salt and pepper

Once you have collected a full jar of the critters, take 'em home. Boil a saucepan of salted water and drop your woodies into it. This will kill them instantly.

In another pan, gently heat the butter, and mix the teaspoonful of flour into it. Slowly add the water and milk, stirring constantly to ensure a smooth consistency. When it's nice and thick, drain your woodlice and mix them in. Yumski. I've had these deep-fried in Bangkok, and they were delicious.

Quick 'n' Easy Termites

No mucking about here. If you can lay your hands on termites in any great number, it probably means that your house is about to fall down. Gather them all up, my friend, and indulge in an orgy of schadenfreude while you still can.

I must admit that this is one of the few recipes in this book that I haven't yet tried—not for lack of interest, but rather for lack of ingredients. I stole the recipe from Vincent M. Holt's *Why Not Eat Insects?*, so I do hope it works.

Serves 4

2 cups termites

3 tablespoons vegetable oil

pinch of Maldon salt

Remove the wings of the termites and spread on a baking sheet to dry—preferably in hot sunshine. Pour your oil into a small frying pan and heat until it's smoking. Toss your termites in the hot oil until crisp. Drain them on paper towels and sprinkle with Maldon (a rarified English salt in beautiful, crumble-able crystals) salt, which has just the right consistency.

A spikey combination of Public Image Ltd, Bloc Party, the Future-heads, and Franz Ferdinand.

Frogs' Legs

L et's just get a few things straight: Frogs' legs do not taste fishy. In fact, they're a bit like chicken and have a very delicate texture. They are utterly delicious. I know this because I'm sitting here eating some.

The French do eat them, but not for every meal. Despite that, we are still entirely within our rights to call them "froggies" in much the same way as they call us (in their endearingly clumsy way) "rosbifs."

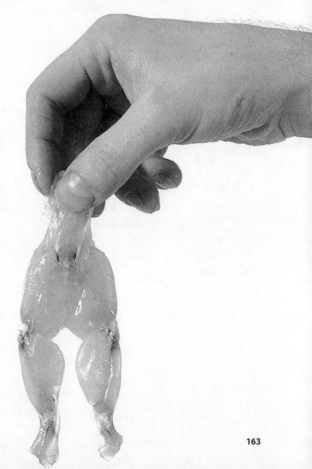

Most of the frogs' legs eaten in France are bought frozen and imported from Taiwan and Indonesia. Their French name is *grenouilles*.

Not being able to find them is a poor excuse for not cooking them. Raise your game by buying them online or through the mail (see list of suppliers on page 241).

Serving frogs' legs does raise eyebrows, but even your wettest friends should enjoy them after their initial revulsion. If you do have any problems, try Escoffier's trick—he called them "nymphs" because he thought that "frog" was a vulgar word. And where was Escoffier from? Nuff said.

They're disarmingly easy and quick to cook. The legs come already prepared—there's no frog peeling involved, which is a relief, even for me. They're usually wrapped in little individual plastic sleeping bags to keep them separate.

The idea with this recipe is to sauté them in a light dusting of seasoned and slightly garlicky flour. It's important to keep it delicate—a KFC coating won't do them justice.

Making the Frogs' Legs

Serves 4

20 pairs of frogs' legs

2 ounces flour

2 cloves of garlic, crushed

a small handful of fresh parsley, chopped

salt and pepper

4 ounces butter

lemon quarters, to serve

⌀ Gently defrost your legs and pat them dry.

⌀ Put the flour in a bowl, add the crushed garlic and chopped parsley, season with salt and pepper, and mix well. Dip your legs into the flour to give them a good dusting.

⌀ Heat the butter in a sauté pan or frying pan on a medium heat until it's bubbling.

⌀ Fry your legs until they're lightly browned and crispy all over, turning once. This should take around five minutes. Remove and (if the fat worries you) rest them on some paper towels. Dust with salt and serve with quarters of lemon.

Frog Sauce

Should the ease of the frogs' legs recipe insult your intelligence, and should you feel the need to tackle something more elaborate, try this sauce for pasta.

For the Frog Sauce

12 pairs of frogs' legs

2 knobs of butter

1 small onion, chopped

salt and pepper

1 tablespoon flour

1 cup vegetable stock

1 egg yolk

a small handful of fresh parsley, finely chopped

linguini

⌒Gently defrost your legs and pat them dry.

⌒Gently fry the frogs' legs in a knob of butter with the onion, salt, and pepper. Cook for ten minutes without browning.

⌒Meanwhile, put the flour in a bowl and slowly stir in the stock. Add it to the frying pan and turn the heat down. Simmer very gently for twenty minutes, stirring every now and then.

⌒Pick out the legs (don't throw the liquid away) and let them cool until you can pull the meat off. Sieve the meat and liquid into a bowl, pushing it through using a wooden spoon to make a fine paste. Add the second knob of butter, the egg yolk, and parsley.

⌒Cook your pasta to your preferred consistency, then drain and return it to the warm pan. Stir in the sauce, taking care not to cook it any further, and just warm it throughout.

MUSIC SUGGESTION

La Mauvais Reputation, a collection of songs by Georges Brassens, a French troubadour and national poet/treasure who spent a lot of his time in the southern French coastal town of Sète. He died of cancer in 1981. With lovely lyric-heavy, sweet or funny ballads, and folksy strummings, it's almost poetry, and very, very French. The sort of stuff you might hear in a Jacques Tati film.

Testicles

Oh, yes. Sometimes known as prairie oysters or "fries," it seems most appropriate for us to call them testicles. Specifically lambs' testicles. These are very difficult to lay your hands on, but if you're throwing a bacchanalian orgy (see page 38), you'll want to make the effort. My local butcher can't find them, and in desperation I have occasionally found them at Ridley Road market in east London, but really the only reliable source I've found is—and I say this at the risk of alienating any class warriors or residents outside London—Harrods, and even then they need ordering well in advance.

The problem is that almost all male lambs are castrated soon after birth, which seems a shame. On the other hand, I can imagine that those left uncastrated have experienced the heights of ecstasy more often than any of us could possibly hope for. So eat them with a mixture of schadenfreude, awe, or jealousy, depending on whether you are at peace with yourself.

Serves 1 as a small starter

1 testicle

salt and pepper

1 clove of garlic, crushed

seasoned flour, for dusting

a knob of butter

a handful of fresh parsley, chopped, to garnish

Drop your testicles (the lamb's, not yours) into a pan of boiling water and blanch them for two minutes, before running them under the tap and skinning them to remove any membranes. Slice them in half (come on—be brave). Season them with salt and pepper and crushed garlic. Dip them in a little seasoned flour and fry them in butter until they are nicely browned. Serve with sourdough toast and a sprinkle of chopped parsley.

MUSIC SUGGESTIONS
Bring it on music: Primal Scream's *Give Out But Don't Give Up*, the Rolling Stones' *Exile on Main Street* and *Definitely Maybe* by Oasis.

Rhinoceros Soup

Sadly, this is not a soup made from real rhinos, which are increasingly hard to come by these days. Rather, it's a soup originally made from the rhinoceros bird (*Buphaga Africana*)—a small Indian bird that is often found picking the ticks from rhinos (a precarious operation yielding humble returns, if you ask me). There is, however, a nice mock-food element to this dish, whereby it *kind of* resembles a rhino, and for that reason alone I heartily recommend this recipe, which comes from Bernard Clermont's *Professed Cook*, published in 1767 and made comprehensible by me in 2004.

The slight complication here is that if you can't lay your hands on any *Buphaga Africana*, you need either quails or pigeons with their heads on. These are easily found in even the grottiest *supermarché* in France, but are difficult to lay your hands on anywhere else except by ordering them. Ask your butcher to source some for you. If he tells you to take a hike, try visiting Harrods' food hall.

The dish is basically a good, rich veal stock in which the birds are poached and served with their heads poking above the liquid. The heads are held up by a skewer inserted through the body and up through the neck. It is a striking (some might say shocking) dish, made all the more memorable by the veal stock. This in itself is an amazing substance—all the gelatin from the bones makes it an incomparably unctuous, velvety liquid. If you really can't be bothered to make veal stock, use a good chicken stock instead, and beat yourself with chains at your earliest convenience.

You might like to consider doubling the quantities so that you can freeze half the veal stock to use later.

Making the veal stock

Makes 2 quarts

3 pounds veal bones (feet are particularly rich in gelatin), chopped

1 large onion, halved

2 large carrots, halved

1 stick celery, chopped

a bouquet garni— a bundle of fresh parsley, thyme, and bay leaf tied up with string

6 peppercorns

1 clove

1 clove of garlic, whole, unpeeled

2-1/2 quarts water

🗁 Preheat the oven to 450°F. Roast the veal bones for thirty minutes or so. Add the onions, carrots, and celery and continue roasting for fifteen minutes.

🗁 Find yourself a huge pot, add the roasted bones and vegetables, plus all the remaining ingredients. Bring it to a boil, turn the heat down so the pot just shudders occasionally, and skim the fat off.

🗁 Start whatever ventilation devices you have at your disposal and open all the windows. If you forget to do this, you will be able to enjoy the smell of veal stock for the next month, whether you like it or not. Simmer the stock for four to six hours.

🗁 Strain the stock, set aside to cool, and skim the fat off again.

Making the soup

Serves 4

4 pigeons or 4 quails, plucked and gutted but with the heads still attached

a knob of butter

a splash of olive oil

1 quantity veal stock (see above)

12 whole baby carrots or 14 ounces sliced carrots

🗁 Name your birds.

🗁 Push a skewer through the head and neck of each bird to keep it bent upward.

🗁 In a frying pan, heat the butter and oil and carefully brown the birds, taking care not to destroy the skewered heads.

🗁 In a saucepan, bring your stock to the boil. Season it and slip the birds in. Simmer gently for one hour (for pigeons) or thirty minutes (for quails). Add the carrots, parsnips, thyme, and parsley. Continue boiling for another forty minutes.

12 whole baby
parsnips or 14 ounces
sliced parsnips

4–6 sprigs of thyme

a handful of fresh
parsley, chopped

fresh bread, to serve

🖜 Ladle a good pool of broth into each bowl with a few vegetables, and add a bird, with the head floating nicely above the liquid.

🖜 Serve with hunks of fresh bread.

MUSIC SUGGESTION
The Peter Sellers Collection

Drisheen
Irish Blood Pudding

A speciality of Cork, this type of black pudding is made with sheep's (or lamb's) blood, breadcrumbs, and suet. Again, it's a question of finding the raw ingredients—a good butcher will try to get these things for you, but don't drop in (as I invariably do) in the vain hope that obscure substances might be in stock. You'll invariably be disappointed (I invariably am). There are several ways of making this— some say that a delicate mixture of sheep and beef blood is what's needed, but here's a simpler version.

Serves 8

1 quart sheep's blood

1 quart milk

2 cups water

5 ounces breadcrumbs

7 pounds mutton suet

salt

✐ Strain the blood into a bowl and add all the remaining ingredients. Leave it to stand for an hour or so. Bring it to a boil in a pan, then simmer for thirty to forty-five minutes and leave to cool— it should turn into a solid block.

✐ Drisheen is traditionally eaten with tripe, but it can be served with a buttery white sauce with lots of pepper.

MUSICAL SUGGESTION
The Pogues' *Rum, Sodomy, and the Lash.*

Ears

I tried my damnedest to write a recipe for lambs' ears for you, but I just couldn't find the raw materials. Unless you have a good friend who happens to be a sheep farmer, it's impossible to get hold of them, so I have plugged for pigs' ears instead. Luckily, they're also very good, packed full of gelatin, ridiculously cheap, and they have a strong pedigree. Dishes like pigs' ears used to be extremely popular, so why we've become so pathetic about offal is beyond me. I'm no great daredevil with food, but I like to try everything for fear of missing out. I'm not a massive fan of tripe, I'll admit, but that's because of the musty flavor, not just because it's made from stomach lining.

I think that a lot of our wonderful old recipes using offal have died out because they take a lot of time. Whereas the more expensive cuts cook very quickly, offal often needs care and extra attention, and will usually have a shorter shelf life. But it makes for a much more interesting meal, so I hope that you'll try recipes like these every now and then. Fantastic guides to offal are Fergus Henderson's *Nose to Tail Eating* and Jane Grigson's *Charcuterie and French Pork Cookery*.

Incidentally: It may come as a surprise to you that around 25 percent of the world's sheep are of the fat-tailed variety, and that the fat stored in said tails is a very important cooking ingredient, with a gratifyingly low melting point. Alan Davidson's *Companion to Food* maintains that it has a "texture somewhat like bacon, though of course with a muttony aroma," and shows a diagram of a rather chuffed-looking ram sporting a marvelous example sitting on its own little trailer to keep its tail off the ground.

One word of warning: You can make this reasonably swiftly, but it's better if you brine the ears for two to three days in advance.

Serves 4

4 pigs' ears

4 ounces butter

4 ounces breadcrumbs

For the court bouillon

1 quart water

2 onions, with 3 cloves stuck into each

2 carrots, roughly chopped

1 clove of garlic

1 stick of celery

1 cup white wine

10 peppercorns

➴ Firstly, put all the *court bouillon* ingredients together and simmer for thirty minutes, strain, discarding the vegetables and peppercorns and reserving the liquor.

➴ Place the pigs' ears in a pan and cover with the *court bouillon* liquid. Simmer them gently for one and a half to two hours, then carefully remove and place them between two plates in your fridge with a few cans of food on top to act as a weight.

➴ Melt the butter in a saucepan. Cut the ears in half (lengthways), coat them in the butter, then dip them in the breadcrumbs to get a good covering. Put the crumbed ears under a medium grill to crisp up.

➴ Serve with bread. They are also great with a mixture of chopped cornichons, Dijon mustard, and oil.

MUSIC SUGGESTION

The Lemonheads' classic track "Big Gay Heart" and anything from the album *It's a Shame About Ray*.

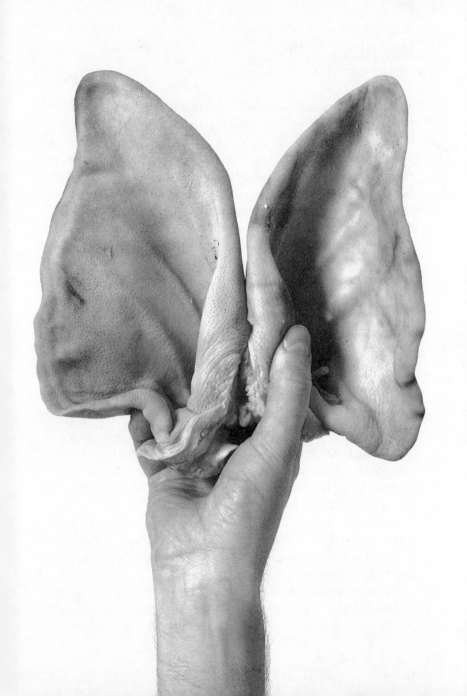

Reindeer Stew

I was Santa Claus once. Not in a dream, but in the central Milton Keynes Shopping Center, winter of 1986. My sister Sam worked the grotto as an elf, which was by far the better deal because you didn't get paid any extra as a Santa and it was bloody sweaty work. It was also oddly traumatic—I was quite intimidated at the idea of wearing an old fella's beard, and on top of that I'm only 98 percent sure that Santa doesn't exist, so I felt very much the impostor. I countered the discomfort by throwing myself into the role with vulgar enthusiasm, so if you were a child living in Milton Keynes around then and had a scarred childhood due to my inept roaring of "Ho ho ho" and my cross-my-heart promise that you'd get *everything* you asked for on Christmas Day, I can only apologize. I was only nineteen—how was I supposed to manage infant expectations?

Anyhow, I managed last year to achieve a kind of closure with Santa. I was very privileged to go to Lapland to meet Sami herdsmen and discover what Father Christmas really ate for Christmas lunch. It was, of course, Rudolph—or at least one of his friends—and it was absolutely delicious.

This dish is called *malis* in Sami, and should you find yourself in possession of any reasonable amount of reindeer, this is the only way to do it justice. At first glance it may sound a little boring—the only ingredients are water, salt, and lots of bits of reindeer. But have faith: Something magical happens in the pot, as befits a creature that comes pre-loaded with the hopes and dreams of a billion children. I can only describe the taste as deeply luxurious—rich and really fatty. The nearest comparison is with mutton, but that description alone could never do it justice. You eat the delicious, gelatinous broth alongside the meat, in a *pot-au-feu* style.

Reindeer stew is best eaten at −22°F sitting on a bed of reindeer skins in a tepee. Whatever you do, don't eat the tip of the tongue as this, apparently, makes you lie. Incidentally, reindeer are sensitively farmed and utterly free-range due to their migratory needs. Smoked reindeer heart is a great delicacy in Swedish Lapland, and the skins (collected with sound ethics as a meat by-product) are glorious. I've managed to convince the nice people at Renprodukter in northern Sweden to sell them to me mail order over the phone (see page 243).

Serves 4

2 quarts spring water

a tablespoon of salt

4 reindeer ribs

1 reindeer tongue

4 reindeer saddle chops

4 reindeer shinbones

To serve

Flat bread—you can get some authentic stuff from Ikea

grated reindeer liver (optional)

✐ Put your water, salt, and reindeer ribs in a saucepan and heat slowly. Bring to a boil and simmer for thirty minutes, making sure that the meat is always just covered by water (top up if necessary), then add the tongue and saddle chops. Simmer for another thirty minutes, then add the shinbones, simmer for another fifteen minutes, and turn the heat off. Do *not* discard the broth—this is an essential part of the meal.

✐ Carefully crack the cooked shinbones with a tough knife to extract the bone marrow. Eat this on some flatbread and alternate each mouthful with a sip of the broth. Then dig into the rest of the meat, bread, and broth.

MUSIC SUGGESTION

Sigur Rós—unfathomably strange yet breathtakingly beautiful music from Reykjavik (it's not in Lapland, I know, but it's the best music to listen to when you're there). Try *Ágaetis Byrjun* or the album entitled ( ) [sic].

Stargazey Pie

The Cornish fishing village of Mousehole plays host to "Tom Babcock's Eve," a curious event that takes place every year. Picture the scene: The village is plagued by storms each winter, with the harbor often barred with wooden beams for protection. Years ago, so the story goes, the storms had stopped the boats from putting out to sea for so long that the village was on the verge of starvation. In a brief lull, however, one Tom Babcock (or Bawcock) managed to nip out and catch enough fish to save the villagers from perishing and they baked a pie with protruding fish heads to celebrate. True or not, Mousehole celebrates the story on December 23 every year, and the owners of the quayside inn produce a spectacular *Stargazey Pie* using pilchards.

It's hard for a *Stargazey Pie not* to be spectacular—the heads of the fish poke through the pastry as though they're a sleepy piscine family all tucked in under a cosy duvet. The traditional reason given for this arrangement is that the fish drip their delicious oils back into the pie—a claim that experiments have shown to be entirely baseless (according to Alan Davidson's *Companion to Food*). So the only real reason for the slightly gruesome appearance is presumably to scare the kids—which is good enough for me.

The pie is delicious cooked with any oily fish, such as herring, sardines, pilchards (which are just grown-up sardines), or small mackerel. Bear in mind that the small mackerel are the easiest to fillet if you or your guests are nitpicky about those little pinbones that are usually very edible. And trying to bone sardines and herrings entirely is a fool's game—trust me, I've tried it. Ask your fishmonger to fillet the fish, but leave the heads attached. He'll raise his eyebrows. Ignore him—you're paying.

Serves 4

2 whole eggs

2/3 cup crème fraîche

8 fish (sardines, pilchards, herrings, or small mackerel), gutted, boned, and rinsed

a handful of freshly chopped herbs, including tarragon, parsley, and dill

salt and pepper

8 slices of bacon

1 pound shortcrust pastry

1 red onion, chopped

a splash of milk

For the egg glaze

2/3 cup milk

pinch of saffron (if you've got it)

1 egg yolk

a pinch of salt

Preheat the oven to 425°F.

First make the egg glaze. Heat the milk in a small saucepan and when it starts to boil, remove it from the heat and add the saffron. When it's cooled slightly, mix in the egg yolk and salt and leave it to infuse.

To make the filling, beat the whole eggs, crème fraîche and herbs together in a bowl. Season the insides of the fish with salt and pepper, and wrap a slice of bacon around each one.

Grease a dish that looks large enough to fit your fish. Divide your pastry into two chunks. Roll the first lump out and line the dish with it. Blind bake for fifteen minutes. Lay your fish in a circle, with the heads poking out over the sides. Scatter the chopped onion over the fish and pour the herb mixture over it. Season with salt and pepper.

Dampen the edges of the pastry with milk (this will help the two pieces stick together). Roll out the other half of pastry to the size of the dish and carefully lay it on top (you'll cover the fish heads to begin with). Either tuck the pastry around the heads or cut around them—whichever you find easiest. Press the two pieces of pastry together to seal the pie.

Brush the pie with the egg glaze. If you have the energy, cut some starfish shapes, anchors, or pastry rope, and brush these with the glaze, too. Slash the top of the pie to let the steam escape.

Bake the pie in the oven at 425°F for fifteen minutes, then reduce the temperature to 350°F for another twenty-five minutes, or until the pie looks nicely golden.

Serve with celeriac and potato mash and glazed carrots, and, if you're feeling greedy, spinach with almonds.

MUSIC SUGGESTIONS

Supergrass—most tracks will do, especially "Alright," "Pumping on Your Stereo," or anything else from the album *I Should Coco*, recorded at Sawmills Studio in Cornwall.

Stuffed Fish Heads

Just as most butchers chuck out their pigs' trotters, you'll find that most fishmongers throw away their fish heads, and it's a tragic waste. On the positive side, this means that fish heads are very cheap—or even free if you smile nicely at your local supplier. Fish cheeks are a moist delicacy—the best part of many fish, and rightly seen as the piscine equivalent of a chicken's "oysters." Whenever I serve fish, I try to nick the cheeks when no one is looking.

On this occasion, however, we are trying to stem the waste of fish heads, so I'd strongly encourage you to let everyone else have a taste. Get the biggest heads you can—I sent my mum out to get some heads and she came back with a couple of massive conger eel heads given away by my local fishmonger. They were utterly delicious and there was a huge amount of meat on them. Two of these will easily feed four of you.

Serves 4

For the stuffing

14 ounces breadcrumbs

4 ounces melted butter

1 small onion, finely chopped

2 eggs, lightly beaten

a handful of fresh parsley, chopped

2 sprigs of thyme

salt and pepper

⌒ Name your fish.

⌒ Preheat your oven to 350°F.

⌒ To make the stuffing, mix the breadcrumbs with the butter, onion, eggs, parsley, thyme, and seasoning. Stuff this mixture into the cavity behind the fish heads and lay them flat (not upright) in a baking dish or roasting pan.

⌒ Slather the softened butter over the fish and sprinkle with the breadcrumbs. Add the remaining ingredients straight into the pan so that the fish sits in a pool of flavored water. Cooking times vary according to the size of your heads, so check frequently—two huge conger eel heads should take one to one and a half hours. Check them every twenty minutes, and if they are looking dry, baste with some of the liquid.

For the fish

4 ounces softened butter

2 vast conger eel heads or 5-1/2 pounds any large meaty fish heads, cleaned thoroughly

4 ounces breadcrumbs

a splash of vermouth or white wine vinegar

a squirt of Worcestershire sauce

3 cups water

✏ To serve them to full effect, place the whole tray on the table so everyone can see what they are eating. Guests can scoop the flesh of the fish themselves. There should be ample juice in the pan—use this as gravy—and serve with something crisp and green.

MUSIC SUGGESTIONS

I feel a murder ballad coming on. I'd play some of Nick Cave's more tender tracks, both with and without the Bad Seeds: "Love Letter" and others from *No More Shall We Part*, most of *The Boatman's Call*, and some of *Abattoir Blues/The Lyre of Orpheus*.

Stone, Stepladder, and Bucket Cream

This is an ancient Lancashire method for aerating your cream without using a whisk. Why you wouldn't want to use a whisk is anyone's guess—maybe in years to come we'll discover that whisks are carcinogenic. Perhaps best to do the crucial messy bit outside.

Serves 6

1 piece of leaf gelatin

1-2/3 cups heavy cream

1 tablespoon sugar

4 drops of vanilla essence

3 tablespoons jam (flavor of your choice)

¾ cup dry sherry

juice and zest of 1 lemon

✑ Soften the gelatin in a few drops of warm water, then add it to a saucepan with the cream, sugar, and vanilla essence. Simmer gently for five minutes, then leave to cool slightly.

✑ In a large, deep mixing bowl (preferably glass)—the "bucket" of the title—spread the jam on the bottom, add the sherry, lemon juice, and zest.

✑ Place the mixing bowl on a stone floor, or anywhere that's easy to hose down—perhaps the garden. Next to it, place a suitable stepladder. Ask a trustworthy, easy-to-clean friend or family member to steady the ladder for you. Ascend your ladder (with the cooled cream) to a height that balances maximum vertical drop with acceptable accuracy and pour the cream into the dish to create as much bubblage as possible.

✑ Put the resulting frothy mess in the fridge overnight and try to withstand the temptation to dip into it until the next day.

MUSIC SUGGESTION
Charles Mingus's *Mingus Mingus Mingus*.

Fourteenth-century Blancmange

The most important cookbook of the fourteenth century was *Forme of Cury*, which had nothing to do with curries, but everything to do with the cooks of King Richard II. Roughly translated, it means "The Proper Method of Cookery." Last year I held in my hands Samuel Pegge's 1780 edition of the text in the British Library, which was a magical moment. Why they let monkeys like me touch things of such beauty, I know not.

It's a fascinating, if rather irritating, read. Here's the famous (well, as famous as a historical recipe gets) transcript of the blancmange recipe, which we can only presume was one of Richard II's favorites. Of course, it's nothing like the sweet-jellied, milk-based dessert we knew as kids. In fact blancmange is one of those foods that has had a startling development through history, starting in one form—here a sophisticated and delicate blend of chicken and almonds—and ending in quite another as a sloppy dessert. It's generally agreed that blancmange derives from the Middle East, from where we used to import our rice and almonds, and it was to be found on many medieval and Renaissance menus across Europe.

FOR TO MAKE BLOMANGER

Nym rys and lese hem and wasch hem clene and do thereto god almande mylk and seth hem tyl they al to brest and than lat hem kele and nym the lyre of the hennyn or of capouns and grynd hem small kest therto wite grese and boyle it. Nym blanchyd almandys and afroun and set hem above in the dysche and serve yt forthe.

Here's my version of how to cook it, so you can put away that degree in medieval literature. Timing note: Some preparation is required one to two days beforehand.

Serves 4

4 ounces whole almonds

4 ounces basmati rice

7 ounces chicken breast, chopped into chunks

1 tablespoon sugar

2 ounces whole almonds, for decorating

1 tablespoon ground almonds, for dusting

◎ First, you need to make almond milk. Spread your almonds on a baking sheet and dry-roast them until they are lightly browned (this brings out the flavor). Put them in a sealable jar, cover them with water, and leave them to soak for twenty-four to forty-eight hours.

◎ Before the day of cooking, put the rice in a saucepan and cover it with water to soak overnight. In the morning, drain and rinse the rice.

◎ Pour the water and almond mixture into a blender and whiz the living daylights out of it. Place a fine sieve (or a muslin, if you have one) over another pan, strain, and reserve the liquid, discarding the pulp. This is your almond milk.

◎ Poach the chicken in boiling water (ten minutes ought to do—test regularly and take care not to overcook it). When it's done, chop it finely.

◎ Place the rice in a pan and add just enough of the almond milk to cover it. Bring to a boil, simmer for five minutes, then add the meat and sugar and set aside to cool. When it's not too hot to touch, transfer batches to a food processor and pound them to bits.

◎ Pour the mixture into a flat dish and decorate with the ground and whole almonds.

MUSIC SUGGESTION

The Hilliard Ensemble performing Cipriano de Rore's *Le Vergine*. It's early sixteenth century rather than fourteenth century, but there you go.

Chapter 6
Grands Projets for Men and Women of Destiny

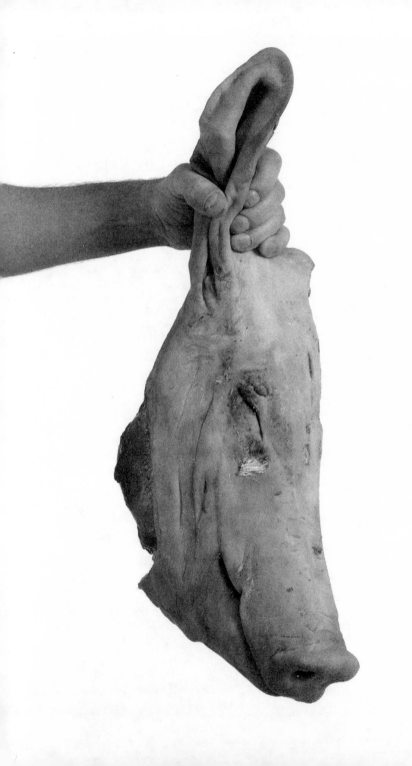

Headcheese

'm rarely at home when Mr. Existential Angst comes calling, but I'm happy to admit that making *Headcheese* is a journey of guilt and redemption, a quest to discover and conquer inner fears. The fact that out of this you get a delicious meat and jelly terrine (sometimes known as brawn) made from all the edible bits of a pig's head is, in the scheme of things, merely incidental. This adventure is similar to that with the suckling pig (see page 194) but without the cost implications. So for those with an eye to both their spiritual and financial budget, cooking *Headcheese* will make you better more cheaply.

On a practical level the idea is to buy, commune with, and cook a pig's head. But before you flick to a recipe that sounds less gruesome, hear me out: I promise that I'll take you firmly by the hand and guide you with care and compassion through all the icky bits. It's simple really: You'll emerge from this quest blooded. You'll be a braver cook, more honest in your relationship to food, and with a deeper understanding and respect for the animals that give their lives to feed us.

This is a relatively simple recipe in that there's no real art involved, but it's still a major project to undertake, and all the culinary bravado in the world can't conquer the sheer primal carnivorousness of dealing with a pig's head. On the simplest level, *Headcheese* is made by soaking the head in brine for a couple of days, boiling it for half a day, and then picking through the resulting gloop for all the edible bits, which are then left to set with some of the gelatin-rich broth left over from the boiling process. The *Headcheese* then chills firm and tastes sweet, rich, and intensely porky, like a healthy *Rillette* (a French concoction of pork belly and fat), or a very fancy pâté held together with jelly instead of lard.

The most important element is that you relate to your head. When you get it home, the first thing you need to do is give your pig a name— it's such a graphic part of the animal that you're bound to feel some anthropomorphism, and hence a relationship will develop, which is best dealt with head-on. Also, building a sense of respect for the animal should make you slightly less scared of it. For the purposes of this recipe, we'll call our pig *Martha*.

When you take your pig out of the bag, it may be a good idea to pause for a moment. You're likely to feel light waves of guilt, remorse, and disgust. Suck it up. It will pass. This may be a good moment to thank and apologize to Martha for her sacrifice.*

I recommend that you read the whole recipe before you start. First a few general points:

❦ Get a butcher to prepare everything as mentioned on page 190. It's dead easy for him, but a bugger to do it yourself without the right tools (bitter experience available on request).

❦ Some time-planning is required: You need to source your pig's head (which may need ordering, but should cost you no more than $3.50), then soak it in brine for a few days before cooking. It will need to cook for half a day, then be left to set for a good few hours.

❦ Infrastructure required: a large bucket, pot, or crock (large clay pot) with a lid. If you are making this in summer, you'll need a cool cellar or enough space in your fridge to fit the bucket. At any other time of year you should be fine leaving it outside (as long as it's protected from slugs, cats, kids, etc.). You'll also need a huge saucepan large enough to fit the head, which is rather an awkward shape.

❦ Bear in mind that you need only a proportionately small amount of extra effort, time, space, and heat to make other dishes with similar cooking requirements at the same time. I recommend pigs' ears, which needs similar work (see page 171 for the recipe).

For any of you who are hardened, ruddy-faced children of the land scoffing at this wimpy urbanity while squinting into the wind, skip this part and turn to the recipe for Pickled Chinaman *on page 63.*

Shopping for your pig

Shopping

Makes enough to salt 2 pigs' heads

1 pig's head

2 pigs' trotters

For the brine

6 quarts water

2.2 pounds sea salt

2.2 pounds sugar

2 tablespoons ascorbic acid or saltpeter or the juice of 4 lemons

1 teaspoon black peppercorns

5 bay leaves

1 tablespoon juniper berries (optional)

1 whole nutmeg, chopped in two or a teaspoon of mace blades (optional)

1 teaspoon cloves (optional)

Give your butcher a call before visiting—mine always has heads in stock, but if you live somewhere posh, they're likely to be few and far between, and you'll need to put an order in. You want one pig's head (chopped in half by the butcher) and two trotters.

Now would be a good time to purchase all of the ingredients listed below especially the (optional) ascorbic acid (pure vitamin C) for the brine solution. Apparently, Walgreens won't sell it because naughty people buy it to cut naughty drugs with, but your local druggist probably stocks it. If not, they'll happily order it for you to arrive the next day. If you really can't find any, you could use the juice of four lemons, though this will alter the taste. Saltpeter is what you're really after, but it's very hard to find.

While you're out spending, buy a plastic tub or bucket with a lid (if you don't already have one) from your local Dollar Store.

Brining

Before collecting your head, first prepare your brine. It's dead simple but it'll need a couple of hours to cool. You'll need to soak the head in brine to tenderize it and bring out the flavor. You could skip this part of the process, but the flavor is nowhere near as good, and you would lose a large chunk of the ritual.

Put all the ingredients into a large pan and bring to a boil—this is to sterilize everything and ensure that the salt and sugar dissolve properly. Simmer for five minutes, then cover it, put it outside to cool, and go to collect your pig's head.

For cooking the head

1 onion

4 cloves

bay leaves

peppercorns

Last bits

juice and zest of 2 lemons

a bunch of fresh parsley, chopped

At the butcher's discuss an appropriate name for the pig, then ask Butch to chop the pig's head in half to help it fit into your saucepan and to give you easy access to the meat inside. Many butchers sell half heads—if so, buy two halves. Ask him to chop the ears off, but keep them. If you have only a medium-sized pot to boil it in, tell him as much and ask for the snout to be chopped off, too. Don't do this unless you absolutely have to as a snoutless pig can look a bit grim. You can ask the butcher to remove the eyeballs as they are particularly vivid, but bear in mind that this is cheating.

When you've unpacked Martha, commune with and apologize to her, as discussed earlier. Rinse her under the tap, brace yourself, then brush any oomskah from her nostrils and teeth. Pour your cooled brine into a large tub or bucket and add Martha. Well done—it's not easy doing this for the first time. Put the brine somewhere cool and leave it for a minimum of two days, up to a maximum of twelve. She'll seem a bit sinister sitting there, especially if she's in one of those opaque plastic tubs like mine through which you can just make out her face.

Cooking

Makes about 3 pounds

Take Martha's head and the trotters out of the brine, rinse thoroughly, and put her in a large saucepan. Stud the onion with the cloves and add it to the pan. Cover with cold water and add an inch of water on top. Bring it all to a boil with a couple of bay leaves and a few peppercorns.

Gently simmer everything for four to six hours with a lid on the pan, remembering to open the window to let the smell out, otherwise your home will reek of pork stock for weeks to come.

🕭 After four to six hours, turn the heat off, and leave everything to cool for a while. Pour off and reserve the broth, leaving all the trotters and parts of Martha's head (these may have disintegrated a bit). This is where you have to get your hands dirty learning how a pig's head works, but it's not as grim as you might think.

🕭 What we need to do here is pick through the remains of the head and trotters, finding all the flesh—and in the process you'll get a lesson in anatomy. Just get in there and find all the meaty pockets, including the brain. The easy bits are the cheeks and tongue, which will separate quite readily. Beyond that, it's really a case of trawling through the goo to find slivers of meat. Take out as much as you can—it will be quite easy to sift through. You may find yourself picking over teeth and the like, which can be a bit stomach-churning, but you should be feeling bolder by now. Dice or shred the meat thinly, then place it in a bowl, cover, and set aside.

🕭 Put all the remaining bones and skin back in the pan with 2 quarts or so of the reserved broth and simmer for another hour until it's reduced by half (you don't have to do this, but if you've got the time, it'll make a stronger, firmer gelatin). Strain the resulting broth and mix two cups of it with the meat from the head, the lemon juice and zest, and the parsley. It should have a porridgy consistency.

🕭 Line a few deep dishes with plastic wrap and spoon in the meat and broth mixture. (The plastic wrap will help you to turn out the brawn neatly.) Leave it to cool, then put it in the fridge overnight.

Eating

❰ In the morning, Martha will have set to a wonderful jelly-and-meat headcheese. If you feel like it, thank her for giving her life for this delicious food, and breathe a sigh of relief. It hasn't been pretty, but you've made delicious and respectful use of a head that might otherwise have been thrown away. Unlike those who shy away from the truth about their food, who prefer not to think about the role of death in sating their appetite, you've built a relationship with the object of your carnivorous appetite. And maybe, by understanding how pigs work, you'll feel slightly closer to these fantastic animals. Of course, you may have become a vegetarian, but either way it's probably good for the pig world. You never have to do this again, but you've broken through the barrier that exists between your food and an understanding of where it came from. It's not pretty, but it's honest and real. Well done.

❰ The *Headcheese* will keep in the fridge for a week. Serve with English mustard and some good bread, and feel justly proud.

The Compleat Cook from 1658 has this recipe:

TO BAKE BRAWN

Take two Buttocks and hang them up two or three dayes, then take them down and dip them into hot Water, and pluck off the skin, dry them very well with a clean Cloth, when you have so done, take Lard, cut it in peices as big as your little finger, and season it very well with Pepper, Cloves, Mace, Nutmeg, and Salt, put each of them into an earthen Pot, put in a Pint of Claret wine, a pound of Mutton Suet. So close it with past let the Oven be well heated; and so bake them, you must give them time for the baking according to the bignesse of the Haunches, and the thicknesse of the Pots, they commonly allot seven hours for the baking of them; let them stand three dayes, then take off their

Cover, and poure away all the Liquor, then have clarified Butter, and fill up both the Pots, to keep it for the use, it will very well keep two or three moneths.

MUSIC SUGGESTION

Holst's crowd-pleaser *The Planets.* Press play as you unpack the head and you'll be accompanied by all the terrifyingly jingoistic bombast of "Mars, the Bringer of War" as you face the horror of your pig's recent death and your own shock

Incidentally: The word "headcheese" may well come from its traditional circular mold shape (which we haven't replicated here) or from its French name, Fromage de Tête, but I like to think that the process of trawling through the disintegrated head is in some way similar to hand-churning curds in the cheese-making process. The etymology of the word "brawn" (from the Middle English by way of Old German) reveals an original meaning of "muscle" or "meat," which developed to refer to meat from a boar.

at having to deal with it so viscerally. Mars is then juxtaposed against "Venus, the Bringer of Peace" as you come to terms with these emotions and realize that you are paying the respect that your pig deserves, by making something positive, useful, and therefore beautiful from it. The rest of *The Planets* becomes a bit of a roller coaster to which you can assign whatever emotions you please. The London Symphony Orchestra's version conducted by Sir Colin Davis is particularly good.

Suckling Pig

This isn't a meal. It's a spectacle. An adventure. A voyage across the twin seas of exhilaration and extravagance, skirting the rocky coasts of shock and horror and washing up on the shores of epicurean ecstasy. It's also pretty easy.

Of course, there are moral issues to deal with: Should you eat an animal that's still a baby? How will your guests feel about you bringing an entire uncloven-hoofed ruminant to the table, nose, ears, tail, and all? Tempting though it is, I won't argue in favor of doing this: You're on your own. All I will say is that if you decide to cast your inhibitions aside and reach for the culinary skies, this recipe will catch your outstretched hands and carry you off to glory. When I cooked this for my friends, we had the most wonderful, raucous, enlightening Sunday lunch I've ever experienced, and I'm sure that it was all due to that delicious, cheeky little pig and its heavenly crackling. Interestingly, we had lots of small children eating with us, and they were delighted rather than appalled at the sight of the entire animal.

This is pretty basic as long as you've done your groundwork. The following recipe looks like a long list of tasks, but that's because I want to give you as much info as possible to make sure you're confident. So plan your meal a week ahead and follow these directions:

In advance

⌒ First, measure your oven. If it's a three-foot range oven, you'll be able to fit a twenty-pound pig in without too much bother. If it's a single two-foot oven, you'll need your pig cut in half (by the supplier). In this case, reduce cooking time by a third and put it back together at the table.

⌒ Next, find your suckling pig. You can make this hard for yourself and convince your butcher to order one, but I wouldn't even bother—

much better to call Pugh's Piglets (see page 241). The folks at Pugh's are incredibly helpful and chatty, giving you recipe tips, advice on how large a piglet you'll need for your number of guests, and generally oozing confidence when you're feeling a little scared about the whole shebang. These guys really know what they're talking about, selling 14,000 suckling pigs every year, mostly to Chinatowns around the UK. Give them at least a week's notice. Your pig will arrive by parcel post in good time in a large polystyrene box with some ice to keep it cool. It's not cheap—mine cost about $135 including delivery—but it fed about ten people, and no one's claiming that this is just a snack. In the U.S. try D'Artagnan in Newark, New Jersey or online at www.dartagnan.com.

✑ When your pig arrives, put it somewhere cool—on a shelf in your fridge if it's summer. Then you'll have to find a roasting tray with a rack that's big enough for your pig. Few people will have a proper one—I use the grill tray and give it a damn good scrub beforehand.

✑ Your pig will come prepared for the oven and, in case you're worried, its eyes will almost definitely be closed. I can't lie: If you're squeamish, it can be a slightly gruesome sight, at least until you can smell how good it is while it's cooking. I didn't mind too much seeing the little thing lying there, but the wife wasn't keen. Now for the cooking . . .

Cooking

Serves 8–12

olive oil

1 pound sausages (for stuffing)

1 pound black pudding (for stuffing)

1 suckling pig 13–20 pounds (size depends on the number of guests)

✑ Name your pig, then reason with it or apologize, depending on your view of the food chain.

✑ Preheat the oven to 400°F.

✑ Add a small splash of olive oil to a frying pan and quickly brown the sausages and black pudding. They don't need to be cooked all the way through, just seared a bit. Set aside.

✑ Lay your pig on its side on the rack over your roasting tray. Stuff the stomach cavity with the sausages and black pudding, then tie up the cavity with string. (This makes manhandling the pig a little easier.)

2/3 cup rum

4 teaspoons salt

pepper

half a bottle of white wine

Cooking time

Approx 10 minutes per pound plus 20 minutes—a 20-pound piglet needs about 3-1/2 hours if stuffed

For the apple sauce

2.2 pounds cooking apples

6 cardamom seeds

To garnish

fresh curly parsley

1 small red apple

*Mix the rum with 2/3 cup olive oil—it looks like a lot, but you need it for basting throughout. Rub this mixture all over the piglet, then rub in the salt and pepper. Cover the ears and tail with foil to stop them from burning. Pry open the little fella's mouth and wedge a stone or similar solid object in—you'll replace this later with the apple.

*Put the piglet in the middle of the oven and cook for three to four hours, depending on the size of your pig. Baste every fifteen to twenty-five minutes with the rum and olive oil mixture. Halfway through the cooking process, turn your pig over. This is a bit tricky, so you may need someone to help you. At this point you could also slip your potatoes under the pig to roast.

*While the piglet is cooking, peel and roughly chop your cooking apples. Crush your cardamom seeds in a mortar (if you have one) and remove the outer husks. Put the apple and cardamom in a small saucepan over a very low heat. Cook slowly, stirring every now and then, for about twenty minutes until the apples have reduced to a mush. Pop the sauce into the oven to reheat before serving.

*When the suckling pig is done, check the crackling. If it's not perfect, slip it under the grill to zap it up. Keep a close eye on it so that it doesn't burn.

*Lay lots of curly parsley on a large serving plate or chopping board and set the pig on top. Leave it to rest, but don't cover with foil in case it sweats and softens the crackling. Remove the stone from its mouth and replace it with the small apple. If you're proud of your creation, take a photo and send it to me at photos@thegastronaut.com.

To make the gravy, pour most of the oil out of your roasting tray and add the wine. Put it on a moderate flame and stir all the gooey bits around until it tastes heavenly.

Carving

This is the one bit that always used to worry me—do you need a butcher's knowledge to carve the little fella? Oh, no. Almost all of it is edible, including most of the head—it's been entirely eviscerated except, perhaps, for the liver and kidneys—also delicious. At the table (don't even *think* about bringing it to the table already-carved) cut into the stomach cavity and allow the sausages and black pudding to spill out dramatically. Working on one side of the pig at a time, carve around the shoulders and take off the entire front and back legs. A front leg is too much for one person to eat, but great to share. Now for the main body: Cut into the backbone either side of the spine and chop the entire torso into segments—serve bones and all. Keep going with all the other sections up to the head. All of this can be served, though you can leave the spine if you fancy. When the head is the last remaining piece, it should be presented to the most honored guest—the one with a strong enough constitution. Your guests should eat the delicious crackling; and pick at the tender meat in the pig's large cheeks.

Serving

Serve with the apple sauce, roasted potatoes, glazed carrots, and perhaps some roasted beets. Take your place at the table to great acclaim. You may now die happy.

Some tracks of heartbreaking beauty would seem relevant here, to pay tribute to your pig. I would choose from Allegri's *Miserere* (in which a small boy is brought out to hit a haunting top C), Wagner's *Parsifal*, the second movement from Tippet's *Concerto for Double String Orchestra* (buy the Scottish Chamber Orchestra's version and you get the glorious *Fantasia Concertante on a Theme of Corelli* thrown in for free), and the Kronos Quartet's recording of Samuel Barber's *Adagio for Strings*. They should all be played deafeningly loud.

Turducken
Three-Bird Roast for a Gastronautical Yule

Turducken has nothing whatsoever to do with duck turds—this isn't that kind of book. The rather unpoetic name comes from a version of this adventure that involves stuffing a turkey with a duck stuffed with a chicken. Basically, it's a Russian doll of a meal, and it involves boning three birds (some butchers will do this for you and some won't). I've made a number of variations, including this mini version using a chicken stuffed with a poussin stuffed with a quail, which seems to work very well.

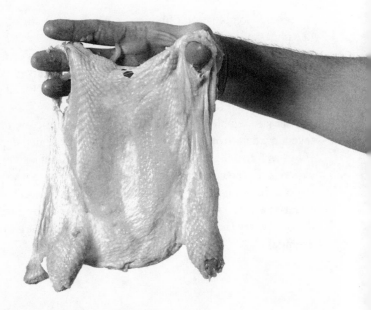

I've experimented extensively with different versions of this, initially thinking that it's just a noble but unnecessary folly. However, after several disasters (including one that cost me $230 and the respect of my father-in-law) I've now cracked it, and not only is it spectacular, it's also delicious.

This is a slow-roast method of cooking, which keeps everything at maximum succulence. The crucial thing is never to let your creation dry out during roasting, which is why you should always cover it with foil and keep adding wine and water so it gets both roasted and braised (incidentally, if slow roasting scares you, just use normal turkey roasting times, but you're making a big mistake). It's a very festive affair and, in the absence of any recognizable Christmas traditions from my side of the family, I've managed to make this our regular Yule extravaganza.

Actually, the other crucial thing is to learn how to bone a bird, which is a bizarrely enlightening experience. Experiment using quail and plan on screwing a few up before getting the knack. (Do eat the birds, though. It would be terribly disrespectful to throw the meat away.)

Use any combination of birds you like (but not strong game birds like pheasant), and adjust the roasting times (see page 202). I've given the recipe for a not-too-enormous version—it's just as complicated to make as the classic chicken-stuffed-duck-stuffed-turkey version, but the ingredients are cheaper. (And given the relative blandness of turkey, I'd save that for Christmas.)

Timing: Assemble your *Turducken* the day before cooking. This can take anywhere from forty-five minutes to three hours, depending on your level of skill, but don't let that put you off—it's an enlightening experience. The cooking time is around six hours, too, so you'll need to do some good planning to get it ready for Christmas lunch.

Equipment: You will make your life easier if you buy a trussing needle or a pastry lacer from a specialist cookshop, but it isn't absolutely essential.

Boning your birds

⌀ Have faith and don't leave it until Christmas morning without practicing. Boning birds is all about teasing the meat away from the bones, and it's hardest around the legs and wings, where the tendons make it tricky.

⌀ First cut the skin along the backbone and then whittle away to ease the skin and meat off as best you can. When you get to the legs and arms, you must separate them from the body by hacking apart the ball joints, and then pushing and scraping the meat down the bones, cutting whichever tendons get in your way. Get as far down them as you can before tugging the bone through the skin and turning the whole limb inside out. It's a lesson in destructive anatomy. As long as you keep the skin intact, it doesn't really matter what the meat looks like, as no one will ever see or care except you. I can now do most small birds in about two to four minutes and I have to admit that I rather enjoy it.

Chicken-stuffed-poussin-stuffed quail

Serves 8–14

3 birds

4 oranges or nectarines or satsumas, peeled and thinly sliced

8 ounces ham, preferably Parma or Bayonnne, but English cooked ham is also good, thinly sliced

salt and pepper

1 sausage link (optional)

9 ounces softened butter

two-thirds of a bottle of white wine

⌀ When you've boned all the birds, lay the largest one out on a chopping board, skin down. Season the inside of it, and lay some slices of orange (or other fruit) on top, followed by a layer of ham. Season again. Lay the middle bird on top (skin down again), season it, add another layer of ham and orange slices, and season this. Lay the last bird on top (skin down), season, and cover with ham and more slices of orange. Put something in the middle of your creation, such as a sausage link, if you fancy.

⌀ At this stage, the whole affair will look like a scene out of a Sam Peckinpah bloodbath. Be strong. Roll the whole mess together, and it will look like a medieval rugby ball or a country dancer's pig's bladder. Resist the temptation to whack small children around the head with it as this is rarely appreciated and quite possibly illegal.

(2 cups water will do if necessary)

🖙 Preheat the oven to 225°F. Truss up the parcel of birds with string (sew it if you have the where-withal, or bind it like a parcel if you don't). Weigh it so you can work out the roasting times.

🖙 Place it in a roasting dish, slather the butter over the top, cover it with foil, and add a couple of glasses of white wine to the dish. Put into the oven for six—yes *six*—hours. After the first few hours, it's a good idea to check your creation every hour to make sure it hasn't dried out. It's best to set a kitchen timer to remind you—I'd hate for you to mess it up after all that effort. If it dries out at any stage, just add more wine and water as required. It should rest, covered, for at least thirty minutes before carving.

There are many variables with slow cooking, so to be sure of success, you should really invest in a meat thermometer. The internal temperature of the thing should be 140–150°F when done. If you lack a meat thermometer, here are a few pointers:

Cooking times

Chicken+poussin+quail totaling about 5-1/2 pounds unboned: six hours at 225°F plus thirty minutes' rest

Turkey+duckling+chicken totaling about 24 pounds unboned: nine hours at 225°F plus one hour's rest

Standard turkey roasting times (if slow cooking scares you) are twenty minutes per pound at 375°F.

MUSIC SUGGESTIONS

Come Yule, we play three CDs on heavy rotation for ten days solid: the Blue Hawaiians' *Christmas on Big Island*, Dean Martin's *Making Spirits Bright* and a multi-CD compilation of *Carols from Trinity College*.

Imu

Pit-cooked Pig, Lamb, Deer, or Goat

I f you have a burning need, as I sometimes do, to indulge your friends with the twin gifts of brutal exhibitionism and grand-scale feasting, this baby is for you. Imu is an ancient method of cooking in a large hole, popular in Polynesia, where it's also known as a *hangi, hakari,* Maori barbecue, or pitbake. There are many ways of using an *imu,* but it's ideal for cooking whole pigs, lambs, deer, or goats, and is an excellent method of feeding anywhere from ten to two hundred people in one go.

But before you run for the spade, it's best you know the pros and cons. The disadvantages are as follows: It's a massive project that requires a garden, enough space in it to dig a pit, a ton of iron, three shopping baskets, a heck of a lot of food, grit, determination, several hours of hard manual labor and three spare days in which to do everything. The advantages are that with a little application, these things are easy to come by, and though the journey is long and tough, at its end you will find a spectacular meal and the awe of your peers. Added to that, I will take you through the whole process with love and kindness.

In brief: You dig a large pit. Build a big fire in it. Throw in lots of old iron (or volcanic rocks, if you have any at hand). When it's red hot, wrap lots of food in wet cotton sheets and foil and put this on top of the iron. Throw the earth back over it and retire for six to fourteen hours (depending on the size of your food) while it effectively steams inside the pit. Dig it out. Unwrap and eat it to rapturous acclaim.

But what's with the iron? Well, in Polynesia volcanic rocks are used—they heat easily, they retain heat well, and don't explode (a problem with many rocks found in the UK and the U.S.). The idea is that you heat the rocks with a fire and put the food on top of them to cook.

Direct fire isn't used because the flame is initially too hot, but soon dies out when buried and deprived of oxygen. Big hunks of iron will work like volcanic rocks, retaining heat for a long period.

In some ways it's a simple affair, but it does take work and careful planning. I draw up a timetable on a spreadsheet to do mine. I've broken the whole process down into its constituent parts and given you a suggested timetable for cooking a lamb. It's a lot to read, but it should make you feel confident enough to tackle it yourself.

Before you start

It really would be best if you read this entire project first, then plan your *imu* like a military operation. Do a spreadsheet if you need to. Factor in enough time and resources (i.e., your friends) to do all the following: Visit your nearest scrapyard, locate and buy the food, prep it, dig a big pit, cook it for half a day, dig it out, eat it, and finally repair the damage you've done to the garden.

A few tips

- ◖ Plan ahead—two weeks ahead if you can. If you want to cook a whole animal, your butcher may need a week's notice, too.

- ◖ You can make this in winter, but it's easiest as a summer feast— the ground is warmer (good for cooking) and lighter to shovel, there's more daylight, etc.

- ◖ Best cooked for supper rather than lunch, otherwise you need to get up very early to light the fire.

- ◖ Don't undercook it whatever you do. You really don't want to dig the thing up and then have to bury it again. I've given some cooking time guidelines, but you should always err on the long side.

- ◖ I know the temptation is strong, but don't get carried away with the digging. If your hole is too big, the fire will be less efficient and your back will cause you untold grief the next day.

- ◖ Don't forget to plan some extra time after your feast to put the garden back together.

◖ If you're cooking a whole pig, it will weigh almost as much as you and be very heavy to carry. Take some strong friends when you pick it up.

You will need

◖ An area in your garden big enough to dig a hole, dump the earth, store a load of wood, and a bit more; sixteen feet x sixteen feet should do it, but more would be useful. Keep away from trees and neighbors or anything else combustible—the fire will be pretty big. Be sensible and careful, and if there's any risk of setting light to other dry matter, choose another site.

Obviously, rocky soil will make your life hell. Plan to make the *imu* somewhere that needs a compost injection—you'll be leaving behind some buried charcoal.

If there are any workmen nearby with a backhoe, you would do well to invite them along to the feast in exchange for their digging talents. This approach is common around Newbury, interestingly.

◖ Fuel: newspaper, kindling, firelighters, and dry logs for your fire. A lot of logs. Dry timber and some big, thick, seasoned, hardwood logs would be ideal (they burn long and hard), but most wood will suffice. You could do with a pile of them—about the size of a small garden shed would be ideal—though if you really can't find any, buy a *lot* of charcoal. Some extra bags of charcoal and a few old pallets would also be a good idea.

◖ A car trunk-load of heavy iron or steel from your local scrapyard. Say you are after "ballast," otherwise they might charge you too much. You really need half a ton or so if your cooking time is six hours (see pages 207–8), and more like an entire ton if it's closer to fourteen hours (for a large animal)—and best to put it in a pickup truck. The scrap merchants will probably let you root around for it yourself—you're after thick hunks of heavy metal, such as brake drums (without asbestos linings), axles, etc. The denser and thicker, the better. Our scrapyard charges about $17.50 for a carload of the stuff, which is probably well over the normal cost, but hey.

◁ Wire shopping baskets or similar, mangled into a shape that will fit your food and lined inside with three layers of good foil. It sounds odd, but you really do need this. You'll probably find something that fits the bill exactly in your scrapyard, but it can be irritatingly tricky to find, so start looking early. (My local Turkish shopkeeper kindly donated his baskets for my *imu*. Oddly enough, I also found something that fit the bill perfectly at Ikea.) It's possible to chop, whittle, or cobble together several wire baskets into a single basket of adequate size if you have some wire cutters, extra wire, and patience. If any of the baskets are covered in plastic, this will need to be burned or cut off. The baskets are lined with foil and used as cages to hold the food so that it isn't in direct contact with the heat and can easily be removed from the pit.

You also need

◁ Large roll of foil. Not the useless lightweight stuff.

◁ A long hoe or similar that will act as a nonflammable poker for shifting red-hot bits of metal around.

◁ The following gardening tools: two spades, a garden fork, a simple tarpaulin, string, and four twigs. A wheelbarrow will also come in handy.

◁ Three cotton sheets (they must be undyed, scrupulously clean and 100 percent cotton). These are dampened and wrapped around the food both to protect it from burning in the ferocious heat and to provide the moisture to steam it with. If you are using individual baskets of food, you'll need a sheet per basket plus two extras. The authentic approach would be to line the baskets with banana leaves, which can be bought at Asian supermarkets. A more North American version of this would be to use large cabbage or chard leaves, which would add some good flavors, too.

◁ A cover or gazebo (you can get a cheap one for around $50) to go over the pit if it looks like rain (only to be used overnight, for instance—not while the fire is burning).

◁ A hunk of corrugated iron to protect the grass in case you need to remove burning logs or iron at some point (not absolutely necessary, but handy).

◁ A water container for adding extra water to the food.

◁ Unless you collect your meat from the butcher on the day you're cooking it (by far the best option) you'll need somewhere big enough and cool enough to store it before use.

Food

The culinary exhibitionist is likely to want to cook a whole animal, though cooking separate bundles of joints or even individual packages is possible. Bear in mind that a normal-sized pig is likely to feed seventy people or so. It really is essential to discuss this with your butcher—more often than not you'll find him enthusiastic and helpful when you're trying something ambitious like this. The following information comes from Richard Douglas at Moens, the legendary and very lovely butcher's in Clapham, south London.

Free-range pig	WEIGHT	130 pounds
	COST	$315
	FEEDS	70–80*
	COOKING TIME	10–14 hours
Lamb	WEIGHT	45–55 pounds
	COST	$95–105 late winter
	COST	$175–$210 spring
	FEEDS	40*
	COOKING TIME	9–10 hours
Goat	WEIGHT	65 pounds
	COST	$105–$210 as above
	FEEDS	30* (more bony)
	COOKING TIME	10 hours

Venison	WEIGHT	220 pounds
	COST	$880
	FEEDS	100–120*
	COOKING TIME	12–14 hours
Suckling pig	WEIGHT	11–20 pounds
	COST	$125–$130 whatever size
	FEEDS	6–12*
	COOKING TIME	6 hours
Mutton	WEIGHT	45–55 pounds**
	COST	$105–$125
	FEEDS	40*
	COOKING TIME	10 hours

Good butchers may be able to source the more common animals the next day, although three to seven days' notice is best, and a week is usually needed for goat or venison.

In addition to the main meat, you can add some escorts. I'm a sucker for the decadent Trimalchio approach (see page 39), which is why I've used a suckling pig—named Percy, and utterly delicious, if you're interested—stuffed with partridge, pigeon, quails, and sausages. We covered him in a dusting of paprika that gave a nice smoky flavor and also helped him look a little less pallid—the steaming method can leave the skin looking a little pale, but no less delicious for that.

There are short cuts. You'll make your life a darn sight easier if you don't go for a whole carcass and instead cook joints of meat, such as whole legs and shoulders of pork and lamb, with a few whole chickens scattered around—they will all do well in this braising type of cookery. This should cut the cooking time down, too—if they are all joints, stick to six hours.

*This really depends on how good the carver is—these are maximum servings from someone who understands a bit of butchery. Beginners may be able to yield only 60 percent as much.

**Because of health regulations, the backbone in older animals can't be sold, hence whole cow and mutton carcasses aren't available.

You'll need herbs and vegetables, too. Solid vegetables that come in big hunks work best: pumpkins, parsnips, potatoes, squashes, celeriac, corn cobs, and turnips are good, if not exactly Polynesian. You'll find that they soak up flavors from the meat and are invariably overcooked to the point of being spoonable (in a good way). I suppose you could make a vegetarian version of the *imu*, though I must admit that I've never tried one. You'd need a lot less cooking time for starters.

So, to recap, here's a potential ingredients list—I'm afraid that exact amounts are really up to you, and the combinations are whatever you like the sound of.

Ingredients

Main meat:	Pork and lamb are most cost-effective.
Extra meats:	Chickens, partridges, quails and sausages as you see fit.
Hefty vegetables:	Pumpkins, squash, parsnips, celeriac, carrots, turnips, corn cobs, etc.
Alliums:	Halved onions, leeks, whole garlic bulbs for lamb.
Herbs and spices:	Don't mix too many different ones, but use lots of them. Rosemary is good with lamb, sage and parsley go well with pork, and thyme and bay leaves are good with both.
Spices:	Nutmeg, whole peppercorns, cardamom seeds, coriander seeds. Don't mix too many, now.
Fruits:	Can be a good addition: If you throw some apples in with the pork, they'll turn into a lovely tasty mash. Depending on your spices, apricots and figs can be good with lamb. Berries and redcurrants would be great with the venison.
Optional fripperies:	Whole pineapples, raisins, orange-water, etc.
Olive oil	
Salt and pepper	
Water	

Food preparation

This really is the easy bit. Remove your meat from the fridge several hours in advance of use.

⁋ If you're adding small fowl and sausages, it's best to sear or sauté them first in a frying pan with a little oil and salt to get some flavor out of the skins. Don't bother cooking them through—just brown them.

⁋ Clean the cavity of your animal with water and dry it out with paper towels. Do the same with any of your extra meats. Using your hands, massage a little oil all over it (inside and out), and rub in salt and pepper.

⁋ Chop your vegetables into big hunks. Leave the skins on where possible (this will help stop them from disintegrating).

⁋ Stuff the meat with herbs and any aromatics you may be using and place some vegetables inside the meat.

How it works

Assuming that you have sourced everything I've mentioned and assembled all the tools and ingredients, you'll need to do the following:

⁋ Get everybody together and whip up a shared enthusiasm for the project. Group hugs may be required.

⁋ Pick up your food from the butcher, supermarket, etc.

⁋ Visit your scrapyard and pick up as much thick iron and steel as your car can safely carry. Avoid asbestos, things full of engine oil, and the like. Some paint and oily ick is okay—as long as you ensure that the fire burns it all off before the food is added. Bring it to the garden and place it close to the location you've chosen for the pit.

⁋ Make your food basket, the size of which will be determined by the size of your ingredients. You need to know how big this basket is before digging your hole. Line it thoroughly on the inside with three layers of good foil.

⁋ Place your basket(s) on your chosen spot and mark out an area the size of it plus twenty inches all around. Mark this with sticks and string.

❧ The day before you're planning to cook, cut out the sod (if there is any) using a spade. Cut along the string markings to a depth of one to one and a half inches and roll it. This is easy, but best done with two people.

❧ Lay out the tarpaulin next to the hole. Between all of you, dig a hole five feet deep, throwing the soil onto the tarpaulin to create an adjacent mound (it will need to be thrown back in soon). This should take one to three hours, depending on your strength, the type of soil, etc. Square it off and make the floor of it level before patting yourselves on your aching backs.

❧ Cover the hole so that neither small children nor clumsy, short-sighted wildlife can fall into it.

❧ Assemble your wood, charcoal, or other fuel adjacent to the pit and double-check that everything is ready for the next day.

❧ Do all your food preparation.

❧ Light the fire. When it's burning well, add the bigger logs to get a huge fire going that covers the whole base of the hole. Let this burn for about one and a half to two hours and feed it with extra logs to get a huge heat going, creating a bed of hot coals. Never leave it to burn on its own and keep a bucket of water or a garden hose nearby to deal with any problems.

❧ When you think that the fire is peaking, drop the iron hunks onto it in the places where the fire is strongest and hottest.

❧ Heat the iron for two hours or so, stoking and feeding the fire constantly. You want the metal to be red hot (or near enough).

❧ Put your three sheets in a bucket of water to soak.

❧ While this is going on, finish preparing your food. Take one of the wet sheets and fold it four times. Line the bottom of your (foil-lined) basket with this fourfold sheet and lay your food on top. Start with the vegetables, herbs, and spices, then your meat, and scatter more herbs and spices on top. Wrap the ends of the sheet over the food and lay another folded sheet on top of this. Tuck it around very carefully. Cover this with two more layers of foil and tuck the foil in. You should have one sheet left over.

◖ Carefully pull out three to four big hunks of red-hot iron (to go on the top) and keep these safely next to the pit. Level off the fire and spread the remaining hot iron into as neat a bed as you can.

◖ Place the food basket on top of the hot coals and pour a few quarts of water onto them. Fill in the space around the basket with earth until it's level with the top of the basket. Cover with a few shovels of earth, then place the spare hot iron on top of this layer of earth. Cover these with another layer of earth, lay the last wet sheet on top of the whole lot to seal in the moisture, and finally shovel all the remaining earth on top until it's nicely packed and no smoke or steam is escaping. (It doesn't matter if the mound of earth is higher than the ground around it.)

◖ For the next six to fourteen hours (depending on your choice of ingredients) you need to keep checking the mound and stopping any gaps where the steam may be escaping with extra soil. Check every fifteen minutes to start with, then every half hour. Try not to get too drunk.

◖ When the time is up, carefully dig out the earth. Remove the first sheet and the iron. Bear in mind that these may well be very hot. Scrape the earth off the second sheet—be very careful here as you don't want the food covered in muck.

◖ Remove the basket and cover the pit with something for safety.

◖ Carefully peel back the top sheet.

◖ Carve the meat, spoon out the vegetables, and serve.

◖ After the meal, remember that you'll need to fill in the hole (with or without the iron still in it).

Suggested timetable for an 8:30 PM whole-lamb dinner

2 weeks before	Write a schedule and decide what food you're going to cook.
	Recruit as many friends as you can to help—at least four of you.
	Locate a good butcher and make contact.

Find a friendly scrapyard and a garden space that meets the appropriate criteria.

Start looking for a basket to fit your main course.

1 week before

Order meat from your butcher.

Check that your friends are still free.

Order or borrow a gazebo.

Buy a tarpaulin and, if the weather looks bad, start covering your chosen site with it to keep it dry.

Find your basket if you haven't done so already.

Make the full-sized basket.

Assemble three sheets.

Purchase your wood.

2 days before

Pick up/buy your ingredients.

Pick up the iron from your scrapyard.

1 day before

Dig your pit.

Assemble a woodpile and keep it dry.

Put the sheets in a bucket of water.

Build the base of the fire with kindling, firelighters, paper, etc.

***Imu* day**

Timings here are dependent on what food you cook and its appropriate cooking time. This version assumes a lamb.

7 AM

Start the fire—it needs to burn for a good one to two hours to get up to the right heat—so build it big and stoke it hard.

Remove the meat from its storage place.

8:30 AM

Rake the fire flattish and drop your iron on top. This now needs to heat up for about two hours while you continue to stoke the fire.

While the fire is going, prepare your food baskets.

10:30 AM

When the iron is as hot as can be, rake it all flat and place your food on it and fill in the pit as described above.

1 PM

Wait. Have a picnic lunch, but try to avoid drinking too much.

8 PM	Dig your food out.
8:20 PM	Carve it.
8:30 PM	Serve it.
Day after	Fill in the hole, remove the iron if necessary and replace the turf.
	Feel good.

Huge thanks to everyone at Orchard Cottage for helping with this, but thanks especially to Ned, Jenny, and Julian.

MUSIC SUGGESTIONS

You'll need a lot of music to last the cooking time, but let's assume it's a lovely sunny day so that you'll be spending that time relaxing with your friends in the garden. As such, you will require the following: Shuggie Otis's *Inspiration Information*, Aim's *Hinterland*, Charlie Mingus's *The New York Sessions*, Morelenbaum2/Sakamoto's *Casa*, Cymande's *The Best of Cymande*, *The Songs of Cole Porter (various artists)*.

Brillat-Savarin's Truffled Turkey

In December 1825 the great French gourmand Anthelme Brillat-Savarin published one of the best food books ever: *The Physiology of Taste*, a funny, meandering, and delightfully pompous celebration of fine eating. In the tradition of great writers he then promptly died (from pneumonia rather than overeating, which seems like a missed trick).

There aren't many recipes in Brillat-Savarin's book—he was an eater, not a cooker—but instead it's packed with anecdotes and ridiculous quasi-scientific assumptions about taste, digestion, dreams, and the like. I'm particularly fond of his concept of sensual predestination—the idea that gourmands were born to be gourmands—and he points to several physical traits that identify great appreciators of the luxuries of the table. Apparently, "they have round or square faces, bright eyes, small foreheads, short noses, full lips, and well-rounded chins. The women are buxom, pretty rather than beautiful and a tendency to run to fat." Brilliant stuff.

His favorite food seems to have been truffled turkey—it crops up so often in the book that he sounds obsessed. He doesn't give us a proper recipe for it, but he does mention that the wealthy should eat a seven pound fowl "stuffed with truffles, so that it has become spheroid."

We might not see the turkey as a delicacy anymore, but I'm happy to trust Brillat-Savarin with my palate—he was a gastro-

A note on truffles: Although almost unbearably and magically delicious, truffles are painfully expensive, but whatever you do, don't bother buying those Chinese things that don't smell of anything. (They don't taste of anything either, as I found out.) If you can afford white truffles, buy them and use them quickly. If you find yourself in southern France or Tuscany between October and January, you should search out the early morning markets where a basket of truffles can be had for a song. Whatever you do, don't blow your entire truffle stash on the cooking stage of this recipe—save at least a quarter of them to shave onto the finished dish.

nomic genius writing in a golden age of gastronomy. The bourgeoisie were experimenting with the teeming wildlife that was available at the same time as restaurants were bursting onto the scene, and aestheticism was very much the order of the day. It is an age we'll never see again, which, although sad, is probably a good thing.

If you are absolutely loaded, stuff your turkey to the gills with truffles and pop it in the fridge for four days before you plan to eat it. On the day of cooking, discard the truffles and be ready to stuff it with more. Everyone else, read on . . .

Serves 6–8 gourmands

truffles—as many as you can afford

salt and pepper

7 pound turkey

12 slices unsmoked bacon

a splash of Madeira or Sauternes

For the stuffing

1 pound fresh best pork fat

9 ounces raw foie gras

a pinch of dried fennel

1 teaspoon fresh thyme

1 bay leaf

salt and pepper

more truffles

a splash of brandy

✑ The night before you plan to eat your turkey, slice half your truffles and slip them under the skin wherever you can to start the aroma seeping into the bird. Place the turkey in its roasting tin, cover, and refrigerate.

✑ To make the stuffing, combine the pork fat and foie gras and whiz to a smooth paste in a food processor. Place in a saucepan and add the herbs and seasoning (but only half the truffles). Heat very gently for ten minutes. Add a splash of brandy and leave to cool.

✑ Stuff the turkey with the stuffing and truss it with string. Cover it with buttered greaseproof paper and put it back in the fridge overnight.

✑ Heat your oven to 325°F. Open the greaseproof paper and cover the turkey with the bacon. Cover with the paper again and pour a wineglass of water into the pan.

✑ Roast for twenty to twenty-five minutes per pound, then remove the paper and bacon, push the heat up to 400°F and put the bird back in to brown for fifteen minutes.

✑ Remove the turkey and set it aside to rest, retaining the juices in the pan. Put the pan on a medium flame and add a good splash of Madeira or sauterne to deglaze it, scraping all the bits into a gravy. Reduce it to your preferred consistency.

✐ Serve the turkey with shavings of all the truffles you have left over.

MUSIC SUGGESTIONS

Find a recording of the sweetest song ever recorded—George Shearing playing *"It Never Entered My Mind"*—and play it over and over again. Failing that, Bizet's *Carmen* (Maria Callas's 1964 version) would fit the bill.

Guinea Pig
and other pets

I know the slaughter of much-loved family pets can be a sensitive issue, so let's get one thing straight right from the start: We all make sacrifices. I'm sure I did once. And anyway, the husbandry of household pets is all very well for the urban child, but for the parent it's torture—an agonizing and constant reminder of our glorious past as hunter-gatherers. That's livestock out there in the hutch.

I think it's only fair, however, to sound a note of caution. Before running into the garden waving your spear willy-nilly, remember that children have feelings, too. This may be a good opportunity to "blood" them and thereby ease their passage into adulthood. Ask yourself: Is it fair to deny them that chance?

On the other hand, children of a nervous disposition may be upset at the loss of a loved one, and this is why I strongly urge you to be sympathetic. Leave at least an hour between slaughtering your pet and serving it up to the family. Wailing at the table is intolerable. A low, constant sobbing I can handle. After the meal, you may find another opportunity to educate your offspring, this time in the pleasures of drowning one's sorrows in cheap brandy. Don't bother with the good stuff—they won't know the difference until they're in their early teens.

Warning—Pet shops generally don't see themselves as livestock suppliers and may even frown on the idea. Avoid asking for "a brace" of guinea pigs or requesting that they be "off the bone" as this may give the game away. Also, please bear in mind that if your cat is acting up and you feel you've drained all the companionship out of him that you ever will, this recipe should not be adapted—there are much better recipes for cat around, though mostly available only in the Cantonese original.

And don't come over all cute on me about eating pets. Just because they're furrier than chickens doesn't mean they should get special privileges. Guinea pig is particularly popular in South America, especially

Peru, where they go through about twenty-two million of them annually. A stunning painting of the Last Supper by Marcos Zapata hangs in Cusco Cathedral in central Peru, and it clearly shows a roasted guinea pig as the centerpiece of the feast, sitting squarely in front of Jesus.

The following recipe comes from the Andes, where it's known as *cuy*. It was originally served at ceremonial occasions and is still standard fare at marriages and first hair-cuttings. These days it's more common, and it's estimated that in some Peruvian communities almost 50 percent of all animal protein consumed is from *cuy* meat.

Peruvian Grilled Guinea Pig

Serves 2

1 guinea pig, gutted and skinned and, if you can be bothered, soaked for a few hours in brine

2 red onions, chopped

4 cloves of garlic, chopped

2 teaspoons cumin

1 teaspoon white pepper

2 teaspoons salt

2 tablespoons water

2 tablespoons vegetable oil

◯ Drain your guinea pig and pat it dry.

◯ Mix all the other ingredients well and spread over the inside and outside of the pig. Put it somewhere cool to marinate for as long as you can bear, up to twenty-four hours.

◯ For ease of cooking, skewer the guinea pig, then tie the front and back feet, stretching out the legs. Grill it, turning frequently (if you've got a rotisserie, that would be even better). If it looks like it's drying out, splash on some extra oil. It's ready when the skin is close to bursting.

◯ This dish is usually served with buttered boiled potatoes sprinkled with cilantro and finely chopped chili.

For extra Andean authenticity, try this peanut sauce for dipping your pig into.

Peanut Sauce

Makes 3 cups

2 tablespoons lard or butter

2 white onions, chopped

2 cloves of garlic, chopped

a pinch of salt

a pinch of cumin

9 ounces roasted, ground peanuts (substitute a good peanut butter if you must)

2 cups milk

Melt the lard or butter in a pan and fry the onions until golden brown. Add the other ingredients and cook on a low heat for thirty minutes.

MUSIC SUGGESTION
Afro-Peruvian classics: *The Soul of Black Peru.*

Chapter 7
Leftovers

A Beginner's Guide to Gastronautics

This book is all about encouraging experimentation and adventure, but I admit that it doesn't necessarily come easily: Trying out new recipes can be stressful. For those of you standing on the sidelines feeling anxious and pressed for time, I'd like you to know that I feel your pain.

It can take quite a leap of faith to experiment in the kitchen because whatever airy-fairy stuff I might say about the transmutation of food into poetry and love and all that, at some point in the process it's still fuel, and you've got to eat your 2,000–2,500 calories a day, otherwise you'll fall over. And if you've got four hungry friends coming for supper, you can be as groundbreaking as you like, but you still have to feed them.

However, I can offer you this from my experience: It's *extremely* rare to screw up a recipe so badly that it's disgusting, and it's almost impossible to make something actually inedible. Hopefully, I've made all the worst mistakes for you already. On the other hand, it's so enlightening when you try something new that the odd disaster is merely collateral damage on the road to glory. That's why the Gastronaut's Creed states that "culinary disaster does not equal culinary failure."

But for those new to experimentation in the kitchen I'd like to offer the following as a nice, calm, easy way of starting out—a route to gaining confidence so that maybe, come the summer, you'll feel ready to make that *imu* for sixty people.

Of the recipes in this book, the *Bum Sandwich* is an easy little adventure to start with, as are *Mumbled Mushrooms*, *Red and White Soup*, *Clapshot*, pizzas, poussins, *Fish Sperm on Toast*, *Frogs' Legs* and *Ears*. *Headcheese* is utterly foolproof, if time-consuming. If even these are beyond you, but you need to impress, here are six recipes that *sound* exciting and unusual but are, in actual fact, dead easy. A way of getting your feet wet, if you will, but still mildly impressing your friends.

Beef Carpaccio

In literal terms, this is thinly sliced raw beef, but in figurative terms it's a fleeting visit to nirvana. One of my favorite dishes of all time—*Carpaccio* is to me what the *Truffled Turkey* was to Brillat-Savarin.

Buy a small piece of the finest beef fillet you can afford. Cut your fillet into slices as thin as you can manage—$1/8$ inch would be good. Flatten these out with the back of a knife (or between two sheets of plastic wrap if that proves too difficult). Pour a small puddle of fine olive oil onto a plate and place a layer of beef in it. Season with salt and pepper and continue making layers until you've used all the beef. Cover the plate with plastic wrap and leave to marinate for half an hour. Meanwhile, toast some pine nuts in a dry frying pan. When the time's up, place the beef on plates to serve, cover with some pine nuts and shavings of Parmesan, and some spots of truffle oil, if you have any.

Ten-hour Leg of Lamb

For a sensible slow-cooked meal, roast a leg of lamb for ten hours or so at the lowest temperature your oven will go, with roughly chopped carrots, onions, garlic, and 1-1/4 cup of water. Keep covered and baste every thirty minutes. Best to use a timer in case you get distracted.

Roast Partridge

You can easily get partridge from your butcher and even in many supermarkets. For people unfamiliar with game, partridge meat is less taxing (sweeter and less strong) than pheasant. Allow one bird per person.

Preheat your oven to 400°F. Wrap the bird in bacon slices and roast for fifteen minutes, then turn the heat down to 350°F for another fifteen minutes. Leave to rest for fifteen minutes and serve with mashed potatoes and gravy.

Chicken with Forty Cloves of Garlic

Throw forty unpeeled garlic cloves, some herbs and a glass of wine into a casserole dish. Add a chicken, breast side down, and scatter some vegetables around it. Cover and cook at 400°F for one hour. Increase the heat to 425°F and brown for ten minutes.

Calf's Liver

Delicious, delicate, and swift to boot, but beware: Overcooking calf's liver is one of the greatest tragedies that can befall a cook.

Pour a little olive oil and a knob of butter into a heavy-based frying pan. Sauté the liver at a high heat for one minute (*one* minute, you hear?) on each side. Remove it to your warm plate. Add a glass of *vin santo*, Madeira, or Marsala or some other dessert wine to the pan, reduce the liquid by half and use this for gravy. Don't, whatever you do, be tempted to follow any of the thousands of recipes that advocate a mixture of onions and vinegar for, although classic, they are all a tragic waste.

Whole Roasted Pineapple

In a small saucepan, melt ten ounces sugar in 3/4 cup water with a couple of vanilla pods and a handful of fresh cilantro (stalks and leaves) and simmer gently for half an hour. Preheat your oven to 350°F. Peel and core a nice ripe pineapple and dig out the eyes, then sit it upright in a roasting tin. Add a generous splash of rum to the sugar mixture and pour it over the pineapple. Roast for one hour, basting it with the mixture every fifteen minutes. Before serving the pineapple, scatter some more cilantro over it and add a dusting of icing sugar.

Seasonal Oddments

Although we may kick against it with all of our might, every gastronaut needs a little order to his or her eating, and this is provided by the changing seasons. Here is a short list of the culinary delights that are with us only briefly each year, but are all the more precious for it and should be pounced upon before the moment has passed.

January: Rhubarb Shortcake

Forced rhubarb kicks the year off, with its outdoor-reared cousin failing to appear until April. The British are world leaders at making forced rhubarb, an operation that is carried out partly nocturnally and produces what's known as "champagne rhubarb" with light, slender stalks. It allows the gastronaut the opportunity to make shortcake sandwiches.

Serves 8

7 ounces rhubarb

2 tablespoons powdered sugar

For the shortcake

3 ounces butter

10 ounces plain flour

2 ounces sugar

1 teaspoon baking powder

1 teaspoon salt

1 large egg, beaten

1/4 cup whole milk

⊘ Preheat the oven to 400°F. Chop the rhubarb roughly and put it into a casserole dish with a splash of water and the powdered sugar. Simmer it gently, uncovered, for about thirty minutes until the rhubarb is tender, but not dry.

⊘ To make the shortcake mixture, rub the butter into the flour using your fingers, then add the sugar, baking powder, and salt and mix thoroughly. Whisk the beaten egg into the milk and add this to the flour mixture a little at a time, mixing it with a fork. Stop adding when you have a good stiff dough. Roll out the dough on a floured surface to a thickness of about 1/4 inch, then cut out pairs of shapes.

3 ounces crème
fraiche

◇ Grease a baking sheet, lay the pieces on it and bake for ten to fifteen minutes until nicely browned. Allow to cool, then just before serving, sandwich the pairs of shapes together with a splodge of rhubarb topped with a splodge of crème fraîche.

February: Pickled Eggs

The thing about pickled eggs is that they give me ferocious, terrifyingly pungent wind. Before I was married, I used to view this as a positive thing. These days I tend to indulge only when I'm either on my own or in the company of someone I'd like to offend and, for those purposes, it's always useful to have some of these little fellas brewing somewhere in the back of your cupboard.

You'll need a good, big jar for these.

Makes 12

12 eggs

1 quart white vinegar
or pickling vinegar

2 large, thumb-
sized knobs of fresh
ginger, peeled

1/2 ounce mustard
seeds

1/2 ounce whole
white peppercorns

2 dried red chilies

◇ Fill a large saucepan half full of cold water and add the eggs to it. Bring it to a boil and simmer for ten minutes. Drain and allow to cool. Shell the eggs.

◇ In another pan, heat the vinegar, ginger, mustard seeds, and peppercorns until boiling, then simmer for five minutes. Strain and leave to cool.

◇ Put the eggs in a sterilized jar, pour over the vinegar, and add the chilies. Seal it tightly and leave for at least four weeks before using.

March: Sweetbreads

Contrary to popular opinion, these are neither brains nor testicles. They are, instead, the thymus gland, taken from the neck or heart of young calves or lambs.

Sweetbreads are utterly delicious. I'm not entirely sure why people are so scared of them when they are happy to eat liver, which by any stretch of the imagination has fulfilled a pretty rank function while still within its host. That said, I have to admit that eating eyeballs makes me feel a bit funny deep down inside.

Pan-fried Sweetbreads

✑ As soon as you get home from the butcher's, soak the sweetbreads for two to three hours in cold water, changing it and rinsing them every half hour. When all signs of blood are gone, put them in a saucepan and cover with cold water. Bring it to a boil and simmer very gently for five minutes—the sweetbreads will turn white and feel firm to the touch.

✑ Drain them and leave to cool for five minutes. Peel off any membrane around them and discard any extraneous gristle or odd ducts. Put the sweetbreads in a bowl, cover with plastic wrap and chill in the fridge for an hour or so to firm them up. They can then be sliced into thick pieces, dusted with seasoned flour, and sautéed in butter. Serve on a bed of delicate vegetables, such as beans with a light vinaigrette.

April: Carrot Jam

Although carrots are in season for a good six months, they are best eaten from the first spring crops.

In case you're interested, carrots originated in Afghanistan and used to be purple. They crop up in Greek literature from around 500 BC but were not highly regarded. The Romans thought the turnip a far superior vegetable. The fools.

I love buying bunches of carrots with their luxuriant tops still attached. The leaves look so delicate and fresh that it seems crazy to throw them away, so I've tried many different ways of cooking them. All have been unmitigated disasters. If anyone knows how to make them edible, I'd love to know.

Makes 1-3/4 pounds

1 pound carrots

1 pound sugar

juice and zest of 1 lemon

20 round almonds

1 tablespoon brandy

✑ Wash and scrape the carrots, then cut them into chunks. Throw them in a steamer and steam for about forty minutes until completely soft (if you don't have a steamer, boil them in as little water as possible). Drain well and whiz in a food processor until very smooth.

Place the puréed carrots with the sugar, lemon juice, and zest in a thick-bottomed pan and stir over a very gentle heat until all the sugar has dissolved. (Don't worry—there should be enough moisture for this.) Simmer the mixture for ten minutes. Add the almonds and brandy and stir thoroughly. When cool, spoon into some sterilized jars, seal tightly, and store in a dry place.

May: Elderberry Flower Cordial

There's a moment in every year, just at the point that spring thinks it might actually be summer, when everything is right with the world. It's also that brief moment when elderberry flowers are ripe for plucking. They make a wonderful floral cordial that's very concentrated and freezes very well, so it's criminal not to make use of them.

Elderberry grows everywhere—riverbanks are often rich picking grounds—so keep an eye out for the flattish heads of yellowy-white flowers. (The best elderberry bush in the world clings on for dear life to a run-down housing estate in eastern Islington, the location of which I'm afraid I can't divulge.) The flowers are highly perfumed, so sniff a few different bushes until you find the right one. The flowering season is quite short, so you must catch them before they start to turn brown and go rotten. If you find them past their best, don't persevere—the results are rather revolting.

Makes 2-1/2 gallons

2 large shopping bags stuffed full of fresh elderflowers

4 lemons

1-1/2 gallons water

10 pounds sugar

6 tablespoons citric acid

Sift through your elderberry flowers to discard anything too scraggy or greenfly-ridden, and strip off any extraneous leaf-twiggery. Put them in a large pan or bucket and squeeze the juice of the lemons over them. Chuck the skins of the lemons into the bucket for good measure. Pour in six quarts of water (or enough to cover the flowers). Put a lid on the pan and leave somewhere cool for three days. Stir it once or twice a day.

Strain the water through a clean muslin (a dish towel will do) into a pan and roughly measure it. Add a tablespoon of citric acid and one and one-half pounds sugar to each quart. (Citric acid is available at pharmacies.)

✑ Heat the pan gently and stir the mixture to dissolve the sugar. Let it boil for one minute, then leave to cool. Pour the liquid into sterilized bottles—it will keep in them for up to a month. If you want to freeze your cordial, use plastic bottles.

June:

Herring Sperm on Horseback (Kromeskies)

I've already given a recipe for fish sperm (see page 157), but this is even more fun. It's just the soft roes of the male herring, best used around June, just before they have spawned. Ideally, use a deep-fat fryer for this.

Serves 4

4 good tomatoes

a splash of olive oil

8 soft herring roes

8 slices bacon

For the batter

3-1/2 ounces plain flour

a splash of warm water

a splash olive oil

1 egg white

sunflower or groundnut oil for frying

8 small sections of French bread

✑ Preheat your oven to 375°F. Cut the tomatoes into eight thick slices, discarding the tops and bottoms. Toss the slices in a little olive oil and lay them out on a baking sheet. Roast them in the oven for thirty minutes.

✑ Meanwhile, to make the batter, gently mix the flour, water, and oil together (don't worry about lumps and don't beat too much). Beat the egg white in a bowl until stiff, then fold it in with the batter.

✑ Preheat your deep-fat fryer to maximum or heat up your pan of oil. Wash the roes and wrap each one in a bacon slice. Toast the bread. Dip the roes in the batter and deep-fry them for two minutes.

✑ Serve by laying a slice of roasted tomato on each piece of toast and putting a bacon-wrapped, fried roe on top.

July: Pickled Walnuts

Opinion is divided on the merits of pickled walnuts, but after extensive work on the subject, I've found out that anyone who says they don't like them is wrong. You need to pick your walnuts around mid-July otherwise the shells will be too tough to eat. Be warned: This is another of those two-week-long projects, so don't plan to go on your summer vacation too early.

Makes 4-1/2 pounds

4-1/2 pounds green walnuts, or as many as you can find

2 quarts water x 4 lots

1/2 pound salt x 4 lots

1/2 pound brown sugar

1/2 quart red wine vinegar

2 cups port

2 red onions, chopped

6 cloves

20 black peppercorns

2 thumb-sized pieces of ginger, peeled

a pinch of mace

3 bay leaves

🗁 Using a bradawl or sharp skewer, prick the shell of each walnut in several places. This is a tricky operation that is likely to cause extensive staining. I'd wear rubber gloves if I were you, otherwise you'll look like you've been out shoplifting from Charlotte Russe.

🗁 Mix the first lot of water and salt in a bucket and stir until the salt dissolves. Add the pricked nuts and place the bucket somewhere safe and cool. Change the brine on Days 3, 6, and 9. On Day 10 drain the walnuts and spread out on baking sheets. Leave these for three days, during which time they will turn black.

🗁 Combine all the other ingredients in a large pan and heat them until boiling. Simmer for five minutes. Leave the mixture to stand for three hours, then strain it and boil again.

🗁 Put your nuts into sterilized jars and cover with the hot spiced vinegar. Seal tightly and leave for ten weeks before using.

August: Marsh Samphire

I love samphire. It's an odd-looking plant, with a succulent, crunchy texture in the mouth and a delicious saltiness to it; it's also the only vegetable I ever see at the fishmonger's. It grows in salt marshes and estuaries all around Europe, and the season can stretch from June to September, though it's pretty much at its best in August. For you

North Americans, you'll just have to fly over and come pick some with me. The famous hunting grounds for samphire are East Anglia and Lincolnshire, though I've found lots of it around the Bristol Channel and in Sussex.

It makes very fine salads, either on its own or with smoked mackerel and boiled new potatoes.

To prepare it, throw the samphire into a bowl of water and pick through it to remove any gack. Pull off and discard any woody stems that it may have at the base of each sprig—these get woodier as the season progresses. Boil a pan of water, turn off the heat, and add the samphire. Leave for two minutes to blanch, then drain it and serve. Resist the temptation to salt it, because it will provide all the saltiness you need, though a grind or two of pepper won't hurt.

September: Dandelion Coffee

Why this is called coffee is anyone's guess—it tastes nothing like it—but it's fun to make nonetheless. It's made from the roots of dandelions, dried and ground. After picking, wash the roots thoroughly, then spread them out in the sun to dry, taking care not to leave mounds of them, as they will take too long to dry and have a tendency to rot. If the weather's not playing fair, put them in your oven at the lowest possible temperature for five hours or so and keep a careful eye on them as they dry out. They need to be completely desiccated. At this point you will realize that your wizened roots don't add up to many cups of coffee, but that's just tough. Grind them finely and use them as you would use instant coffee.

October: Fragolina Grapes

I first ate these when I took my mum for a tasting course at the legendary London cheese shop La Fromagerie. We were each given a small sprig of knackered sultanas. The moment I tasted one, however, I practically fell off my chair. It was heavenly. They are perfect little lozenges, sweet, gummy, and intensely fruity, with a hint of strawberry. I immediately asked for more, only to be devastated by the news that there weren't any left. I resolved to track them down, but, tragically, the three- to four-week season had just ended. So now, every year, I wait with bated breath for the season to begin so I can spend all the housekeeping money on them. I encourage you to do the same.

November: Mushroom Ketchup

When the air turns damp, it's time to forage for mushrooms.

Makes 2-1/2 cups

2-1/4 pounds mushrooms

2-1/2 ounces salt

2-1/2 cups white wine vinegar

1 teaspoon allspice

10 black peppercorns

a thumb-sized piece of ginger, peeled

4 cloves

a stick of cinnamon

Chop the mushrooms into marble-sized pieces. Place a layer of them in the bottom of an ovenproof bowl and sprinkle with salt. Continue making layers of mushrooms and salt until they're all used up. Cover with a cloth and leave somewhere safe at room temperature for five days. It sounds odd, but this makes the juices leach out of the mushrooms. Stir a few times every day.

Heat your oven to 275°F, cover the bowl with foil, and cook for one and a half hours. Strain the mixture through a muslin or fine sieve, leaving it to drip for two hours.

Place the liquor in a pan with the vinegar and spices and simmer until it has reduced by half. Strain it again and pour into sterilized bottles.

December: Homemade Ginger Beer

Strictly speaking, there's no seasonality to this drink. But I do associate ginger with Christmas, so please indulge me.

Makes 5 quarts

5 quarts water

2 ounces fresh ginger

1 pound sugar

3 lemons

2 teaspoons tartaric acid

1 tablespoon brewer's yeast

In a large saucepan, bring the water to a boil, then turn off the heat. Meanwhile, grate the ginger using a cheese grater and put it in a spotlessly clean bucket with the sugar. Carefully pour in the boiled water and stir to dissolve the sugar. Squeeze the lemons into the water, and throw the rinds in, too. Add the tartaric acid. Let it cool for thirty minutes, and when it's still just warm, add the brewer's yeast. Cover with plastic wrap and something solid (perhaps a spare chopping board) and stash somewhere for two days.

Get another large pan or clean bucket and strain the beer into it through a muslin or clean dish towel. Using a siphon, transfer it into your bottles, and then jam the corks in. If you really promise that you're going to drink some of it within a week, you can fill a few small screw-cap bottles. Leave for three days, then drink.

A safety note: Save some wine corks and bottles for storing your beer because, over time, the pressure can really build up with explosive results. I used to terrify the neighbors with forgotten plastic bottles exploding. Use corks instead of screw-caps, and the pressure will only pop the cork out, causing a lot less damage. You really ought to drink the beer within a couple of weeks anyway, thereby avoiding any grief.

A Brief History of Washing-up

I t's safe to say that the history of washing-up probably began shortly after the invention of cooking and that the invention of cooking probably coincided with the domestication of fire back in the Paleolithic era. The Paleolithic is a bit of a catch-all, beginning 3.5 million or so years ago, and extending to around 8000 BC, so the exact date remains a source of much back and forth. Recently, however, a group of Harvard scientists settled on 1.9 million years ago, when nutrition appears to have suddenly improved.

The distinguished Victorian essayist Charles Lamb paints a wonderful picture of the moment that a Chinese swineherd stumbled across the concept of cooking. In "A Dissertation Upon Roast Pig" he imagines the poor bloke burning his father's herd by accident. He is naturally distraught—until he tastes the crackling . . .

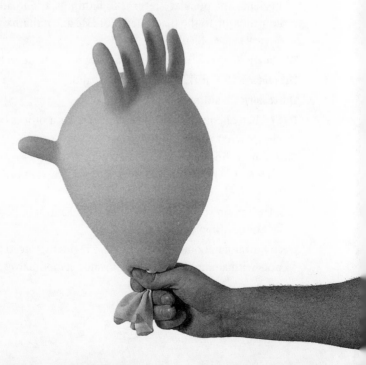

What Lamb failed to picture, however, was the short-lived joy of the Paleolithic bloke's girlfriend, whose view of gastronomy was tempered by the accompanying realization that someone was going to have to clean this bloody lot up, and she had a pretty bloody good idea who that someone was going to be. And so, an aeon of domestic servitude—mainly women's—began, and it would be only mildly alleviated 1.9 million years later, in 1850, with the invention of the dishwasher by Joel Houghton. In the meantime, billions of people have indulged in the inevitable ritual of washing-up, and I've always wondered if there's any beauty in the process, or if it really is just a chore.

Of course, the invention of detergent made it easier, and this was all bound up with the development of soap for bathing. Here are a few of the main events associated with washing up:

2800 BC: Earliest evidence of soap making in ancient Babylon.

1500 BC: Ancient Egyptians start making soap as we know it, combining animal and vegetable oils with alkaline salts.

312 BC: The first Roman bath is built. The populace begins to get clean.

AD 467: The fall of Rome and the concomitant fall in standards of hygiene. The populace returns to filthiness, eventually contributing to the Black Death of 1348 and culminating in the Great Plague of 1665–66.

7th century: Soap making becomes a recognized trade in Europe.

12th century: Soap making begins in England.

17th century: Cleanliness back in fashion.

1791: French chemist Nicholas Leblanc invents a process allowing cheap, large-scale commercial soap production.

1813: Soap technology forges ahead, with discoveries by Michel Chevreul (who also paved the way for the invention of margarine).

1853: The tax on soap in Britain is abolished and standards of cleanliness improve.

1900s: Edwardian domestic servants are regularly forced to clean pots with ammonia, boiling hot water, lemon halves, and salt using their bare hands. Wives, too: In 1903 *The Way to a Man's Heart* advises them to use washing soda or ammonia.

1916: A synthetic detergent is developed in Germany—used mainly for dishwashing and laundry.

1953: Synthetic detergent sales overtake those of soap.

1960: The first sales of Fairy Liquid in Britain.

1990s: The invention of the world's twelfth best soap joke. Two nuns are bathing. One says, "Where's the soap?" The other one says, "Yes, it does, doesn't it?"

And mechanical dishwashers? Well, although the dishwasher was patented in 1850, it wasn't until 1893 that one Josephine Cochrane launched the first marketable, hand-operated version at the World's Fair. Her company eventually became the legendary KitchenAid Corporation. Even then, it wasn't until the 1950s that the machines were produced in a convenient size and at a reasonable price, and not until 1988 that my family bought its first one.

But dishwashers have no place in the most curious washing-up ritual of all—the Eucharist (the Communion service). The communicants eat bread and drink wine, either enjoying transubstantiation (the transformation of the bread and wine into the actual body and blood of Christ) or not, depending on which side of the ecumenical fence you sit. And then the priest carefully and very publicly does the dishes—or chalices, to be exact. I've always thought that this is a highly symbolic act. A cleansing ritual, perhaps related to absolution for sins or to the cyclical nature of death and rebirth. However, my adviser on all things Christian, the lovely Father Evan Jones, says that it's just a simple practical chore—it's got to be cleaned by someone, and the priest must finish all the remaining bread and wine because it would be a sin to waste Christ's body. So the congregation sits while he gathers all the crumbs and finishes off the wine, swilling it out with water to make sure there's none left.

Of course, Father Evan is very thorough in front of an audience, but what about at home where no one's watching? Well, I'm glad to report that he made me a cup of coffee a few weeks ago, and I did check very closely. It was spotless. On the other hand, my favorite mug sports an all-round tea tan that I can never quite bother to scrub off. Maybe Father Evan has got it right—I like to see spiritual patterns in my food (perhaps to justify my unnatural obsession with edible matter). On one level washing-up is simply a chore, but just as the misery of death becomes, through the immutable, unshakeable cycle of life, inextricably linked to the wonder of birth, so the misery of washing-up is part of the cycle that leads inevitably to the miracle of lunch.

Useful Web Sites and Suppliers

Food Suppliers

Butchers

Butcher shops in America are pretty much a thing of the past, unfortunately. To find specialty meats, try one of these online meat retailers:

D'Artagnan: www.dartagnan.com

Exotic Meats: www.exoticmeats.com

Omaha Steaks: www.omahasteaks.com

The following butchers supplied meat for this book:

M. Moen & Sons: The legendary and very lovely butchers in Clapham, south London are good for suckling pig and other butchery fun. 020 7622 1624 www.moen.co.uk

Frank Godfrey & Son: of Highbury Barn, north London, is also fantastic, and supplied most of the meat for the recipes in this book. 020 7226 9904

Pugh's Piglets: Based in Preston, Lancashire. 01995 601728 www.pughspiglets.co.uk

Canned insects

Thai Tastes: www.thaitastes.com

Frogs' legs

Cajun Grocer: www.cajungrocer.com or Amazon.com

Cheese and cheese making

La Fromagerie: A wonderful spread of great cheeses. I have never felt welcome here, but the fact that I still visit on a fortnightly basis is a testament to the quality of their stock.

30 Highbury Park, London N5 2AA 020 7359 7440

If you don't have a local cheese shop, try one of these online cheese retailers:

igourmet.com: www.igourmet.com

French cheese: www.fromages.com

Cheese making equipment:
The Cheesemaker: www.thecheesemaker.com
Moorlands Cheesemakers: www.cheesemaking.co.uk

Chickens
Wholesome Harvest: Free-range, organic chickens.
www.wholesomeharvest.com

Farmers markets
Find a Farmers Market in your state: www.ams.usda.gov/farmersmarkets

Japanese food
Asian Food Grocer: www.asianfoodgrocer.com

Laver bread
The Welsh Barrow: A Web site for obsessives (there's a rather lovely video clip of some laver lying on a very cold-looking Welsh beach), and they tell you where you can buy it. PO Box 218, Mumbles, Swansea SA3 4ZA 020 7793 7085 (mail order) www.laverbread.org

Tokaji—the finest liquid on the planet
To find Disznoko Tokaji:
Dotcom Wines: www.dotcomwines.com
Wine Zap: www.winezap.com

Weird stuff
They don't ship to the States, but the site is worth a quick window-shop.
Edible: www.edible.com

Other Suppliers

Brewing
The Amphora Society: www.amphora-society.com
Homebrewers Outpost: www.homebrewers.com
Homebrew Heaven: www.homebrewheaven.com
Home Distillation of Alcohol: www.homedistiller.org
Hop Shop: www.hopshopuk.com

Gold and gilding equipment
Chef Tools: www.cheftools.com
Habberley Meadows: www.habberleymeadows.co.uk
E. Ploton (Sundries) Ltd: www.ploton.co.uk

Margarine info
National Association of Margarine Manufacturers: www.margarine.org
The Margarine & Spreads Association: www.margarine.org.uk

Reindeer meat and skins
Exotic Meats: www.exoticmeats.com
Renprodukter: Based in northern Sweden. 00 46 980 1008

Smokery designs
Charcoal Grill Depot: www.smokergrills.com
Fish & Fly: www.fishandfly.co.uk/jbedit1201.html
Hastings Fly Fishers' Club Ltd: www.hastingsflyfishers.co.uk/smoker.htm

Speeches and poetry on CD
The British Library: www.bl.uk or Amazon.com

Food-related music
The First Vienna Vegetable Orchestra: www.vegetableorchestra.org
Matthew Herbert (Accidental Records): www.magicandaccident.com

Food Information

In case you want to know what the government thinks is safe to eat, visit the *Food and Drug Administration's Web site*: www.fda.org

The other side. *The Food Commission*: www.foodcomm.org.uk

And in the U.S., try *Center for Science in the Public Interest*: www.cspinet.org

Recipes, Chat And That

foodreference.com: www.foodreference.com
rivercottage.net: www.rivercottage.net
Slow Food: www.slowfood.com
Annals of Improbable Research: www.improb.com
Malcolm Gladwell: A wonderful writer with some witty, in-depth and beautifully crafted pieces on food. www.gladwell.com
Project Gutenberg: Free electronic books. www.gutenberg.org

Cheap or free ordination into the clergy
Spiritual Humanism: www.spiritualhumanism.org

Bibliography

Some of the following books are out of print, but can be found very easily through second-hand booksellers. If anyone ever fancies buying me a Christmas present, all they need to do is find me another book on food.

The one book everyone should have
Davidson, Alan. *The Penguin Companion to Food* (Penguin, 2002)

Practical books for gastronauts
Food in Vogue: Six Decades of Cooking and Entertaining (Conde Nast, 1976)
Blumenthal, Heston. *Family Food: A New Approach to Cooking* (Penguin, 2003)
Bourdain, Anthony. *Anthony Bourdain's Les Halles Cookbook: Strategies, Recipes, and Techniques of Classic Bistro Cooking* (Bloomsbury, 2004)
Carroll, Ricki. *Home Cheese Making* (Storey Books, 2003)
Cradock, Fanny. *Time to Remember: A Cook for All Seasons* (Webb & Bower, 1981)
Davidson, Allen. *North Atlantic Seafood: A Comprehensive Guide with Recipes* (Penguin, 1980)
Fearnley-Whittingstall, Hugh. *The River Cottage Meat Book* (Hodder & Stoughton, 2004)
Grigson, Jane. *Charcuterie and French Pork Cookery* (Michael Joseph, 1967)
Henderson, Fergus. *The Whole Beast: Nose to Tail Eating* (Macmillan, 1999)
Howe, Robin. *The International Wine and Food Society's Guide to Poultry and Game* (Drake Publishers, 1971)
Innes, Jocasta. *The Country Kitchen* (Frances Lincoln, 2003)
Jones, Evan. *The Book of Cheese* (Pan Macmillan, 1980)
Levy, Paul. (ed.) *Penguin Book of Food and Drink* (Penguin USA, 1998)
Mabey, Richard. *Food For Free* (HarperCollins Publishers, 2002)
McGee, Harold. *Food and Cooking: The Science and Lore of the Kitchen* (Scribner, 2003)
Norrman, Ola. *Home Distillation Handbook* (Bokforlaget Exakt, 2003)
Seymour, John. *The Complete Book of Self-Sufficiency* (Dorling Kindersley, 1996)
Steingarten, Jeffrey. *It Must've Been Something I Ate* (Vintage, 2003)
Steingarten, Jeffrey. *The Man Who Ate Everything* (Vintage, 1998)

Time-Life series—various editions published in the 1960s and '70s

Warhol, Andy and Suzie Frankfurt. *Wild Raspberries* (Bulfinch Press, 1997)

Willan, Anne. *Great Cooks and Their Recipes: From Taillevent to Escoffier* (Pavilion, 2000)

Strange foods

Hopkins, Jerry. *Extreme Cuisine* (Bloomsbury, 2005)

Lucan, Medlar and Durian Gray. *The Decadent Cookbook* (Dedalus Ltd, 1998)

Schuyt, M. and Foy, S. *Phantasievoller Ratgeber für vergnügte Köche* (DuMont Buchverlag Köln, 1995)

Schwabe, Calvin. W. *Unmentionable Cuisine* (Virginia University Press, 1998)

Food history

Bottero, Jean. (Fagan, T. L., trans.) *The Oldest Cuisine in the World: Cooking in Mesopotamia* (Chicago University Press, 2004)

Boyd, L. (ed,) *British Cookery: A Complete Guide to Culinary Practice in the British Isles* (Croom Helm, 1976)

Edwards, John. *The Roman Cookery of Apicius* (Rodale Pr, 1984)

Fernandez-Armesto, Felipe. *Food: A History* (Pan Macmillan, 2002)

Fletcher, Nichola. *Charlemagne's Tablecloth: A Piquant History of Feasting* (St. Martin's Press, 2005)

Hartley, Dorothy. *Food in England* (Time Warner Books UK, 1999)

Kelly, Ian. *Cooking for Kings* (Short Books, 2003)

Kurlansky, Mark. (ed.) *Choice Cuts: A Savory Selection of Food Writing from Around the World and Throughout History* (Penguin, 2004)

Richardson, Tim. *Sweets: A History of Candy* (Bloomsbury USA, 2003)

Strong, Roy. *Feast: A History of Grand Eating* (Harcourt, 2003)

Historical gems

Beeton, Isabella. *Mrs. Beeton's Book of Household Management* (Oxford University Press, 2000)

Brillat-Savarin, Jean Anthelme. (Drayton, A., trans.) *The Physiology of Taste: Or, Meditations on Transcendental Gastronomy* (Penguin, 1994)

Francatelli, Charles Elmé. *A Plain Cookery Book for the Working Classes* (Pryor, 1993)

Glasse, Hannah. *The Art of Cookery Made Plain and Easy: Excelling at Any Thing of the Kind Ever Yet Published* (Applewood, 1998)

Holt, Vincent M. *Why Not Eat Insects?* (Intl Specialized Book Service Inc, 1988)

Arcana

Barnett, Beatrice. *Urine-therapy: It May Save Your Life* (Lifestyle Institute, 1993)

Douglas, Norman. *Venus in the Kitchen: Or Love's Cookery Book* (Bloomsbury, 2002)

Garwood, Nigel and Rainer Voight. *Food Mania: An Extraordinary Visual Record of the Art of Food, from Kitchen Garden to Banqueting Table* (Three Rivers Press, 2001)

Habets, B. *The Complete Incontinence Handbook* (Carnell, 1993)

Leckie, Ross. *The Gourmet's Companion: Curious Fables, Facts and Folklore from the World of Food and Drink* (Edinburgh Publishing Co., 1993)

Petits Propos Culinaire—a thrice-yearly journal (Prospect Books)

Pond, Caroline M. *The Fats of Life* (Cambridge University Press, 1998)

Rolls, Edmund. *Emotion Explained* (Oxford University Press, 2005)

Saulnier, Louis. (Brunet, E., trans.) *Le Repertoire de la Cuisine* (Barron's Educational Series, 1976)

Schott, Ben. *Schott's Food and Drink Miscellany* (Bloomsbury, 2003)

Cannibalism

Abler, T. I. *Cannibalism: Fact Not Fiction* (Ethnohistory, 1980)

Arens, W. *The Man-eating Myth: Anthropology and Anthropophagy* (Oxford University Press, 1980)

Barker, Francis, Peter Hulme and Margaret Iversen, eds. *Cannibalism and the Colonial World* (Cambridge University Press, 1998)

Boucher, Phillip P. *Cannibal Encounters: Europeans and Island Caribs, 1492–1763* (Johns Hopkins University Press, 1992)

Chong, Key Ray. *Cannibalism in China* (Longwood Pr Ltd, 1990)

Clastres, P. *Cannibals* (The Sciences, 1998)

Conklin, Beth A. *Consuming Grief: Compassionate Cannibalism in an Amazonian Society* (Texas University Press, 2001)

Dornstreich, M. and G. E. B. Morren, *Does New Guinea Cannibalism Have Nutritional Value?* (Human Ecology, 1974)

Elgar, Mark A. and Bernard J. Crespi, eds. *Cannibalism: Ecology and Evolution Among Diverse Taxa* (Oxford University Press, 1992)

Goldman, Laurence R., ed. *The Anthropology of Cannibalism* (Bergin & Garvey, 1999)

Harris, Marvin. *The Sacred Cow and the Abominable Pig: Riddles of Food and Culture* (Touchstone Books, 1987)

Harris, Marvin. *Cannibals and Kings: Origins of Cultures* (Vintage, 1991)

Lestringant F. *Cannibals* (California University Press, 1997)

Petrinovich, Lewis. *The Cannibal Within* (Aldine, 2000)

Sanday, Peggy Reeves. *Divine Hunger: Cannibalism as a Cultural System* (Cambridge University Press, 1986)

Seabrook, William. *Jungle Ways* (Harcourt, Brace and Co., 1931)

Takada, Shiguro. *Contingency Cannibalism: Superhardcore Survivalism's Dirty Little Secret* (Paladin Press, 1999)

Tannahill, Reay. *Flesh and Blood: A History of the Cannibal Complex* (Little, Brown, 1997)

Yue, Gang. *The Mouth That Begs: Hunger, Cannibalism, and the Politics of Eating in Modern China* (Duke University Press, 1999)

The Gastronautical Survey

Before I started writing this book I wanted to get a better understanding of people's relationship with food, so I drew up a list of simple questions and sent it to as many people as I could. I didn't really expect anyone to fill it out, but the response was astounding. People loved being asked about food and enthusiastically detailed all their grubbiest eating habits. I had originally assumed that the British, though a lovely and huggable tribe, were pretty conservative eaters. Oh, how wrong I was. We've all had some insane culinary experiences, complex cannibal desires, and bizarre physical reactions to food.

My task of creating a snapshot of the nation's murkier eating habits is not yet complete, and these results have been compiled from the first five hundred replies. The survey now rests on the *Gastronaut* Web site at www.thegastronaut.com. I'd really appreciate it if you would send me your thoughts and maybe help with some other culinary questions. And I'm dying to hear from my American cousins.

Here is what I learned.

What best defines food for you?

Love	57%
Fuel	29%
Power	14%

What's your relationship with food?

Eater	39%
Foodie	34%
Cook	21%
Gourmand	3%
Chef	3%

Do you love eating turkey at Christmas?

Love	71%
Hate	29%

Do you genuinely like your pasta *al dente*?

Like pasta *al dente*	62%
Don't like pasta *al dente*	38%

What's your favorite food?

Cheese	8%
Lamb	7%
Fish (general)	6.5%
Chocolate	6%
Curry	5%
Sushi	5%
Bacon	4.5%
Meat (general)	4%
Pasta	3.5%
Scallops	3%

2.5% or fewer included these highlights: testicles, Korean-style beef, raspberries, roast chicken dinner, mango, apple tart, olives, micro-elephant on toast, poached eggs, fish eggs, crème Anglaise.

What's your *least* favorite food?

Fast food	8%
Liver	7%
Fish	6%
Beets	3.5%
Offal	3%
Anchovies	2.5%
Meat	2%
Brussels sprouts	1.5%
Tripe	1.5%
Celery	1%

Other leading figures of hate included: broad beans, courgettes, marzipan, olives, oysters, peas, rice pudding, and yogurt.

Have you ever made a recipe you've seen on a TV program?

Never	43%
Occasionally	41%
Once	10%
Often	6%

After you've picked out food trapped between your teeth, do you eat it?

Yes	66%
No	32%
Depends on certain factors	2%

What food or drink last made you sick?

Wine	12%
Fish	6%
Beer	5%
Prawns	3%
Vodka	2.5%

Are you tasty?

Tasty	54%
Not tasty	28%
Don't know	18%

If you were a cannibal, which famous person would you most like to eat?

Brad Pitt	5%
Kylie Minogue	3.5%
Nigella Lawson	3%
Ainsley Harriott	3%
Wouldn't eat a famous person	3%
Cameron Diaz	2.5%
Delia Smith	2.5%
Britney Spears	2.5%
George Clooney	2%
George W. Bush	2%

The remaining 71% offered no clear favorites but included Dawn French, Lisa Riley, the Reverand Iain Paisley, Vanessa Feltz, Luciano Pavarotti, Napoleon Bonaparte, Chris Tarrant ("if I can kill him first"), Roseanne Barr, the Rock, and Hattie Jacques.

If you were a cannibal, which body part would you most like to eat?

Thigh	17%
Buttock/rump/bottom	15%
Breast	6%
Cheeks	5%
Ear	4.5%
Leg	4.5%
Arm	4%
Liver	4%
Baby's bottom	3%
Testicles	2%

The remaining 35% offered no clear preference.

Have you ever eaten or drunk … ?

Nails	53%
Boogers	44%
Scabs	36%
Breast milk (as an adult)	35%
Ear wax	10%
Urine	6%
Semen	4%
Hair	3%
Feces	2%

Have you ever eaten *any* of the above belonging to someone else?

5%

Which meal, if any, is most likely to end in sexual congress?

Meal with lots of alcohol	11%
Take-out meal	7%
Chocolate	5%
Expensive meal	4.5%
Breakfast	4%
Oysters	3%
Fish (various)	2%
A light meal	1.5%
Cooked by male partner	1%
None/no response/ expression of outrage	18%

Among the remaining 43%, other items that cropped up more than once included: lobster, sushi, crispy duck, champagne, strawberries, fruit, lunch, quick meals.

What food is most likely to make you fart?

Beans	29%
Cruciferous vegetables and asparagus	11%
Jerusalem artichoke	9%
Onion and garlic	5%
Curry	5%
Potatoes/corn/noodles/wheat	5%
Fruit	4%
Cheese	1%

The remaining 31% showed no clear preference, were statistically irrelevant, or just plain stupid.

What food makes your pee smell?

Asparagus	51%
Sugar Puffs	6%
Curry	5%
Alcohol	4%
Artichokes	3%

The remaining 31% refused to answer or offered no clear preference.

Strange foods

As children, many people had experimented with strange foods, including: marbles, toilet freshener blocks, beads, buttons, bleach, pens, coal, lip balm, turpentine, soap, bits of metal, maggots, hair grips, paper, paperclips, and shoe polish. There was one instance of a boy eating polystyrene cement straight from the tube when he was twelve years old, and the most disturbing was the respondent whose mother tried to serve him a Comet crumble.

As adults, most people had been admirably brave with their food. Here are some of the things they said were weird (though most of them are considered run of the mill in one country or another).

Alligator

Animals whose names I knew

Au pair's cottage pie made with half a tub of cinnamon

Beans on toast

Brains

Breadfruit

Catalan food

Cheese

Chickens' feet

Chitterlings

Chocolate ants

Chocolate-covered brussels sprouts

Chocolate pasta

Coal

Cobra (freshly beaten to death with a long stick)

Coconut with blood and spices (in Bali)

Conch meat

Crocodile

Curry

Deep-fried cheesecake

Deep-fried goats' brains

Dog

Donkey ragout

Dried banana

Dried worms

Duck heart (sliced into the shape of an ornamental rose)

Ducks' tongues

Durian fruit

Eel pie

Eel's penis

Ethiopian food

Fish eye

Fried grasshoppers

Fried pigs' guts

Fugu (the poisonous Japanese blowfish)

Goat's face pâté

Gizzards

Goose hearts

Grass soup

Guinea pig

Hare in chocolate sauce

Hotdog filled with cheese by hypodermic needle

Insects

Intestine

Jellyfish

Kangaroo

Konnyaku ("little squares of rubberiness")

Ladies' fingers

Larks' tongues

Live lobster

Lizards

Maggots in tequila

Marmite scrambled eggs

Monkey-brain dim sum

Musk ox

Pigs' trotters

Puntarel

Putrefied shark

Rare sashimi

Roasted magpie

Rosemary sorbet

Sea-urchin sushi

Shark-fin soup

Sheep's eyes

Snails

Snake

Something in Kerala

Sparrow kebabs

Stingray

Sugared beet sandwiches

Surstrooming ("bulging tins of fermented stinky herrings")

Swan

Tête de veau (calf's head with brain sauce)

Tilapia from Uganda

Tongue

Toothpaste sandwich ("when I was eight")

Traditional Icelandic pickled whale

Tripe

Weevils

Weird Chinese shellfish

Whale blubber

Whole rabbit

Worms in Fiji

100-year-old egg

Index

Aberdeen Nips, 51
aftershave, 95–7
alcohol
    communion wine, 35
    moonshine, 13–14
almonds, Fourteenth-century Blancmange,
    182–3
Amursanu-pigeon Broth, 159
ancient recipes, 158–9
aphrodisiacs, 73–8
Apicus, De Re Coquinaria, 39, 40, 158
apple sauce, for Suckling Pig, 196
army worms, 48–9
asparagus, 82, 88
Assurnasirpal II, palace-warming feast
    of, 31–2
aubergines, 137

Babcock, Tom, 176
bacchanalian orgies, 38–46, 146, 166
    menu for Trimalchio's feast, 40–1
    music, 44, 45–6
    slaves, 42–3
    vomitoria, 42, 45
Bacchus, god of wine, 38, 39
bacon, Buckinghamshire Bacon Badger,
    118–19
bananas, Heartbreaker sandwich, 116
Barrett, Samuel, 48–9
Bartnett, Dr. Beatrice, Urine Therapy, 71
beans, and flatulence, 79, 81
beef
    Beef Cecils, 51
    biltong, 15–17
    carpaccio, 41, 226
    Carpetbagger Steaks, 129
    Monkey Gland Steak, 127–8
    Pigeon Pie, 151
Beeton, Mrs. Isabella, The Book of
    Household Management, 141, 152–3
beets, 88
    soup, 101

Berliner, David, 75
the Bible
    and cannibalism, 56
    and insects, 160
    and the Last Supper, 33–4, 37
biltong, 15–17
Bischinger, Dr. Friedrich, 68
biscuit-tin smokeries, 25–6
black pudding
    and Clapshot, 130–1
    Drisheen, 170
    Suckling Pig, 194–8
Blancmange, Fourteenth-century, 182–3
boogers, 65, 68–9
Boiled Prisoner, 63–4
boning birds, 199, 200
Bottero, Jean, The Oldest Cuisine in the
    World, 159
Boyd, Lizzie, British Cookery, 52
Brandes, Bernd Jürgen, 56
Brassens, Georges, 165
brawn (Headcheese), 187–93, 225
bread, pumpernickel, 81
breast milk, 69–70
Brillat-Savarin, Anthelme, 42, 52, 96, 226
    Truffled Turkey, 215–17
British food, culinary decline of, 50–2
Brotherly Love, 52
Buckinghamshire Bacon Badger, 51, 118–19

Caligula, Roman emperor, 39
calf's head, 152, 153
Calf's Liver, 227
calves' feet, Mock Turtle Soup, 152–5
cannibalism, 55–72
    the human harvest, 65–72
    and the law, 58–60
    recipes, 61–4
    survey on, 55–7
Carême, Antonin, 52
Caroll, Ricki, Home Cheese Making, 19
Carpaccio, beef, 41, 226

Carpetbagger Steaks, 129
carrots, 89
    Carrot Jam, 230–1
Cass, Mama, 32
Celeriac Soup, 102
ceviche, salmon and Issey Miyake, 97
Chaplin, Charlie, 31
Chaucer, Geoffrey, Canterbury Tales, 79,
    81
cheese
    and dreams, 87, 88–9
    and flatulence, 79, 83
    King Edward's Chippenham Cheese Savory,
    108
    Welsh, 111
cheese-making, 18–20
    and breast milk, 69–70
Cheetos
    golden, 7
    with gruel, 126
Chevreul, Michel, 238
chicken
    14th-century Blancmange, 182–3
    with 40 cloves of garlic, 226
    Chicken-foot Stew, 109–10
    chicken-stuffed-poussin-stuffed
    quail, 201–2
    Picasso's Poussin, 133–4
    Turducken, 199–202
chickens, and eggs, 10
China, and cannibalism, 56, 62
Chocolate Balls à la Chambord, 138
Chong, Key Ray, Cannibalism in China, 63
Christmas Day, 90
Clapshot, 51, 130–1, 225
Clermont, Bernard, Professed Cook, 167
Cochrane, Josephine, 239
Communion (the Eucharist), 35, 239
conger eel, Stuffed Fish Heads, 179–80
cooking, invention of, 237
Cow-heel Soup, 149–50
Cox, Peter, 13
Cradock, Fanny, 98
cream
    The Dean's Cream, 51
    Stone, Stepladder and Bucket Cream, 181
cream cheese, 19
crickets, 160
cruciferous vegetables, 79, 82

Dandelion Coffee, 234
Davidson, Alan, Companion to Food, 171,
    176
The Dean's Cream, 51
Deep-fried Mars Bars, 143
detergent, history of, 238–9
Dickens, B. M., The Control of Living Body
    Material, 59
Dio Cassius, 39
Dionysus, god of fertility, 38, 39
dishwashers, history of, 238, 239–40
dormice, 40, 41
    stuffed, 158–9
dreams, and cheese, 87, 88–9
Drisheen (Irish blood pudding), 170
duck, Turducken, 199–202

ear wax, 65, 70
ears, pigs', 171–2, 225
Edward VIII, King, 108
Edwards, John, The Roman Cookery of
    Apicus, 40
eggs
    and chickens, 10
    egg-sucking, 9–11
    Mumbled Mushrooms, 103–4, 225
    pickled, 229
    scrambled eggs and laver bread, 112
Elagabalus, 40
Elderberry Flower Cordial, 231–2
Erox, 75
Escoffier, Auguste, 163
Eucharist (Communion service), 35, 239
Euripedes, The Bacchae, 39
eyeballs, 229–30

Fanny Sandwich, 98–9, 225
fat-tailed sheep, 171
Fearnley-Whittingstall, Hugh, River
    Cottage Meat Book, 123
feces, 65, 72
fish
    Fish Sperm on Toast, 157, 225
    Mackerel Tartare, 113–14
    Stargazey Pie, 176–8
    Stuffed Fish Heads, 179–80
fish-tweezers, 113
Fisher, M. F. K., 98
Fitless Cock, 51, 152
flatulence, 79–86
Flaubert, Gustave, 73

Fleming, Elise, *The Compleat Cook*, 192
Fletcher, Nicola, *Charlemagne's Tablecloth*, 146
Flummery, 51, 141
foie gras, *Truffled Turkey*, 215–17
fondue, toffee, 144–5
food poisoning, 103
forcemeat quenelles, 154–5
Forme of Cury, 182
14th-century Blancmange, 182–3
fragolina grapes, 234–5
Francatelli, Charles Elme, *A Plain Cookery Book for the Working Classes*, 149
Frankfurt, Suzie, 138
French food terminology, 50, 52
fries, golden, 7
Frogs' Legs, 163–5, 225
fruit
    and flatulence, 79, 83
    and pit-cooked meat, 209
    Toffee Fondue, 144–5
Frumenty, 146

garlic
    Chicken with Forty Cloves of Garlic, 226
    and flatulence, 79, 82
Gastronautical Survey, 248–51
Gastronaut's Creed, xiv, 225
Gibson, Glenn, 79
gilded food *see* gold (gilded food)
ginger beer, homemade, 235–6
Girdle Sponges, 51
Glasgow Magistrates, 51
Glasse, Hannah, *The Art of Cookery Made Plain and Easy*, 152
GM (genetically modified) crops, xiii
goat, pit-cooked, 207
gold (gilded food), 3–8
gold leaf, 4
The Gold Rush, (film) 31
Gold Wasser de Danzig, 3
Goodyer, John, 81
goose, 152
grapes, fragolina, 234–5
grasshoppers, 48, 160
gravlax, homemade, 105
Grey, Elizabeth, *Secrets in Physick and Chyrugery*, 3

Grigson, Jane, *Charcuterie and French Pork Cookery*, 171
gruel, 125–6
guinea pigs, 219–20

haggis, nettle, 121
hair, 65, 72
Hartley, Dorothy, *Food in England*, 50
Hasty Pudding, 51, 139–40
Headcheese (brawn), 187–93, 225
heart
    ox, 148
    smoked reindeer, 175
Heartbreaker sandwich, 116
Henderson, Fergus, *Nose to Tail Eating*, 171
Henry IV, King, 146
herring roes
    Fish Sperm on Toast, 157, 225
    Herring Sperm on Horseback (Kromenskies), 232–3
herrings, *Stargazey Pie*, 176–8
hiccups, 89
Holt, Vincent M., *Why Not Eat Insects?*, 47, 161
Houghton, Joel, 238
Huffkins, 51
Human Sauce, 64
Hunters' Buns, 51

Inky-pinky, 51
Innes, Jocasta, *The Country Kitchen*, 19
insects, 40, 47, 48–9, 160–2
Interactive Pizza Engineering, 135–7
Irish Blood Pudding (Drisheen), 170
Irish potato famine, xii

Jerusalem artichokes
    and flatulence, 79, 81, 82–3
    mackerel tartare, 113–14
Jesus Christ, 56
    and the Last Supper, 33–4, 220

Kaswell, Alice Shirrell, 10
ketchup, mushroom, 235
Kid Stew, 159
King Edward's Chippenham Cheese Savory, 108
koalas, xii

Kromenskies (Herring Sperm on Horseback),
    232–3
Kurlansky, Mark, *Choice Cuts*, 98
kuru, 56

lactose, and flatulence, 82, 83
lamb
    sweetbreads, 229–30
    ten-hour leg of, 226
    Testicles, 166
Lamb, Charles, "A Dissertation Upon
    Roast Pig", 237
Lancashire Nuts, 51
the Last Supper, 33–7, 220
Laver Bread, 40, 111–12
Leblanc, Nicholas, 238
leftovers, 223–40
lemon grass, *Smug Homemaker Iced Pea and
    Lemon Grass Soup*, 106–7
lemons, *Flummery*, 141
Leonardo da Vinci, painting of the Last
    Supper, 34
liver, calves', 227
Livingstone, David, *Zambesi*, 55
locusts, 160
Loubert, Émil, 30
Love in Disguise, 52
Lucius Verus, 39
Lumpydick, 117

McKeith, Dr. Gillian, 75
Mackerel Tartare, 113–14
Mao Tse-tung, 37
margarine, 21–4
Marinated Criminal, 64
Mars bar, deep-fried, 143
marsh samphire, 233–4
Medical Law (Kennedy and Grubb), 59
Mège-Mouriès, Hippolyte, 22
Meiwes, Armin, 55, 56, 62
Mesopotamian cuisine, 159
Middle Ages
    Fourteenth-century Blancmange, 182–3
    gilded food, 3
    Mystery Plays, 34–5
milk, breast milk, 69–70
mineral supplements, 90, 91
Mitterand, François, 32
Mock Turtle Soup 40, 152–5
Monkey Gland Steak, 127–8

moonshine, 13–14
Mousehole, Cornwall, 176
Mumbled Mushrooms, 103–4, 225
mushrooms
    mumbled, 103–4, 225
    Mushroom Ketchup, 235
mutton, pit-cooked, 208

nails, 65, 67
Napoleon III, French emperor, 22
Nero, Roman emperor, 33, 39, 56
Nettle Haggis, 121
Nettle Soup, 120
nutmeg, 89

onions, and flatulence, 79, 82
Ordinance of Pottage, 3
ortolans, 32
Osborne, Charles, 89
ox heart, 148
oysters, 40
    Carpetbagger Steaks, 129

paleolithic era, 237
Pan-Fried Sweetbreads, 229–30
Papua New Guinea, cannibalism in, 56
partridge
    roast, 226
    suckling pig stuffed with, 208
peanut butter, *Heartbreaker* sandwich, 116
peanut sauce, for guinea pig, 221
peas, *Smug Homemaker Iced Pea and Lemon
    Grass Soup*, 106–7
Peking Man, 55
Pepys, Samuel, 121, 123
Peruvian Grilled Guinea Pig, 220–21
Petronius, *Satyricon*, 33, 39
physiological effects of food, 87–90
Picasso's Poussin, 133–4
Pickled Chinaman, 63
Pickled Eggs, 229
Pickled Walnuts, 233
pies
    pigeon, 151
    rabbit, 123–4
    stargazey, 176–8
pig
    pigs' ears, 171–2, 225
    pig's head, 187–93
    Pigs' Trotters, 40, 189, 191

pit-cooked pig, 203–14
Suckling Pig, 194–8
see also pork
pigeons
    Amursanu-pigeon Broth, 159
    Pigeon Pie, 151
    Rhinoceros Soup, 167–9
    suckling pig stuffed with, 208
pilchards, Stargazey Pie, 176–8
pineapple, whole roasted, 227
pit-cooked pig, 203–14
    food preparation, 209–10
    ingredients, 206–9
    music, 214
    suggested timetable, 212–14
pizzas, 135–7
placenta, 63
Pliny the Elder, 75
Ploton's, 4–5
Plum Duff, 118
Pollio, Vedius, 39
Poor Man's Goose, 152
pork
    Mock Goose, 152
    see also pig; sausages
potatoes, xii
    Clapshot Fries, 130–1, 225
    Golden Fries, 7
poussin, 225
    chicken-stuffed-poussin-stuffed
        quail, 201–2
    Picasso's, 133–4
Presley, Elvis, 116
Priddy Oggies, 51
Pugh's Piglets, 195
pumpernickel bread, 81

quails, 133
    bacchanalian orgy, 40, 41
    chicken-stuffed-poussin-stuffed
        quail, 201–2
    Rhinoceros Soup, 167–9
    suckling pig stuffed with, 208
quenelles, forcemeat, 154–5
Quick ' n' Easy Termites, 161

rabbit, 61
    pie, 123–4
Raffald, Elizabeth, 3
Red and White Soup, 101–2, 225

Reindeer Stew, 174–5
rennet, 19
Rhinoceros Soup, 40, 167–9
rhubarb
    leaves, 89
    shortcake, 228–9
rice
    Fourteenth-century Blancmange, 182–3
    Gruel, 125–6
Richard II, King, 182
Roast Partridge, 226
Roasted Placenta Loaf, 63–4
roes see herring roes
Roman aphrodisiacs, 75
Roman feasts, 32–3, 39, 158

Sade, Marquis de, 76
St. John restaurant, London, 148
salmon
    biscuit-tin smoked, 26
    Homemade Gravlax, 105
    and Issey Miyake ceviche, 97
samphire, 234
sandwiches
    Fanny Sandwich, 98–9, 225
    Heartbreaker, 116
    Venus Sandwich, 99
sardines, Stargazey Pie, 176–8
Saulnier, Louis, Le Repertoire de la Cuisine,
        52
sausages
    Gilded Sausages and Mash, 6–7
    and pit-cooked meat, 208, 209–10
    Suckling Pig, 194–8
Savoy Hotel, 34
scabs, 65, 69
sea urchins, 148
Seabrook, William Bueler, Jungle Ways,
        61–2
seasonal oddments, 228–36
seaweed, Laver Bread, 111–12
semen, 65, 71–2
serotonin, 89–90
sheep
    fat-tailed, 171
    see also lamb
shortcake, rhubarb, 228–9
silver leaf, 4
Singing Hinnies, 52
Slot, 51

smokeries, biscuit-tin, 25–6
Smug Homemaker Iced Pea and Lemon Grass Soup, 106–7

soapmaking, history of, 238–9
soup
    Amursanu-pigeon Broth, 159
    Chicken-foot Stew, 109–10
    Cow-heel, 149–50
    Smug Homemaker Iced Pea and Lemon Grass, 106–7
    Mock Turtle, 40, 152–5
    Nettle, 120
    Red and White, 101–2, 225
    Rhinoceros, 40, 167–9
Spanish fly, 76
sperm, 71
    Fish Sperm on Toast, 157, 225
    Herring Sperm on Horseback (Kromenskies), 232–3
Spiritual Humanist Church, 36–7
Spotted Dog, 118
steaks
    Carpetbagger, 129
    Monkey Gland, 127–8
Strike, John, 25
Strong, Sir Roy, *Feast*, 42–3
Stuffed Fish Heads, 179–80
Stufffed Dormouse, 158–9
Suckling Pig, 194–8
    pit-cooked, 208
suet puddings, *Buckinghamshire Bacon Badger*, 118–19
Sugar Puffs, 88
sushi, mackerel, 113
swede, *Clapshot*, 130–1, 225
sweetbreads, 229–30

Ten-hour Leg of Lamb, 226
termites, quick 'n' easy, 161
Testicles, 166
Tigellinus, 39
Titanic last dinner, 29–30, 30–1
Toad in the Hole, 152
Toffee Fondue, 144–5
toothpaste, 90
Trimalchio's feast, 32–3, 39–41
tripe, 171
Truffled Turkey, 215–17
truffles, 215

Turducken, 199–202
turkey
    and sleepiness, 89–90
    truffled, 215–17
    Turducken, 199–202
turnips, *Clapshot*, 130–1, 225
Turtle Soup, 152

urine, 65, 70–1, 87–8
urokinase, 71

veal
    Mock Turtle Soup, 152–5
    Rhinoceros Soup, 167–9
    sweetbreads, 229–30
vegetables
    cruciferous, 79, 82
    pit-cooked, 209–10
venison, pit-cooked, 208
Venus Sandwich, 99
Viagra, 76
vitamins, 90–1
Voodoo Stew, 63

Wallace, Danny, 36
Wallis Budge, E. A., *The Divine Origin of the Craft of the Herbalist*, 64
walnuts, pickled, 233
Warhol, Andy, 138
washing-up, history of, 237–40
Welsh food, *Laver Bread*, 111–12
Wet Nelly, 51, 118
wheat, *Frumenty*, 146
Whim-wham, 51
Whole Roasted Pineapple, 227
Wild Raspberries (Warhol and Frankfurt), 138
wine, Communion, 35
Woodlice (Oniscus muriarius), 161
Woolton, Lord, 56
worms, 48–9
Wow-wow Sauce, 52

York, George Neville, Archbishop of, 31

Zapata, Marcos, painting of the Last Supper, 220

Acknowledgments

This book has been some time in the making. To everyone whose lives have been blighted by its gestation, thank you. To everyone who never quite understood what I was going on about, thanks for forcing me to get it right.

Thanks to the gorgeous Michelle Kass for her love, honesty, and strict guidance; the lovely Borra Garson who makes stuff happen; Nicky Ross who wasn't really sure if such an august organization as the BBC really ought to publish a book about scabs and boogers, but persevered nonetheless; and Isobel Gillan and Christopher Tinker, who've managed to fashion a silk purse without losing the sense of sow's ear. A huge transatlantic thank-you to Jen Charat and David Hough at Harcourt for their kindness and wonderful editing—and for letting this weird English bloke keep his weird English turns of phrase and never once using the word "quaint" to describe him. Not within earshot, anyway.

Some nice people from the telly helped make this book happen in various ways, including Richard Johnson (the most huggable man I've ever met), Mandy Cooper, Jeremy Daldry, Gary Hunter and Vanessa Fry, the only posh Australian in the world. Thanks to Nick Ghirlando for helping the wife with the photography, and to Danny Eccleston for suggesting some brilliant music.

And in no particular order: the entire Trier family (the finest, truest gastronauts I know)—Ned, Caroline, Jenny, Emma, and Julian; also Mickey Richardson, Ewan Bailey, the British Library, Tante Mimi Leotard, Bob and Moo Wilson, Graham Smith, Isaac, Lilly, Tom, Olive, Tess, Millie, Isaac and Belle, Jean-Anthelme, Jeremy and Manon, the Fish Society, Father Evan Jones, Dan and Erika, Erica Sutton, Mark McAlindon, Stevie Lee, and Danny Wallace's mum, who knew how lucky he was when I gave him a sausage.

Thanks to my wonderful mum, Jean Gates, for checking my recipes and helping me sift through the remains of pigs' heads. She can, at least in genetic terms, be blamed for much of what I've written. Sam Gates for her love and tireless enthusiasm; Tom, who keeps my keyboard warm when I'm trying to type on it; Daisy, for rejecting every normal meal I've ever made and only eating the weird stuff; and the glorious Georgia Glynn Smith who inspires me, is a Babe and a Sauce, takes wonderful photographs, including the ones in this book, gives me kisses, and leaves me alone every now and then to write.

London, July 2005